Consciousness and Truth

in *Don Quijote*

Juan de la Cuesta
Hispanic Monographs

Series: *Documentación cervantina*, Nº 28

FOUNDING EDITOR
Tom Lathrop
University of Delaware

EDITOR
Alexander R. Selimov
University of Delaware

EDITORIAL BOARD
Samuel G. Armistead
University of California, Davis

Annette G. Cash
Georgia State University

Alan Deyermond
Queen Mary, University of London

Daniel Eisenberg
Cervantes Society of America

John E. Keller
University of Kentucky

Steven D. Kirby
Eastern Michigan University

Vincent Martin
University of Delaware

Joel Rini
University of Virginia

Donna M. Rogers
Middlebury College

Russell P. Sebold
University of Pennsylvania, Emeritus
Corresponding Member, Real Academia Española

Noël Valis
Yale University

Amy Williamsen
University of Arizona

Consciousness and Truth in *Don Quijote* and Connected Essays

by

JOSEPH V. RICAPITO

Louisiana State University, Baton Rouge

Juan de la Cuesta
Newark, Delaware

ON THE COVER: The inside courtyard of the University of Alcalá de Henares

Some chapters have appeared earlier in these publications:

Chapter 6: "Cervantes y la consciencia: 'Yo sé quien soy," El caballero de los leones y Ricote el Moro." *Cervantes y su mundo*, III, eds. Robert A Lauer and Kurt Reichenberger. Kassel: Reichenberger, 2005.

Chapter 7: "Cervantes and the 'Funny Book' Syndrome," Malve Filer, Dominick Finello, William Schertzer, eds. *A Celebration of Brooklyn Hispanism*, Newark, DE: Juan de la Cuesta, 2004

Chapter 8: "Cervantes, Lepanto, y el cuerpo y el sufrimiento físico," *Volver a Cervantes*, Actas del IV Congreso internacional de Cervantinas. Palma: Universitat de Lles Illes Baleared, 2001.

Copyright © 2007 by Juan de la Cuesta—Hispanic Monographs
270 Indian Road
Newark, Delaware 19711
(302) 453-8695
Fax: (302) 453-8601
www.JuandelaCuesta.com

MANUFACTURED IN THE UNITED STATES OF AMERICA

ISBN: 978-1-58871-112-0

FIRST EDITION

Table of Contents

INTRODUCTION 9

1. Consciousness and Don Quijote 11

2. Cervantes and Consciousness:
   The Christian and Muslim Worlds Juxtaposed................. 17

3. Consciousness, Don Quijote
   and the Muslim World 45

4. The Unending Quest for Truth
   and Objective Reality 57

5. Cervantes's Don Quijote:
   Now You See it and Now You Don't 65

6. Cervantes and Consciousness:
   "Yo sé quién soy," El caballero de los leones
   and Ricote el Morisco 81

7. Cervantes and the "Funny Book Syndrome" 93

8. Cervantes, Lepanto and
   the Concept of Wounding, Pain and Suffering 123

9. History, Society and Economics
   of the 16th and 17th Centuries
   with Reference to Don Quijote 149

Concluding Remarks 179

SELECTED BIBLIOGRAPHY 181

*This book is dedicated to
SAMUEL G. ARMISTEAD,
Mentor, Teacher, Friend,
and Lover of Cats.
With Enormous Affection.*

Introduction

THIS BOOK IS MY third attempt at writing about Cervantes's works. I thought that in order to tackle a book on *Don Quijote* I should work with another genre of Cervantes's work as an introduction to his larger work. To that end I published two works on the *Novelas ejemplares*. That proved to be a useful exercise but not a critical one. The *Novelas ejemplares* have a certain amount of material and thematics that coincide with *Don Quijote*, but in the *Novelas ejemplares* Cervantes was attempting to out-Boccaccio Boccaccio. But *Don Quijote* represents a greater challenge, one that goes beyond the perspective of short fiction, at which Boccaccio (and Cervantes) excelled.

In writing *Don Quijote*, Cervantes had a more complete idea and program of the creation of a new form of literature. As E. C. Riley has shown, Cervantes supersedes with great skill and controlled irony the very sub-genres that he wove into the fabric of his *Don Quijote*. In the course of this challenge, Cervantes created the first modern novel.

In order to carry out this challenge successfully Cervantes had to understand the dynamics of the other genres. In doing so, his creation is founded on a number of variables, not the least of which is Cervantes's own vision and understanding about what life was all about, and a deeply felt existential reaction to his own experiences, which he transfers on to his characters.

Dealing with *Don Quijote* involves handling several threads at a time, and many times these threads are functionally independent and do not lend themselves easily to accommodation; thus my decision to focus principally on the themes of consciousness and the search for objective truth and reality.

During the time that I have researched and written this book, I have consulted many colleagues, and I wish to thank them all, especially Sam Armistead who, over the many years of our friendship lent me his moral support and limitless knowledge of literature, language and many, many other areas of knowledge. In the interstices of the work one can see and feel the presence of M.J. Benardete, my first teacher of Spanish literature and to Américo Castro whom I studied through his students and followers, Joseph

H. Silverman, Samuel Armistead, Stephen Gilman, Manuel Durán, A.A. Sicroff, Francisco Márquez Villanueva and Benito Brancaforte. I also proffer my thanks to Ignacio Navarrete, Luigi Imperiale and Manuel Da Costa Fontes, attentive scholars and friends; to Joseph Kronick, who always had time to direct me along newer theoretical dimensions; to Robert L. Fiore, Narciso Bruzzi Costas, Dominic K. Finello, Jesús Torrecilla, and Bryant Creel, whose intelligence stimulated me to chart new paths to the understanding of literature; to Emily Batinski, my current Chair, who offered me unlimited moral support in this project. Above all, to my wife, Carolyn and our children, Frank Peyton Ricapito and Maria Ricapito who have always understood my passion for literature and have given me much support as I pursued my literary critical ends. To all of you, I say "thank you," and hope that this book does justice to my debt to you.

Baton Rouge, Louisiana
July 6, 2006

Consciousness and *Don Quijote*[1]

IN 1975, J.B. AVALLE Arce published an essay that dealt with consciousness in *Don Quijote*. He presented a balanced picture of what this theme was and meant. He especially took pains to point out that at its base, consciousness was linked with the Orteguian concept of an individual's contact with an experienced vital project (this in the Spanish sense of *vital* as in *proyecto vital*). The *Encyclopedia of Philosophy* defines consciousness as "consciousness or reflection is a person's observing or noticing the 'internal operation' of his mind. It is by means of consciousness that a person acquires the ideas of the various operations or mental states such as the ideas of perceiving, thinking, doubting, reasoning, knowing and willing and learns of his own mental states at any given time" (191b).[1]

---

[1] See Avalle-Arce (Avalle henceforth), *Nuevo*, "El conocimiento se puede definir como la trayectoria que liga nuestra conciencia con una zona determinada de la realidad," p. 40. See also, "Conocimiento y verdad aparecen en la obra cervantina indisolublemente unidos a un tercer término: vida. El problema es, pues, trino y uno." (17-18); Avalle and Riley, "Sin embargo, el punto central del *Don Quijote* es el mismo de Don Quijote…Se lee la novela de dentro hacia fuera, por así decir. Partiendo de un punto humano particular, el sentido de la historia va radiando hacia horizontes infinitos de lo universal…." (*Suma*, 71). "My premise [Gaylord's] in this essay is that Cervantes's novel foregrounds intentions—his own, Don Quijote's, those of a whole host of other characters—not in order to tease us into deciphering his own 'true' authorial purpose but rather to dramatize the difficulties inherent in all intending and meaning. In his exposure of the contradictions at the core of orthodox plotting Cervantes not only foreshadows the Freudian account of a masochistic contest between repressing consciousness and intractable unconscious but anticipates ironically Freud's linking of the work of repression to the idea of civilization itself" (117); see also Cascardi, "From an existentialist point of view, *Don Quijote* represents a successful correction of the heroic ideal insofar as Cervantes is compelled to redirect his hero's failures and succeeds in transforming these into sources of authentic self-creation" (42). Riley says, "Cervantes's ironic vision enables him to put within the pages of *Don Quijote* things that are normally outside

This definition gets at the root of the personal aspects of consciousness, and I shall be using this theme as a key to the understanding of Cervantes's *Don Quijote*. In order do this to my satisfaction and within the purview of the purpose of this book, I shall be extending the definition to include the sense of consciousness not only in the case of Don Quijote but also to that of other characters and of the author himself, in the measure that this can be done deductively from what is known about the man and his life. I realize that I am dangerously crossing boundaries but I believe that to understand *Don Quijote*, the reader and critic must examine how some basic ideas on life and living are proposed and dealt with by Cervantes.[2]

I begin with a treatment of consciousness through the experience of the Captive (I, 39-41). Consciousness is the awareness of more than how a person manages important life experiences through inner mental procedures. Consciousness is based upon the sense a person has about the self and how one responds to profound questions, and this includes how an individual processes emotions and reactions. To have consciousness means an individual has an awareness of life around him/her, and how such

---

books automatically and also to manipulate the story so that the principal characters are actually conscious of the world outside the covers of the book" (*Theory*, 40).

[2] See René Girard who notes that nobility, passion and desire comes from within (116) as well as Efron, "Benedetto Croce spelled out the philosophical and psychological assumptions behind these views when he wrote that all of us are in a state of unshakable sympathy with Don Quijote simply because life is itself a process of necessary illusions" (6). Cfr. Auerbach's definition of what is Cervantean: "First of all it is something spontaneously sensory: a vigorous capacity for the vivid visualization of very different people in very varied situations, for the vivid realization and expression of what thoughts enter their minds, what emotions fill their hearts, and what words come to their lips. This capacity he possesses so directly and stongly, and in a manner so independent of any sort of ulterior motive, that almost everything realistic written before him appears limited, conventional, or propagandistic in comparison" (Lowry Nelson, Jr., 118). Very much to the point, Grinberg and Rodríguez look for the reasons of madness. Freud, they aver, tries to make sense of madness. One must look for the source of "la razón de la sinrazón" (28). Yet, Carlos Feal says, "Don Quijote answers that there is a point in doing something for no reason at all. The reason for his unreason is clear, however: it is the reason of the unconscious, the repressed, which, as we have seen, Cardenio has compelled Don Quijote to face" (187); Márquez Villanueva says, "Su [Cervantes's] mentalidad universalmente crítica desconfía de todas las escolásticas y, en una época de ideologías en pugna, profesa (como sólo él podía hacerlo) una generosa lección sobre la esencial relatividad del hecho humano" (*Personajes*, 13).

awareness leads to action (or, as in some cases, inaction). Being conscious means a person is aware of the self, whence it came and where it is going; how the historical, economic and social factors have molded an individual's world view. Consciousness also means an awareness of the past and how such a memory aims someone in the present or the future.[3]

In a well-argued book, Martínez Bonati surveys the theme of consciousness in the following way: "As the phenomenological school of criticism has assumed, the fundamental meaning of a work of fiction and art lies in the ideal consciousness that is shaped in it. A new frame of mind, an imaginary and artificial self, is adopted by the reader in the process of experiencing literature. It is through this medium of a consciousness transformed however slightly, that a new image of the world can appear" (xii).

Don Quijote is unique because it is almost impossible to grasp a basic notion or idea that embraces the whole. I do not believe that Cervantes intended to isolate one idea that is the root. *Don Quijote* is composed of so many separate threads that it is almost impossible to say that one emotion dominates the work.[4]

---

[3] See Martínez Bonati, "The *Quixote* can be seen as a vast and subtle rhetorical-didactic operation, in the second of the senses of these terms that I have delineated. It begins by seducing readers with the joys of the comical and its devices, or with conventionally romancesque appearances that conceal a problematic depth, in order to carry them along toward growing uncertainties, to perplexities of ethical judgment, and to symbols of inexhaustible meaning. These complications will temporarily suspend the force of readers' convictions, and at the same time will activate their sensibility and their intelligence" (35).

[4] Riley's work should inform us adequately about the theoretical foundations of *Don Quijote*. But the very nature of the work, built on ambiguity and the opposite of the national approach to things, instead brings the reader to certain pitfalls (according to traditional Western canons). As Girard says, "A basic contention of this essay is that the great writers apprehend intuitively and concretely, through the medium of their art, if not formally, the system in which they were first imprisoned together with their contemporaries" (3). Avalle/Riley note, "Se puede decir que si el mundo de don Quijote está gobernado por la lógica del absurdo, los mundos de Sancho y de Andrés están gobernados por el absurdo de la lógica" (*Suma*, 54). According to Márquez Villanueva, "Sirven [técnicas cervantinas] así para introducirnos en un laberinto determinado por la ambigüedad, la aporía y la paradoja, cuya difícil o, tal vez, imposible salida ha de ser buscada por la conciencia personal de cada uno (*Personajes*, 13). He also notes, "No se olvide que la naturaleza ambigua y aporética de personajes y temas del *Quijote* no tiene nada de casual: deriva de una coherencia interna muy buscada y no al contrario" (14). Focusing on Dorotea, Márquez says,

Cervantes's view is wide and subsumes many ideas, hence the difficulty in building a critical view on one single piece. If there were ever an overwhelming central idea, I would say that it would be the theme of truth, which follows this chapter on consciousness.[5]

In interpreting the thought of Martin Heidegger, Quentin Lauer says the following: "Now, the demands that psychology cannot satisfy, phenomenology does satisfy. What phenomenology does is to analyze consciousness, where alone objectivity is absolute. Phenomenology, then, is a study of consciousness, but it is not a psychology, a notion impossible to grasp until one sees consciousness as not a physical something" (10). Lauer adds another observation which is relevant to my position on consciousness and phenomenology: "The confusion here comes from the supposition that there must be absolute uniformity of method in sciences and that the method is that of the empirical sciences. True science, on the other hand, conforms itself to its objects, regardless of methodological prejudices based on the success of one method in other scientific endeavors" (11). We can extend this observation, to see the separate areas of objectivity and human reaction to objects, which is the subject of my present study. Furthermore, Lauer says, "Thus we are not faced with two equal 'realities' that can be studied according to the same 'objective' methods. If

---

"Con Dorotea pisamos, pues, de lleno el terreno de la paradoja irónica en que Cervantes gusta de situar a sus personajes favoritos, amasados de contradicción y de opuestas tradiciones literarias, de Edad Media y de Renacimiento, de novela y de drama" (24). Avalle/Riley suggest, "Conceptualmente, los temas preceden a las historias particulares, cuyo sentido refleja esas verdades por medios ejemplares o simbólicos." (*Suma*, 71). Studying the aesthetics of creation, Márquez Villanueva says, "Digamos de una vez que Cervantes nunca deja de ser profundamente lógico. Pero no hay que olvidar que esa lógica es, en primer término, una lógica *literaria* [Emph. his], regulada por su propia eficacia artística y responsable primordialmente ante ésta" (148). See also Martínez Bonati: "*Don Quijote* cannot be rightly approached without a sense of these multiple dimensions. It is many things. It is the expression of a search for truth and redemption in an age of shaken religious faith, political pessimism and renascent naturalistic thought" (xii). He also says, "This vision has, one must suppose, a natural link with the person and the life of Cervantes. But it is the product of the alienation of his lived experience by the forms of literary tradition in *one* among the various constellations of styles that he tried in an effort to redeem his life in enduring and joyful images" (38).

[5] Martínez Bonati says, "Certainly the *Quijote* is a very profound image of life, and for that reason it is rightly known as *true*, but its image of life is not a *realistic* [Emph. his] one" (5).

spirit is to be studied scientifically (and it must), psychology itself must be reformed and become a science of the human subject; 'objectivistic' prejudices must be abandoned" (19).[6]

Husserl himself broaches the tangibility of experience when he says, "Involved in this, as in any other such analysis, is the complete exclusion of every assumption, stipulation, or conviction concerning Objective time (of all transcendent presuppositions concerning existents). From an Objective point of view every lived experience, like every real being [*Sein*] and moment of being, may have its place in the one unique Objective time—consequently, also the lived experience of the perception and representation [*Vorstellung*] of time itself" (22), as well as "When we speak of the analysis of time-consciousness, of the temporal character of objects of perception, memory, and expectation, it may seem, to be sure, as if we assume the Objective flow of time, and then really study only the subjective conditions of the possibility of an intuition of time and a true knowledge of time" (23).

I have endeavored to plumb the structure of experience *in se*, as well as tied to experience. The bases of the apprehension of experience as tied to an internal, quasi subjective power is the object of this part of my study.

---

[6] When Lauer considers Husserl's thought with that of Descartes, he says, "Unlike Descartes, however, Husserl will not look upon this knowledge of the subject as a first indubitable principle from which all other knowledge can be derived. Instead, taking the *cogitatum* as the objective correlative of the *cogito*, he will see in subjectivity the one and only (transcendental) source of all absolute, objectively valid knowledge, because in the subjectivity of consciousness and only here is the being of objectivity absolute" (20). Lauer further says, "If the experience is fully grasped, its object (the 'noematic' aspect of the act) is fully grasped, which is to say, it is 'known.' No element outside the act enters into this validation; the act itself reveals its own validity or invalidity—based on the necessary a priori conditions or rules for valid thinking: an act completely in accord with the rules for this type of act is valid" (29).

2
Cervantes and Consciousness: The Christian and Muslim Worlds Juxtaposed

WHEN I FIRST BEGAN to be interested in consciousness, I found many books that dealt with neurology and psychology. A good example of this is the work of the Portuguese neurologist, Antonio Damasio. His book, *Descartes' Error,* is an exemplary study of consciousness within a medical framework.

At the same time, I found David Lodge's, *Consciousness and the Novel,* a work that provided me with some very good examples of consciousness-analysis within a literary context.

Lodge attempts to locate consciousness within the person, and uses words like "human awareness" (5), which I find very applicable to literary consciousness studies. He focuses on "Qualia," a word of Latin origin which means "the specific nature of our subjective experience of the world" (8).

Daniel Dennett, another writer on consciousness, believes that "consciousness is a kind of illusion or epiphenomenon" (in *Lodge,* 9). Writers who engage in this investigative mode not only study aspects of consciousness in characters but also in reader response, whereby one can come to understand one's own experiences through the characters that one studies. To strengthen his position, Lodge quotes Joseph Conrad, who writes, " 'My task which I am trying to achieve… is by the power of the written word to make you hear, to make you feel — it is before all, to make you *see* [Emph. Lodge]. That–and no more, and it is everything,' " (13).

The human aspect of consciousness is reiterated by Lodge when he says "It creates fictional models of what it is like to be a human being, moving through time and space. It captures the density of experienced events by its rhetoric, and it shows the connectedness of events through the devices of plot" (14).

Dennett further notes that, "Our fundamental tactic of self protection, self control and self definition is not spinning webs or building dams, but telling stories, and more particularly, connecting and controlling the story we tell others—and ourselves—about who we are' " (quoted by Lodge, 15).

Let it be said that scientific knowledge and consciousness are complementary, as C.P. Snow said (quoted in Lodge, 16). It is in the author's interest to go behind behavior in the same way that Freud sought to understand the substrata of human behavior. Crucial words like "emotions," "ideas," and "consciousness" offer us the clue to this kind of critical insight. Lodge insists the characters, through their manipulation by their authors, project versions of themselves. Point of view, these authors seem to be saying, is localized in sensory and feeling human mechanisms. Joyce did this in both the first and third person narratives (Lodge, 55). Lodge cogently notes the absence of "objective facts" in the work of Virginia Wolff, and we might add, the work of the Spaniard, Miguel de Unamuno. For Lodge, it is "the inner voice of the character himself or herself who is the 'center of consciousness'; rendered in interior monologue or free indirect style, and mingled with the accents of other discourses, written or spoken, which belong to that character's mental world" (65).

A good example that Lodge cites is Graham Greene. Lodge says, "the Catholic Greene did not turn away entirely from depth in order to render the surface of life; he remained interested in representing the consciousness of his characters, partly because he regarded them very literally as having 'souls,' capable of salvation and damnation" (76).

If we begin with the consciousness of the author, of Cervantes, we are forced to enter the workings of his mind, so that the figure of Don Quijote is a reflection of the inner creative impulse of Cervantes and his own "*circunstancia*" regarding his personal history, his vital situation, his experiences, his fears and doubts. Such a mental disposition will affect the whole work and will place it upon a foundation of the author's experience.[1]

I believe that it is valid to make judgments that link deduced intentions and fictional results, so that the reader will notice the contact points

---

[1] Gilman notes the effect that the novel has on the readers: "it presents its fictional world in the same temporal fashion with which we experience our own" (136-137). He says as well: "Rather, the novelists of later centuries who can be perceived as belonging to the Cervantine tradition rediscover, reinvent and give birth anew to creatures who experience their residence on earth in a way comparable to Don Quijote and Sancho" (xvi).

between inner reality of *Don Quijote* and the author. I do not hesitate to attribute certain claims to the author and bounce between the work and the character and the author.[2] Consciousness is a tricky concept and like its cousin, phenomenology, is often difficult to understand in precise terms. Avalle has attempted with some success an understanding between the concept and the work. Avalle's judgments are largely correct, and I shall be following a similar path. Américo Castro examined in his monumental work, *Cervantes y los casticismos,* and noted: "Cervantes desplazó el acento, que hasta entonces apuntaba hacia la 'esencia' de la figura literaria, y lo puso sobre el tenso y problemático proceso vital de aquélla; sobre ésta se proyectan, con sus luces cambiantes, las acciones suyas y las de quienes forman con ella una textura humana de vida ensalzada y entrechocada" (*Casticismos, 21*).[3]

The work begins in a shocking way, a *fait accompli* of the character. We

---

[2] James Parr cautions precisely against the approach I am using when he says, "The rules of the game dictate that the historical author, Miguel de Cervantes Saavedra, be relegated to the periphery in any serious study of narrative. Such a move on the part of the commentator is merely prudent if she is to enjoy the requisite autonomy, avoid the intentional fallacy, and eschew biographical determinism. We do the author no great service, for instance, when we make the captive's tale depend overly much upon lived experience" (13). While I endorse much of his book, I shall try to "unfallicize" the intentional fallacy and show, where possible, that there is a common sense approach to the place of autobiography in literature. Note the title of a paper I presented recently at a conference at the University of California at Santa Cruz: "Autobiografía en la literatura y la literatura en la autobiografía."

[3] Cfr.: Castro: "El *Quijote* no es una obra de tesis, es una novela hecha posible por circunstancias personales y sociales ajenas a la literatura, y transmutadas por el genio de su autor, según vengo diciéndolo en una forma secularizada de espiritualidad religiosa" (*Casticismos,* 156); also "La tensión literaria del *Quijote* es consecuencia de haber logrado el autor que los problemas se transformaran en motivaciones de vida, en lugar de ser expresados en proposiciones lógica o didácticamente formuladas" (*ibid.* 158); Gilman notes: "Here is the really unprecedented capability of the invention: the literary self-consciousness that the author induces in the reader gives birth to the independent and ever-changing self-consciousness of the two protagonists" (122); as well as "Admittedly, both endings are inevitably melancholy, and the consciousness of Huck (and, refracted through it that of Jim longing for his family and prey to remorse for his mistreatment of his deaf child) is as forlorn as that of Don Quijote during and after his sojourn in the Duke's palace. Nevertheless, their consciousness does possess the magic power to transform romance into novel, to infuse adventure with experience" (29).

are introduced to a man who has lost his sanity by having read so many romances of chivalry. But the modern, sophisticated reader knows that you do not become insane by reading too many books; the unconscious reasons are what causes someone to become insane. In the case of Don Quijote, it is books of chivalry. The very beginning of this work stands on this suspicious ground, but Cervantes must begin somewhere with his character. The binomial reality/insanity is established here with a middle-aged man who is suffering a mid-life crisis, and who will tie himself to one part of the binomial, insanity, in the form of a bogus knight of chivalry.

In his composition, Cervantes must know that he is entering difficult terrain, especially since the age of chivalry is long over. When we refer to the age of chivalry, we are thinking of the fifteenth century, the expansion of the great Spanish monarchy in Europe and the New World. Cervantes conceives of a character whose mania will be that of living out a form of life, which no longer exists and, in fact, has been replaced by a monarchy headed for disgrace and loss of power (see *infra*). Cervantes is conscious of this fact and uses this literary character to move in a different atmosphere.

Don Quijote is a landowner and someone who is able to function without the immediate need of money. There is no indication that he is preoccupied with mundane concerns like paying taxes. He has wrapped himself in the myth of chivalry.

After he decides to take up the occupation of chivalrous knight, he searches his house for the accoutrements of a knight. Cervantes then allows the reader to glimpse what the novel will be like. The episode dealing with the helmet (*celada de encaje*) will be the key with which the reader can enter the world of the adventures of Don Quijote.

After having cleaned and repaired the helmet, he checks its efficiency by dealing it a blow, and the helmet breaks. The proof of reality shows that such a helmet will not be functional in a battle. Don Quijote returns and repairs the helmet and the second time he foregoes the test. The message here is clear enough. Perhaps it is better not to test all aspects of reality. This message places the world of the novel on a curious anvil. It is in many ways a house built on sand. At some point there will be a test not only of the helmet but also the principle of reality. The first chapter offers the reader the possibility of seeing the world in a strange light, a world based upon false appearances, but then this is what Cervantes is offering us: a hint of what the world of this displaced knight-errant is.

Interestingly enough, we are getting a case of double vision: the world as seen and constructed by Cervantes and the world that Don Quijote sees.

Part of Don Quijote's vision is to have a beautiful lady that will be his guide, his Beatrice to whom Don Quijote will dedicate his adventures. But this lady, Dulcinea, does not exist. She is a construction of Don Quijote's mind. The closest he has been to a woman of "carne y hueso" is a masculine, sweaty farmhand named Aldonza Lorenzo.

A key to the novel will be Cervantes's use of narrator(s). It is not just one narrator. Cervantes sets up the situation as one of a challenge. Narrators are supposed to describe what happens honestly and truthfully, but when you have several narrators you have different points of view, and for a work that intends to give the reader the truth and all the truth, this becomes a sticky wicket. The use of several narrators is a maze through which the reader will pass trying to find the way to the end.

The first chapter is so important for the understanding of the work. Here we find the themes of regeneration, or to use the words of Castro, "Incarnation,"[4] in the change of character from a comfortable country squire to a committred chivalric knight; the abandonment of an old comfortable way of life to one of battling; the adoption of a new persona; the commitment to an asexual life (the question of his lack of a spouse or lover is glossed over by the author). The closest he comes to a female are his niece and *ama,* as well as Aldonza Lorenzo. One cannot stress enough the fact of his sexually empty life. He is a fifty-ish man who projects his amorous fantasies outward to impossible goals and non-existent women. It is evidently easier to worship a female that does not exist than a living person, and also less threatening to him and his lifetime project (*proyecto vital*).

Don Quijote's beliefs and ideas must be examined in the light of a particular obstacle that Cervantes has placed in the book. The narrator or narrators are not merely communicators of the action of the book. They may be the "omniscient" figures, but in the novel they assume a role very different from that of the neutral observer and communicator, the omniscient third narrator. Don Quijote will be out in life, and his ideals and behavior will be judged by the people he meets along the way, most of whom think he is insane.[5] The narrators must be regarded as critics of Don

---

[4] See this important essay in Flores and Benardete, *Cervantes Across the Centuries,* pp. 136-178.

[5] It is important to note that the world Don Quijote will be entering will be a hostile

Quijote's actions, and many times they are sarcastic and negative critics. In I, 1, the narrator refers to him as "ingenioso Don Quijote," just as in the next chapter he will refer to Don Quijote's horse as "famoso caballo Rocinante" (I, I, 22a).[6] In both cases, there is a negative insinuation toward the characters. There is nothing in the first chapter to confirm that Don Quijote is "ingenioso,"[7] nor that Rocinante is anything other than his name suggests, "un rocín antes," but no longer one. Compare the attitudes of the narrator(s) with that of Don Quijote. He is full of confidence at the beginning of his career. He has no doubts about himself. He says, "—¿Quién duda sino que en los venideros tiempos, cuando salga a luz la verdadera historia de mis famosos hechos, que el sabio que los escribiere no ponga, cuando llegue a contar esta mi primera salida tan de mañana, tan desta manera?" (ibid, 22a). As it has been noted many times by critics, Don

---

one: "Sumamente importantes son esas manifestaciones del punto de vista de cada uno, prisma de la realidad que se ofrece así con muy diversas facetas…Una persona frente a otra representa un problema," Castro, *Pensam.* 70 [the curious reader might ask why I use Castro's 1928 edition of *El pensamiento de Cervantes* and not the later edition of Rodríguez Puértolas. I wanted to preserve the original ideas as they were articulated in Castro's early thought; see also "El personaje quijotizado y un mundo que no lo está, van a enfrentarse. Una aventura literaria de tal estructura carecía de antecedentes, pero urgía hacer posible la conexión entre dos realidades humanas heterogéneas, sin bufonada, haciendo del hecho mismo de tal inadecuación un caso de literatura 'plausible' manteniendo la íntegra realidad del *uno* y la de los *muchos* juntamente con la del medio humano en que todos se mueven" Castro, *Casticismos*, 62; see also his "No teniendo vocación de místico, se construyó imaginativamente una *forma* en que se expresara el proceso penoso y conflictivo de quien aspira a ser persona, e identifica la consciencia de personalidad con la pretensión de realizar el bien en un mundo malignamente dispuesto" (*ibid.*, 130-31).

[6] All textual citations of *Don Quijote* are taken from the edition that has an introduction by Américo Castro, Mexico, D.F. The choice of the horse is more complex than one might think. Castro says, "A cada uno su menester: Rocinante seguirá el rumbo que su 'rocinantismo' le pida, el Caballero se encargará de todo lo demás" (*Casticismos*, 64). See also his "El *Quijote* se inicia en un lugar indeterminado de La Mancha, y despliega su existencia por las amplitudes de aquellos campos, pero don Quijote no tiene más habitáculo que ese libro. Por lo mismo el rumbo de su cabalgar ha de confiarse al instinto—que Cervantes llama 'voluntad'—de Rocinante" (*ibid.*, 58), as well as "No es cierto que Rocinante encarne la locura caballeresca de su jinete, porque él, simplemente, vive su vida lo mismo que el caballero vive la suya" (*ibid.*, 57).

[7] On *ingenio* Gilman says, "The *Quijote*, itself is an exemplary literary lesson for an age of stampeding *ingenio* and farfetched falsehood" (112).

Quijote is endowed with a robust picture of himself and of his career as a knight-errant. He possesses a solid consciousness of his proposed career. Some of the humor, sarcasm and satire of him are the result of the reactions of others toward him, the view of others toward his confidence. Avalle/Riley say, "En esto, precisamente radica la esencia heroica del Quijotismo, y su significado profundamente humano. Tiene que ser evidente para todos el hecho de que este hombre [Don Quijote] ha reconocido, desde mucho antes de la aventura de la Cueva de Montesinos, que su ideal de vida era total y trágicamente inadecuado para vivir en ese mundo" (*Suma,* 59).[8]

But these statements precede his important discourse. This discourse has been mistakenly viewed through the Renaissance lens of the imitation of the Classical Golden Age, but Cervantes had other things in mind. Cervantes, the man, who is the origin of all things in this novel, allows his feelings to penetrate the language of the Knight. In these statements that precede the important discourse of the "Dichosa edad y siglo dichoso," Don

---

[8] See Riquer, (*Suma,* 289), who, focusing on Don Quijote's appearance says, "El arcaísmo del atuendo de don Quijote (cuya ridiculez acrecentará la bacía de barbero) se complementa con el anticuado lenguaje que muy a menudo, sobre todo en la primera parte, emplea el hidalgo manchego, que es un castellano con notas medievalizantes propias de los libros de caballerías." Efron notes that according to some critics, "Don Quijote may be described in positive terms because of his role as restorer of traditional cultural values, or because of his idealistic opposition to the values of his social environment, or because he is seen as an example of modern rather than medieval man, creating his individual personality with the strength of his own will and imagination rather than carrying out the role that his society has defined for him" (4), as well as Efron's "Dulcineism, *or the belief that human life is satisfactorily conducted only if it is lived out in close accord with prescribed ideals of the received culture*" (11). Spitzer offers the interesting insight: "All of Quijote's adventures would show the pattern of the heroic fight of man against the established world order with the subsequent inevitable, heroi-comical, shattering defeat—as when the pathetic Quijote must endure the ordeal of the cheese as it melts and drips down over his eyes and beard, all because his rustic squire Sancho, heedless of knightly propriety, has stowed away the cheese in his master's helmet" (Lowry Nelson, Jr., 83-84). With more of a psychological, social idea in mind, Cascardi says, "Accordingly, Don Quijote attempts to 'reread' the modern world in terms of the categorical oppositions between the noble and the base" (*Quixotic Desire,* 41); he also says, "More important than any alignment of the structures of desire along the historical lines designated by 'caste' or 'class' is Cervantes's ability to locate the hidden mobility of desire everywhere within the societies we may call, respectfully, 'heroic' and 'modern', or 'old' and 'new' " (48).

Quijote reiterates his profound belief in the invincibility of his *proyecto vital*. This may seem excessive to the reader; after all, Don Quijote is at the beginning of his career, but this does not prevent him from externalizing the deep faith he has in himself. This points to a very important aspect of consciousness. Now whether this consciousness will be fulfilled will be shown in his later episodes.[9]

When Don Quijote arrives at the inn, his mania concerning the (mis)perception of reality takes over and individuals, the prostitutes, the swineherd and others are changed in his mind into characters from the genre of the romances of chivalry; his consciousness of this mania is ever present. He cannot lock out the process of change. The process of change occurs in his mind before he perceives it: the mental problem that he has is not something that he can control; it is an automatic reaction on his part, and throughout the novel this psychiatric mania will be in force in his mind and behind his actions.

The arrival at the inn is the first example of the change of reality. It demonstrates Don Quijote's instability, because if he could control such a reaction, he would not be considered insane. This episode is also the beginning of another major theme of the work: the nature of truth.[10]

---

[9] Avalle/Riley say: "En esto, precisamente radica la esencia heroica del quijotismo, y su signicado profundamente humano. Tiene que ser evidente para todos el hecho de que este hombre [Don Quijote] ha reconocido, desde mucho antes de la aventura de la Cueva de Monetesinos, que su ideal de vida era total y trágicamente inadecuado para vivir en este mundo" (*Suma*, 59).

[10] Avalle/Riley say: "Broma, ficción, ilusión transparente y pasatiempo para hacernos reír, por supuesto. Y lo bueno es que quien más se ríe será Cervantes, que precisamente por estos medios ha logrado sugerir —y casi engañar a algunos— que sus cómicos héroes ficticios tuvieron una vida independiente de todas las versiones" (*Suma*, 79). Riley approaches the question of truth in the following way: "It is not hard to arrive at the corollary that, if romance represents a world of dreams, another kind of fiction is needed to deal with the world of waking experience" (*Don Quijote*, 68); and "His [Cervantes's] idea of verisimilitude was certainly not modern realism. Cervantes could never bring himself to reject the idealization of experience, in spite of a rather shaky mistrust of the exaggeration it involves. He drew the vague line that must be drawn somewhere between idealism and fastasy close to the latter. [Cervantes] had "a new sense of the need for art to deal responsibly with the truth" (*ibid.*, 68). Elsewhere Riley notes, "The first is the nature and limits of the work of art. The Knight's confusion of fiction and fact is an extreme case, but the author clearly shows that there is some justification for it. Not only the boundries between what is imaginary and what is real, but those between art and life, are indetermin-

A major episode which reveals Don Quijote's attitudes is the encounter with the Toledan merchants. Don Quijote's unchecked enthusiasm for his career and his belief in his powers of bringing about change get the better of him. Or, to put it another way, Cervantes lets Don Quijote spread his wings as far as he can before he can have him learn something—a limitation. Here Don Quijote comes across as a committed fighter for his cause. This battle between him and the merchant has nothing to do with any fantasies he may have. It is a blood and guts battle. Cervantes disrupts Don Quijote's fantasy by having his horse trip, and Don Quijote falls to the ground, leaving Don Quijote defenseless, and he is beaten. The deconstruction of Don Quijote's understanding of limitless powers is brought to a halt because one of the most important themes of the work is the unpredictability of his actions. Cervantes does not want the character and reader to think that just because Don Quijote says something, that it will be true for all occasions. To have had Don Quijote continue on in this level of unregulated power the book would have ended up being a work of entertainment, which is what the books of chivalry were. It seems as if Cervantes is saying that nothing is inevitable. As is to be seen in the episode of the windmills, the life of the individual is subject to change at any moment.

The latter part of this episode finds Don Quijote beaten and on the ground, unable to get up. A farmer finds him reciting ballads, especially one about the Marquis of Mantua. Don Quijote's answer shows the extent of his consciousness and his control over his person. "Yo sé quién soy—respondió Don Quijote—, y sé que puedo ser, no sólo los que he dicho, sino todos los doce Pares de Francia y aun todos los nueve de la Fama, pues a todas las hazañas que ellos todos juntos y cada uno por sí hicieron se aventarán a las mías" (I, VI, 32a; see *infra* for more on "Yo sé quién soy"). At one point, it was tempting to think that the metamorphosed gentleman has been carrying on in a conscious way and is winking at his reader. But that is not so. When Don Quijote says, "Yo sé quién soy," he is stating a truth about himself.[11] He is aware of the fact that he is imbued with

---

able. Life and art are continually interfering with each other. Inherent in this problem is that of the nature of artistic truth. What truth is to history, verisimilitude is to fiction. But can you by pretending fiction is history, turn verisimilitude into something as potent as historical truth? The question is insistent throughout the *Quijote* and the *Persiles*." (*Theory*, 43).

[11] As J.J. Allen notes, "There is a vast amount of 'acting' in *Don Quijote*, quite apart from the possibility suggested by Mark Van Doren that this is in fact Don Quijote's

a profound commitment to his new persona that has emerged, telling the reader that he knows what he is all about. By having Rocinante trip, resulting in Don Quijote's being beaten, Cervantes is showing that one of the basic characteristics of life, its unpredictability, is greater than his career as a knight-errant. Even the deep belief in himself and his career is not more powerful than life (that is, if we accept the fact that life is an unpredictable force). This episode also shows a conflict between the consciousness of Don Quijote as knight-errant and shows the power of consciousness of Cervantes's craft as a writer of imaginative fiction is greater than his character. Symbolically, "Yo sé quién soy" extols the power of the imagination for both Cervantes and Don Quijote. Cervantes's creation is astronomical in its meaning, and on a second level, the character is saying that he can be even greater than has been seen in literature up to that point.

As a part of the *mis en abîme* of the novel—which some see as the greatest contribution to the creation of the modern novel—, Cervantes insures his presence in the book by putting aspects of himself there, in the manner that Velázquez puts himself in his painting of *Las meninas* or Juan Ruiz in *Libro de buen amor*. By having the priest and the barber enter into his library, Cervantes is insuring the fact that his novel would be unthinkable without the link with literature and also because Don Quijote is conceived within literary art (romances of chivalry, picaresque romance, Moorish romance, etc.).[12] *Don Quijote* is virtually a challenge to other literary works of art. Cervantes exercises his powers as supreme creator and suggests that his work will continue on while the others that are burned come to an end. Here we witness that self-consciousness of the author who no doubt sensed that he had done something important with the work he created, otherwise it would have resulted in a caricature of fame if he thought an inferior work was the best he could do.[13]

---

real profession—actor, and not knight-errant" (69). Girard says, "In the novels of Cervantes and Flaubert, the mediator remained beyond the universe of the hero'; he is now within the same universe" (9). He also notes with respect to Don Quijote's love for Dulcinea, that he exhibits the wish to be absorbed into the substance of the Other (54-55).

[12] Cfr. Avalle/Riley on *Don Quijote*'s link with literary art: "La idea de vivir la vida como obra de arte es norte de don Quijote y fácil será recoger la pista en la segunda parte" (53), or, as C.B. Johnson says, *Don Quijote* "is a book about books" (*Don Quijote*, 71)

[13] As Avalle says, "Es claro que esa guía no es de índole religiosa, sino literaria,

Don Quijote is a work that has numerous individual episodes that can be studied from the point of view of consciousness.[14] One of these is the episode dealing with the windmills. This episode has entered the language

---

puesto que son los libros de caballeros las autoridades que respaldan sus juicios y acciones" (*Nuevos*, 21); elsewhere he says, Don Quijote has "descubierto que intentar vivir la vida como una obra de arte es todo vanidad, porque la vida es una sombra y un sueño" (*Forma*, 213), as well as "Desde un punto de vista simbólico, la penitencia de Sierra Morena nos muestra un don Quijote que piensa haber elevado su vida a las alturas del ideal artístico" (*ibid.*, 174). Within the same work Avalle discusses further the book as *arte*: "Cuando Cardenio tiende la vista hacia el pasado para empezaar a contar su tragedia amorosa, es evidente que ve a su vida como un producto artístico" (*ibid.*, 169; Don Quijote thought that with his life he would have imitated art, "sin pararse a medir las consecuencias" (161); "Pero si volvemos a la literatura, dichos deslindes son un poco más fáciles de efectuar aunque no mucho más. Don Quijote de la Mancha fue un hombre que erigió a su imaginación en credo, fue un hombre que hizo de la ficción la razón de su vida, fue un hombre, en fin, con cuya vida se urdió la primera novela moderna y la más grande de todos los tiempos" (*ibid.*, 146). Avalle does point out a Schopenhauerian link with Don Quijote, in as much as Don Quijote's choice, if it be called that, is a product of his *voluntad* (154). See also *Forma*, 147, and *Nuevo*, 151, for similar remarks on this subject. Levin calls attention to an important facet of Don Quijote, "The method of Cervantes utilized literary conventions and, in the very process, invented a form substantial and flexible enough to set forth the vicissitudes of modern society" (Lowry Nelson, Jr., p. 42).

[14] Avalle has noted several things on this subject: See *Forma*: "Cervantes ha abierto de par en par la puerta que conduce a la plena vida del subconsciente" (185), and, citing a statement by Dilthey dealing with the idea that "la vida es, precisamente, multilateral. Tres siglos antes que el gran filósofo e historiador alemán de nuestra época, Cervantes había cimentado todo su universo poético sobre el mismísimo concepto. En consecuencia, multiplicidad de perspectivas es lo que exige cualquier aproximación a Cervantes, y esta lección debe ser contaminatoria para el crítico" (167), and he says, "Cabe preguntarse otra vez: ¿es lógico que Andresillo acuse a su libertador por la paliza recibida? ¿No parece, más bien, que el mundo de Andresillo está gobernado asimismo por lo irracional y el absurdo?...Como corolario de todo esto podemos decir que si el mundo de don Quijote está gobernado por la lógica del absurdo, los mundos de Sancho y de Andrés están gobernados por el absurdo de la lógica" (172). To the questions raised by novelists, Avalle says: "Sus [Cervantes's] respuestas, por lo tanto, no serán de razón lógica" (*Nuevos*, 18), and he says further, his answers are "Así se explica que sus contestaciones no estén dadas como abstracciones intelectuales sino que aparezcan inextricablemente enlazadas con las vidas de sus personajes" (*ibid.*,18); and, "La vida de Don Quijote, o una vida cualquiera, lleva en sí las formas embrionarias de todas las vidas" (*ibid.*, 20).

with the phrase "tilting at windmills." Once again, we have an instance of Cervantes manipulating his character to be humiliated or, to put it another way, Cervantes is God to his child, Don Quijote. Don Quijote is a character in this strange book, strange because it is unlike any other book of its kind. Don Quijote is a puppet in the hands of his master, Cervantes, and Don Quijote will respond to the urgings of his puppet master. Cervantes has created this episode because he wants to show the character's transposing nature of his perception of reality; and he wants to show the extent to which Don Quijote's messianic nature as a renewed knight-errant has some conflicting flaws when it is placed in direct opposition to the reality which others see. Cervantes seems to be saying that when Don Quijote's mania fails, he is going to pay seriously, just as it happened with the farmer who beats him while he is reciting ballads. There is a serious risk attached to being a knight-errant, as Don Quijote will soon learn in various adventures.

It does take a certain amount of courage for Cervantes to introduce the paradox at the end of the first manuscript, exactly in the middle of the fight between Don Quijote and the Basque. There is where you see the ironic, humorous hand of Cervantes. He is sure of the fact that the only reality we have is the one we are living in. We hear statements like Ginés de Pasamonte's who says that his book is not finished because his life is not ended. This immediacy is prevalent in *Don Quijote*, and Cervantes deals with it in two ways: the first is that he is calling attention to the fact that the book is being carried out in a time parallel to that of the reader's. The reader is the beneficiary of the games that Cervantes plays. The rubric of "Donde se cuenta lo que en él se verá" (II, IX) underscores the temporal expansion of the work as a continuum just like the life of the reader.[15] The second is to call attention to the tradition of literature upon which the satire is based. By pausing in the middle of the battle between Don Quijote and the Basque, Cervantes is performing "surgery" on the action of the romances of knight-errantry. He is dissecting it to show how facile it is. The only change we have is the tangibility of the action by having Don Quijote speak of the injuries he received in the battle. This point can be related to the chapter below on the wound and physical pain, which is made immediate in the episode. While in the books of chivalry wounds are noted, other aspects of

---

[15] Gilman speaks of the effect of the novel on the readers when he says, "it [the work] presents its fictional world in the same temporal fashion with which we experience our own" (136-137).

the knight's actions are being highlighted. It is all a bit of trickery by Cervantes, but at the end he carries out even a bigger trick. He finds the second part just at the point where Don Quijote and the Basque left off. This too is related to the romances of chivalry. Cervantes reflects the silliness and the far-fetchedness of so many episodes by creating another one in another context, so the reader can see the triviality of the episodes of the books of chivalry. And throughout it all Cervantes is standing behind the curtain manipulating everything. The twin consciousnesses peer through the curtain—Cervantes's literary agenda that Don Quijote be made to prove himself.

One should note that the bases upon which Don Quijote's life stand are very precarious, as I have said above. Following the model of the first chapter, things do not happen in a rational way. The described episode can come to an end any time but the resolution of the episode (the finding of the manuscript which begins exactly where the other left off was in itself totally irrational and not worthy of belief, just like the literary genre to which it belongs).[16] Gilman notes the links with other literatures when he says, "in addition to parody and satire of the romances of chivalry, Cervantes proposed to 'reform' the assembly-line fiction of the last hundred years and, at the same time to salvage and reuse whatever was meritorious therein" (108).[17]

One of the ways that Don Quijote enlists Sancho is to promise him the rule of an island. In dealing with Sancho we must assume that the role of Don Quijote is that of a father to a child. There is the sincerity and honesty to Sancho that ingratiates him to all that come in contact with him; that he has the faith of a child. His ambitions and his aims are fairly explicit and are to be seen as being on a relatively low but tangible and practical level. Offering him the governance of an island is superior to whatever ambitions he is harboring.

An aspect of Don Quijote/Sancho partnership is the question of

---

[16] See Foucault who devotes a great deal of writing to the binomial reason-unreason idea.

[17] Gilman also says "How would Cervantes accomplish that aim? Quite simply, by taking advantage of what was wrong with the chivalresque, the picaresque, and the pastoral: the fact that they had been (or would be) produced en masse for a mass public whose collective mind was habituated to—and, indeed, saturated with—the simple patterns of fiction" (91).

contrast. While this relationship does not exist on a high level, it does allow the reader to see the difference in their strivings. These strivings function within the area of the consciousness of each person. Don Quijote's exist on a very high level, and Sancho's on a rudimentary one. Therefore, with whatever psychology Cervantes used, he knew that to expect from Sancho when Sancho is faced with such a choice.

Related to the question of choice is that of freedom. Just as Don Quijote expressed his freedom in adopting the life of a knight-errant, Sancho too chooses to follow Don Quijote. There is an interesting psychological datum to be observed. Don Quijote's choice is linked to some ephemeral object: to be a figure that does not exist any longer in his time. Sancho accepts something that has a ring of contemporaneity and an accessible reality to it, only that it is ironic if not strange that a low-borne person has the ambition to rise above his station. Don Quijote can rise to the level of knight-errant, but Sancho's rising to the level of real governor of an island is simply beyond the level of a simple farmer. But Cervantes need not be hindered by the reality of such a case. He is writing fiction not history.

The "dichosa edad" speech definitely falls within the purview of the theme of consciousness. This is one of the moments of Don Quijote's greatest sobriety and sanity. Some critics have chosen to see this speech as a link with the Classical sense of the Golden Age. Like other writers of the *Edad conflictiva*, who wrote between the lines, e.g., Luis de León in his poems, notably the *Oda a la vida retirada*, Cervantes too joins several levels in this speech, which, the narrator interestingly deconstructs before our eyes: "Toda esta *larga* [Emph. mine] harenga (que se pudiera bien escusar) dijo nuestro caballero, porque las bellotas que le trujeron a la memoria la edad dorada, y antojósele hacer aquel *inútil* [Emph. mine] razonamiento a los cabreros" (I, X, 50b).

Don Quijote's harangue loses its meaning if and when one thinks of the Classical Golden Age. This episode achieves greater meaning if one were to see how Cervantes's life was filled with disappointments, losses, and deceptions. The comparison of the Golden Age to "esta nuestra edad de hierro" makes sense within the understanding of a contemporary scene. When Don Quijote steps out into the world he bears the beliefs and attitudes of a knight who holds himself to rigorous standards of behavior. It is in juxtaposition that one sees the greatness of the age of hegemony which was based on a belief of religion and special conduct become diluted. Cervantes went to Lepanto under the banner of the great monarchy. His return was to a Spain bereft of the values that supported perhaps the greatest monarch that Europe had seen had fallen asunder. There was not to be a return to earlier noble ideas, just the example and ideas of an enfeebled country.[18]

The episode of Marcela and Grisóstomo represents the cross of volition: Grisóstomo's with respect to his love and Marcela's with respect to her independence. Each character represents a consciousness toward life.

Grisóstomo follows the well-worn path of the rejected lover. When he is rejected, he commits suicide (a worthy example of Cervantes's use of other literary genres, in this case, the *novela pastoril*). This reveals a one-sided view of life that Cervantes obviously has; it is either *César o nada*.

Marcela is a different case. She has a more open view of her options. She has rejected not only Grisóstomo, who represents a common-life option, marriage; or a complete withdrawl from the conventional life-patterns offered to her. She chooses the latter. In terms of the novel, she withdraws from the usual cycle. The love groups (Dorotea/Fernando; Luscinda/Cardenio) drive towards a completion, because they choose to follow the conventional mores of life.

The link with the novel is Don Quijote, who is interested in hearing about this tale of tragic love where a character ends his life outside of the strict Catholic morality against suicide. Don Quijote identifies with Marcela because he shares with her the passion for love. Marcela could be Dulcinea, and therefore Don Quijote feels himself involved. Just as Don Quijote would do whatever he could to preserve his love for Dulcinea, so Marcela does—but in reverse. She pushes for an all-out withdrawal in the name of her independence. Essentially, she is exercising her wish *not* to love. This is another point of contact between Don Quijote and Marcela. In fact, both are examples of existential choice.

There is another reason for this tragic dénouement. One of the basic keys of the book and quixotic behavior is as unexpected as an action involving two persons can be. All the social pressure is on Marcela to marry Grisóstomo and cure him of "mal de amores," and that is viewed as a reasonable ending to the episode; and even if it is not Grisóstomo, it could be someone else, but her journey in life is already charted in an essentialist pattern.

---

[18] See below the chapter on history, economics and social life in Spain of the time.

Part of the creative skill of Cervantes is to avoid neat, *prêt à porter* solutions. Cervantes plays with the expected, and just when the reader is ready to predict an outcome, Cervantes deceives the reader and does otherwise. When the reader expects Marcela to cure Grisóstomo's *mal de amores* and their situation resolved conventionally, Cervantes chooses the tragic solution because that too is a part of life. This resolution belongs to the pattern of diversity in human behavior and actions with which Cervantes works.

The resolution anticipates other tragic loves like that of Leandra and Vicente de la Roca that also surprises the reader who is expecting a continuity of life. The purpose of *Don Quijote* is to present human experience in all its diversity.

There is also the indirect text of Cervantes's own consciousness as a writer and a chronicler of human experience. Just as he insisted in the introduction of his *Novelas ejemplares*, he considered himself the first to narrate (*novelar*) in a form that went beyond the Boccaccesque. As the person acknowledged as the creator of the first modern novel, Cervantes is challenged by the conventional pastoral romance and the Greek romance. As with most of the narrative forms at his disposal, Cervantes sees through their shallowness and submits each to correction, i.e., he brings them up to form and date, up to his creative vision, which is to show how such genres as the pastoral romance and the love romance miss the mark, as far as being a barometer of human existence.[19] The novel, Cervantes suggests, should reflect as accurately as possible the everyday experiences of each person. And so, the episode of Grisóstomo and Marcela exists on many levels of Cervantes's consciousness as a writer and as an individual.

What can be considered a minor episode is that of Rocinante's itchiness for physical love. There is here the opportunity to see Cervantes as one of the precursors of what will become Freudian (or even Jungian) symbolism.

There is an undercurrent of sexuality in the work with several female characters being deceived, and the major thread of Don Quijote's chastity as a curious factor.

For García Lorca, the sexuality of his characters is embedded in his texts or overtly expressed. The horse in *La casa de Bernarda Alba* signifies the naked sexuality of Doña Bernarda's youngest daughter—the kicking the horse gives in the stable stall is an example of the power of the *id* as

---

[19] For more information on this subject see Finello, *The Pastoral Form*, 178-192.

indicative of the passion of the youngest daughter who wants to be free to love her sister's boyfriend. Rocinante's friskiness is a symbolic expression of Don Quijote's repression of physical passion, and as master of the horse, one can surmise that there is an extension of Don Quijote's libidinous repressed strivings on the horse. In this, Cervantes proves to be a precursor of sexual symbolism in literature, as he is in so many other ways. The kicking of the horse indicates that in preserving his chastity, Don Quijote is sublimating his normal sexual urgings. One can read this episode as one that also creates comic relief. Against the background of the love example of Grisóstomo and Marcela, the excited Don Quijote, who is saving himself for Dulcinea, must handle his own sexual urges, but cannot do so openly. But Cervantes is too aware of life to have his hero escape the kinds of stimuli that make Cervantes's characters move, so he transfers Don Quijote's reaction and response on to his horse. Symbolically, Don Quijote has sexual feelings and in spite of his devotion to Dulcinea he is a man of "carne y hueso," therefore the horse symbolizes Don Quijote's repressed passions. If, as Don Quijote says later, the life of knights-errant "está sujeta a mil peligros y desventuras" (65b), then one of these is physical passion. But had Don Quijote indulged this passion, then the basic decorum of his character would be flawed. The sense of Don Quijote's chastity will be retained throughout.

The first true example and test of Don Quijote's condition and his mission comes when he arrives at the inn (I, XVI, 67). From the point of view of the reader's expectation Don Quijote is mad, therefore what he does falls within the radius of such expectations. He interprets the inn as a castle, a swineherd as a character of the romances of knight-errantry, prostitutes at the doors of the inn as refined damsels. Here the consciousness of the character is intact. He does what we expect him to do. Cervantes also juxtaposes the opposite with what Don Quijote sees, i.e., the "real" model of the inn, plus characters. The reader is supposed to join the side of the "realists," and does, thinking that Don Quijote is mad. But Cervantes has in place a deconstructing mechanism. Each side goes through its acts. Don Quijote wishes to be dubbed a knight to make "official" his adoption of this new life, and the owner of the inn will do it, to the pleasure and humor of bystanders. But Cervantes obviously does not want either side to win decisively. People go along with the game but at the end the balance seems to go in favor of Don Quijote. Don Quijote moves on, does not pay for his stay, and the prostitutes feel uplifted by someone who treats them decently.

Typically, Cervantes does not approve of either position. But the fact that Don Quijote wins the approval and sympathy of the reader in spite of the fact that such a reader knows that Don Quijote is mad must be seen through the deliberate process of Cervantes who blurs the lines of distinction between the consciousness of the innkeeper and the consciousness of Don Quijote. At the heart of this contention is the question of truth. But suffice it to say that Cervantes is pleased to lead the reader and the characters through a maze which is like a never-ending arabesque. The play between author (Cervantes), narrator(s), characters and readers will continue throughout the book. At the end, the reader is left with a sensation of insecurity, but the instability of the character causes the reader to keep on even though there is no sure endpoint. In I, XIX, Don Quijote and Sancho come upon the *descamisados* and the dead body. The scene must be interpreted in a specular way. It is the kind of theater that Cervantes indulges in. It appears in several instances in his *Novelas ejemplares*.[20]

The scene is significant because it sparks in Don Quijote the *memento mori*.[21] The person in the litter is a sign of death. It must seem very appropriate because Don Quijote talks about his legacy but does not talk about death until the last chapter when he does die. The episode is accompanied by a "grey-ness" of tone, which intensifies its significance along the lines of a consideration of death.

This is one of the few moments when Cervantes succumbs to the demands of the Counter Reformation and its presence in literature and the arts in Spain from the middle of the sixteenth century to the seventeenth century: that literature must serve an exemplary function, using the model of death as the deterrent against sin and the loss of salvation. The atmosphere of the chapter is bleak and the subject matter uncomfortable. It possesses the same negative quality of some chapters of the second part. Don Quijote attacks some of the participants of this death parade. It would seem obvious that Don Quijote is made uncomfortable by the specter of death and therefore handles the anxiety in a violent way. The text says, "así que, muy a su salvo, Don Quijote los apaleó a todos, y les hizo dejar el sitio mal de su grado, porque todos pensaron que aquél no era hombre, sino

---

[20] See my works, *Cervantes's Novelas ejemplares: Between History and Creativity*, and *A Formalist Study of Cervantes's Novelas ejemplares*. See also my essay "La teatralidad en la prosa de *Don Quijote*."

[21] Such a thought is profoundly a part of the consciousness configuration.

diablo del infierno que les salía a quitar el cuerpo muerto que en la litera llevaban" (I, XIX, 82a).

A further example of the discomfort caused by the funeral parade is to be seen when Don Quijote says, "El daño estuvo, señor Bachiller Alonso López, en venir, como veníades, de noche, vestidos con aquellas sobrepellices, con las hachas encendidas, rezando, cubiertos de luto, que propiamente semejábades cosa mala y del otro mundo" (ibid, 82b).

It would have seemed strange that a work of that time would *not* have something like a *memento mori*, especially when one thinks of Tirso de Molina's *Don Juan Tenorio*, and Mateo Alemán's *Guzmán de Alfarache* and other works that were replete with religious symbolism and outright proselytizing. This episode can only be interpreted within the philosophical and religious consciousness of death and not a part of a plan of exemplarity.

The chapter of the galley slaves is one of the most quoted and anthologized parts of *Don Quijote*. Once again, Cervantes manipulates a situation where the side of realism and the side of fantasy are opposed. In this episode, Don Quijote is not just an observer, he is an active participant. The reader by now has become well acquainted with Don Quijote's tendency to behave in a way commensurate with his *proyecto vital*. A scene or a suggestion sparks that part of his mind that is compelled by this lifetime project to interpret things according to the dictates of his mission. The galley slaves are prisoners who have been found guilty of a crime; their punishment is to row in government galleys.

The spark that ignites Don Quijote's action is the expression "gente forzada del rey" (I, XXII, 96-97). The compass of Don Quijote's actions are linked to the concept of liberty and independence. Don Quijote could not imagine that the king would force these men to be galley slaves. The episode becomes the opportunity for Cervantes to exercise his consciousness of justice, and he does this through his character and in an ironic mode. Don Quijote believes in an ideal world, and his consciousness knows no other solution. And just like the situation with Andrés and Haldudo, he believes that he is serving his ambitions by reading only what he wants to read into this situation: that he will not tolerate any infraction of his code.

Unfortunately, the guards realize that Don Quijote is mad, and that is their reality. Cervantes puts tongue-in-cheek to have Don Quijote *think* [Emph. mine] that he has complied with the demands of his obligation as a knight-errant. Seen from a distance, we observe that what Cervantes has done is to have each party carry out its own reality principle, hence the conflictive nature of the two parties' perspectivism and carry them out to their conclusions. Don Quijote will become a criminal for interfering with the arrest of the prisoners. One could look at *Don Quijote* and define it as a series of expressions of which Don Quijote is the subject or the observer. We have witnessed already the string of these adventures. The fantasy principle is only partly fulfilled because although Don Quijote is satisfied that he has done his duty, that satisfaction is qualified by the attack of the very galley slaves who later stone him. Cervantes will do something here that is within the purview of his conception of his character and his world. When Don Quijote resolved the situation with Andrés, he marches off with the feeling that he has done something great. It is only later when Don Quijote chances upon Andrés that Andrés subjects Don Quijote to Andrés's own reality principle. At this moment, Cervantes indulges his consciousness: that nothing in life is determinedly black or white. Every act will have its undoing effect. Was Don Quijote successful? Certainly, in his view. Were the guards successful, thereby invalidating the reality principle? No.[22]

This episode is marked by a presence of several views or consciousnesses. At the end the reader is not sure which is the real principle, if there is such a thing. One could look at *Don Quijote* and define it as a series of adventures of which Don Quijote is the subject or the observer. We have already seen a string of these adventures.

The adventure dealing with Cardenio raises different questions. Cervantes bathes his creation in his own consciousness and to this he adds that of Don Quijote and Cardenio. Within the structure of *Don Quijote*, Cardenio affirms the importance of the metamorphic imperative either by choice (Don Quijote) or by any other means. Cardenio is afflicted with *mal de amores*. He withdraws from society in a form of acute depression because he believes that the woman he loves has married someone else. His

---

[22] Milan Kundera, in an extremely perceptive short essay on Cervantes, highlights the salient idea of ambiguity, which is a foundation piece of *Don Quijote*. He says: "In the absence of the Supreme Judge [God], the world suddenly appeared in its fearsome ambiguity; the single divine Truth decomposed into myriad relative truths parceled out by men...To take, with Cervantes, the world as ambiguity, to be obliged to face not a single absolute truth but a welter of contradictory truths (truths embodied in *imaginary selves* called characters), to have as one's only certainty the *wisdom of uncertainty* [Emph. in both cases Kundera's], requires no less courage" ("Legacy", 6-7).

withdrawal from society is not unlike that of Don Quijote himself and with the same social reaction.²³ When Don Quijote decides to be a knight-errant, people believe he has taken leave of his senses; likewise Cardenio retreats to the mountains and is looked upon as a madman. The reader understands that Don Quijote is mad, but there is something pleasant, affable, about him.²⁴ The picture that the Other has of Cardenio is of this rustic wild man jumping from rock to rock.

Cardenio tells his story, and since it deals with love, Don Quijote is very interested. The stories of this situation involve a second pair of lovers. These belong to the tradition of the star-crossed lovers and is another instance of how Cervantes is jousting with other forms of literature. But in this case there is a difference. The characters of this episode appear more authentically *de carne y hueso*, unlike the characters of the Ethiopian or Greek romance tradition, and just as Cervantes does with other narrative genres, his object is to show their triviality, inanity and their distance from real human situations.

Cardenio's story is that he fell in love with Luscinda, but unbeknown to him his "friend" Fernando takes a keen interest in Luscinda. Later the reader is told that Fernando has seduced a young woman named Dorotea. The two pairs of lovers will occupy the novel for several chapters.

The major themes of this episode are love, requited and unrequited. But Cervantes's approach is to give the reader other insights that link with themes proper to the basic novelistic structure of *Don Quijote*. Cardenio shows no courage regarding Fernando's treachery. There will be no murders in the name of honor here.²⁵

Part of the attraction to Cervantes of this situation is how he creates the adventures of each character. In the case of Cardenio Cervantes shows that Cardenio has no volition. He is playing peeping Tom to the marriage ceremony between Fernando and Luscinda; he merely watches. It would take a strong will to break in and demand that they desist because he considers Luscinda his. This is Cervantes's test of Cardenio as a person and Cardenio fails; Cardenio then departs for the mountains. Had he waited, he

---

²³ Avalle says, "En la Sierra Morena Cardenio funciona como una especie de alter ego de Don Quijote" (*Forma*, 168).
²⁴ One must per force quote Croce here. See his essay in *Cervantes Across the Centuries*.
²⁵ See below for observations regarding Basilio and Camacho.

would have seen that Luscinda faints before she assents to the marriage, and a letter is discovered on her person explaining why she does not want to marry Fernando. This is of course the modus operandi of the Greek romance.

When a beautiful young woman appears dressed as a man, the love situation is revealed. She is Dorotea, the country girl that Fernando has wronged. She comes dressed as a man to ward off any unwanted attentions if she were dressed as a woman.

Dorotea's case is different from Cardenio's and Luscinda's. In order to protect herself, before she succumbs to Fernando's passion, she makes him swear on an image of the Virgin that he will keep his word to marry her; but of course he does not fulfill his promise. This situation is best seen from a distance in which the reader can see what type of manipulation takes place. On the one hand he has two victims—Cardenio and Dorotea; one predator, Fernando; and one victim with a small amount of will—Luscinda.

There are several interesting connections to be revealed here. Cardenio is sincere in his love for Luscinda who, as it turns out, is at least sincere in some measure towards him, her faint being a half-way example of passive aggression.[26]

Typical also of the Greek romance, the writer must find a method of reconciling loose ends. Cervantes will examine the various intentions of the principals. In the case of Cardenio and Luscinda, the intention of each lover is to form a unity. Therefore they will join, even though, based on the literary tradition from which this episode derives, they simply cannot achieve their wishes easily.

In the case of Fernando and Dorotea, Cervantes also is guided by intentions, albeit intentions ruled by irony. Dorotea's intention is clear—she loves Fernando and gives up herself as proof of her love. Fernando feigns sincerity but what he does not know is that Cervantes creates an unscientific and typically un-rational situation. Because we are in the world of love and affect, there may not be room for very much rationality. Cervantes allows a popular commonplace solution to take place. According to popular belief,

---

[26] Cfr. Girard's opinion regarding the triangle model based on the mystery of human relations. These would apply here. See also his "*Askesis* for the sake of desire is an inevitable consequence of triangular desire. It can therefore be found in the work of all the novelists of that desire. It is present as early as Cervantes. Don Quijote does amorous penance after the fashion of Amadis" (158).

Fernando must marry her because he made a promise and, above all, it was made in the presence of a religious icon, thereby investing the promise with certain religious bases. We are not here in a world of lawyers and practitioners of sophistry. The resolution here is on a street-level, so to speak, plus an unstated intervention, a *Deus ex machina*. God or the Virgin must be acknowledged as the intercessor. Once again, a literary consideration enters into the discussion. In the case of Fernando and Dorotea, according to the standards of violation of the honor code, a death will take place. In his exemplary novel, *El celoso extremeño*, the *perulero* falls into a deathly faint when he sees his child bride lying next to Loaysa. The reader expects him to take a weapon, kill both or at least, Loaysa. But it does not happen. Cervantes's disposition against such violence is clear. The agèd, jealous lover dies from a stroke.

In this case, seen as an act of will, Dorotea comes searching for Fernando to force him to comply with his promise. It is an act of pure will, and the religious undercurrents of the promise made before the icon of the Virgin will hold sway. Dorotea wins out because of her will and the "assistance" of the Virgin.

Cervantes is conscious of the fact that in matters of the heart, reason does not always rule, and that in such matters there is a distinct possibility that all may end well, and, as we shall see later in other cases of love, things may come to a tragic end. But not here. Cervantes opts for balance and creative irony (the case of Fernando and Dorotea), solutions that are not unlike the kind one finds in an everyday context.[27]

Consciousness here means being aware of the primacy of love but also to be aware of its multifaceted effects and its unpredictability.

Cervantes attempts to give the reader an ample set of examples, beginning with his own imagined one with Dulcinea. There are other examples that we have touched upon here. But the last love story deals with the experience of Leandra and Vicente de la Roca.

Here Cervantes subjects the amorous romance (*la novela amorosa*) of the genre best represented by *Cárcel de amor* to a shocking end. As in other instances of the challenge to literary forms through his *Don Quijote*,

---

[27] Sullivan, referrring to J.J.Allen, says Allen was the " 'first to see that all of Cervantes's fictional world is governed by a single beneficent Providence that both rewards and punishes' " (55).

Cervantes will submit the chosen work to a breakdown, showing the triviality of the other forms and the immediacy of his own treatment, the very approach that makes *Don Quijote* a current and different narrative more in keeping with what one can experience in life. Vicente de la Roca, like Fernando before him deceives the beautiful Leandra by promising to marry her. This is a replay of the earlier Fernando/Dorotea model. In the Leandra/Vicente case, after convincing her of leaving her father's house, and after taking her father's wealth she gives Vicente the money. He later abandons her, and she returns in disgrace to her father's house.[28] The text reads: "El mismo día que pareció Leandra la desapareció su padre de nuestros ojos, y la llevó a encerrar en un monasterio de una villa que está aquí cerca, esperando que el tiempo gaste alguna parte de la mala opinión en que su hija se puso. Los pocos años de Leandra sirvieron de disculpa de su culpa, a lo menos, con aquellos que no les iba ningún interés en que ella fuese mala o buena; pero los que conocían su discreción y mucho entendimiento no atribuyeron a ignorancia su pecado, sino a su desenvoltura y a la natural inclinación de las mujeres, que, por la mayor parte, suele ser desatinada y malcompuesta" (I, LI, 251b-252a).

This story is the reversal of the "locos amores" by which a woman holds sway over the poor man, much in the manner of the "amour courtois" or the Petrarchan version of it. It is written with stark realism, pointing to the nefarious acts of Vicente and the weakness of any inexperienced woman in the face of the trickery of a duplicitious person like Vicente, which places Leandra in the same class as Dorotea.

In the earlier treatment of the theme using Fernando, Cervantes follows the solution of marriage as forgiving all infractions in the name of love; it ends happily. On the other hand, Leandra's story has a tragic ending. In more than one instance, things do not end happily, e.g., El curioso impertinente.

In order to avoid the pitfalls of the conventional sublimity of the love romance genre, Cervantes also frames the story in very contemporary customs, e.g., when a young lady is victimized in a love situation, the culprit can be killed and/or the young lady sent to a convent if she is pregnant. The important thing for the family is to save face and to take the evidence of her frivolity and/or innocence out of circulation, at least for a time (see "La fuerza de la sangre," of Cervantes's *Novelas ejemplares*).

---

[28] The motif of taking a father's goods is also in the Captive's story.

Beside the realistic treatment he gives to the episode, there is nothing out of the ordinary, none of the silliness of a lover tearing up a love note, placing it in a glass of water and drinking it, as in *Cárcel de amor*. Every detail is verifiable and justifiable in its severe truthfulness—a foolish young woman and a mean, manipulative man. The dénouement, besides being credible, represents Cervantes's wish to show how love works, and also what the results *can* be. It is a Cervantine template that there be happy solutions as well as tragic ones. Cervantes shows that life is an example of every kind of resolution. *Don Quijote* is an example of the vast mosaic that is life, an aspect of Boccaccio's thinking to which Cervantes may have responded. Cervantes is the chronicler of happy loves and tragic ones; no life can be without one or the other. The question of consciousness here is Cervantes's not Don Quijote's, although he is touched by the story, especially when compared with other love stories and calls for a more exact understanding of the tale. Without pointing to specific episodes and generalizing, it is obvious that in creating the novel and dealing with the theme of love, Cervantes could not but think about his own life in which there were happy moments and sad ones. Without falling into morbid silliness, Cervantes is filtering his own self and his own experiences into the substance of his novel. In this Cervantes is writing an existential work; but then what work does not emanate from a writer's interior life? This is the value of having readers see the myriad facets of love presented.

The end of the first part is filled with a mixture of humor and pathos. From the beginning the reader sees that there is an undertow in the work, a deconstructing element, an effort to force Don Quijote to his home, which is synonymous with sanity. The rationalization of his family is to protect Don Quijote by taking him off the roads and byways. But that is their wish, not Don Quijote's. Don Quijote is content to continue along in his mad way, but the act of forcing Don Quijote home is like crippling his *voluntad*, which is his own, and subverting his mission and *proyecto vital*. The negativizing forces in the work come to bear. Don Quijote is placed in a wagon, which is a type of cage. The significance of the episode becomes more and more evident at every step: convince Don Quijote to enter the cage.[29]

---

[29] Placing Don Quijote in a cage to return him to his home recalls methods of dealing with the insane in the Middle Ages and the Renaissance. See Foucault's interesting chapter, " The Great Confinement," pp. 38-64.

There is a further step to be considered. The antagonists of Don Quijote leave nothing up to the imagination of the reader. They arrange their arrival "adonde entraron en la mitad del día, que acertó ser Domingo, y la gente estaba toda en la plaza, por mitad de la cual atravesó el carro de Don Quijote" (I, LII, 256a). There is nothing funny about this episode. Up to this point the reader has been won over by Don Quijote, even when the reader sees the cracks in Don Quijote's person, as well as the rationalizations for his defeats and the strange way he bounces back from his failures. The reader accumulates a certain *simpatía* for him. The ending of the first part has no humor to it (see *infra*, Chap. VII). There is also nothing funny about being turned symbolically into an animal, and such a return also symbolizes a defeated person, just as it will be at the end of the second part, which closes the novel. Don Quijote is the child of Cervantes, just as he says in the prologue. The book is his child and Don Quijote is his child. Such an ending spares no one. If it is not seen as an example of *desengaño* (that is left to the second part), it must be momentarily seen as a painful, ironic ending to Don Quijote's mission, and in the sadness the regretful tension of the author who must not let his novel fall into a maudlin ending.

The power of suggestion can be very urgent, and Don Quijote's relationship toward Amadís de Gaula has a great deal to do with Don Quijote's consciousness. Above all, it has to do with constructing images. Don Quijote says, "que estoy por decir que con mis propios ojos vi a Amadís de Gaula, que era un hombre alto de cuerpo, blanco de rostro, bien puesto de barba, aunque negra, de vista entre blanda y rigurosa, corto de razones, tardo en airarse y presto en deponer la ira" (I, I, 237a). It is probable that Don Quijote may have read this description in the *Amadís*, but what interests us is the construction of Don Quijote's wishes. Amadís is also a creation. Both these characters grow out of Don Quijote's need to believe in a spiritual world. Both, if however superficially in the case of Don Quijote, are members of the world of knight-errantry. In psychology and parapsychology one can read of cases when by sheer will some things are claimed to have happened. It is not possible to think of Don Quijote without his *proyecto vital*, which is an extension of the world of knight-errantry. The process of creation has already taken place when the reader is introduced to him. The delusional world of such matters exists as a reality in Don Quijote's mind. It has a tangible aspect that Don Quijote believes in, but it exists solely in Don Quijote's mind. That is why he can speak about it with such conviction. It is perhaps misleading to use the terms "real" and "reality." The world of knight-errantry is just as tangible as someone else's contact with his/her house or room. This is why it is so difficult to deal intelligently with the topic of Amadís. He is a literary creation but his presence in *Don Quijote* goes well beyond a mere literary associative presence.[30] He is the foundation upon which Don Quijote has built his awareness of himself. On the one hand, Don Quijote inherits him from a literary tradition, but on the other he assumes a "human" presence because Don Quijote's mind makes the change, and it can assimilate non-real things into his consciousness.

Such is not to say that Amadís is a static presence in Don Quijote's imagined fantasies. Cervantes creates an ironic situation in which a twist of the sick mind can create positive happenings outside of Don Quijote's mind. Don Quijote frees Andrés who is being beaten; Don Quijote frees the galley slaves as inevitable extensions of his personal ideology. What he cannot see is how the figments of his imagination do not stand up in any consciousness outside his own. Therefore, to speak of consciousness in *Don Quijote* is to pursue a personal program of complete exclusivity. Amadís is a literary character who exists on paper for most people, but for Don Quijote Amadís comes off the page and assumes a life "de carne y hueso." It is there that one sees how the refractive process works in *Don Quijote*. You have a human being who is mentally disturbed in one way; you have a literary character; this literary character assumes a reality in the mind of the mentally disturbed person. This refractory process continues often linking one series of experiences with others so that the quality of the final product can be challenged as to its "healthy" integrity. That is why writing about *Don Quijote* is so difficult and because of this the composite elements are not all verifiable. When Don Quijote describes Amadís it is because he has built him up in his mind in such a way that he could not be more real, just as Dulcinea, another creation of his imagination, has assumed a "real" place in his mind.

---

[30] When speaking of Amadís and other literary figures, one should recall Avalle's basic point of view, which is built on the concept of *Don Quijote* as an example of art on various levels.

3
Consciousness, *Don Quijote* and the Muslim World

THE INTRODUCTION OF SANSÓN Carrasco is worthy of comment within the examination of consciousness in *Don Quijote*. Sansón is basically a *letrado*, a man of letters, unlike Don Quijote who considers himself a man of arms. Sansón holds a degree from Salamanca. Don Quijote often makes reference to himself as a lover and a soldier. Sansón belongs to the group of pen-wielders, thinkers following certain forms of thinking like philosophy and rhetoric. But these forms of thinking are alien to the rational-less world Cervantes has created. It is to be supposed that Cervantes is creating a situation in which the strength of the pen will combat the strength of bookish knowledge versus the strength of intuition and devotion to an intangible quest. Each one has its pros and cons, but within the discourse of *Don Quijote* it is very important. As it happens, Sansón Carrasco reverts to cheating and fakery with the use of masks and lying in his quest to return Don Quijote to his home.

The description of this episode within the purview of consciousness creates an open field of action. Sansón is sure that he can dissuade Don Quijote from continuing his mission. Sansón departs from a sense of sureness of the efficiency of his preparation. Don Quijote has no idea of this symbolic confrontation between reason and non-reason. Like all mentally disturbed people, Don Quijote cannot see beyond the claim that Sansón's lady-in-waiting is more beautiful than Dulcinea. This is a forbidden area for anyone to tread on.

When it comes to studying the question of "consciousness," especially applied to Cervantes's masterpiece, *Don Quijote*, the most important thing is to understand the whys and the wherefores of a person, in essence, his/her vital substance. The first character in the Captive's Tale (I, XXXIX-XLI) that we meet is the Captive's father. He spent his life as a soldier and blames some of his habits on the soldierly life. Reviewing his father's life is a function of one of the principal exercises of one's consciousness—memory. The Captive recalls all this in an autobiographical fashion, and the episode of the Captive is one of several such interpolated tales throughout the work. Later, his father decides to share his wealth with his sons before it disappears through his spendthriftiness.

Linking this with later episodes each son will follow the dictum of *iglesia o mar o casa real*, and each will contribute part of his inheritance to their father. The Captive begins with his father because it is a link in a chain of similar events. The Captive will opt for the soldierly life. His adventures as a soldier exemplify what we read in the chapter of the discourse on *armas y letras*. While some Christians are freed, he is captured and thus begins his epic as a captive going from one misadventure to another, subject to cruelties and abuse. He ends in a *baño* where the episodes with Zoraida begin. The Captive's life is one of the beginning in relative comfort, passing through subsequent stages of soldiering, battles, war, confinement, and later, freedom.

Zoraida represents another character that indicates a consciousness perhaps more complex than that of the Captive. Her life is wrapped in a series of ambiguities. She is Moslem but was raised by a Christian servant who converts her to Christianity. She is perhaps the greatest *conversa* of them all. She also initiates the relationship with the Captive and will follow Christian beliefs in her heart until the moment when she fully flees with her verbally accepted "husband" and reach Vélez Málaga to take up the Christian life completely.

An important character for our understanding of consciousness is Zoraida's father. In the beginning of the episode he is presented to us as a rich Moor, who has a beautiful daughter. Up to the episode in the garden, Zoraida's father does not suspect that she has been preparing for flight from him to a Christian culture. When her father is put aboard the boat as part of the escape strategy, he realizes the impossible as coming true: his daughter "defects" to Christian life. Such an experience shakes him to the core, and he attempts suicide by throwing himself in the water. He is saved by his caftan which, when inflated by the water, was big enough to be grasped by the hands on the boat. Where his daughter exhibits glee on achieving her goal of going to a Christian country, he exhibits his complete desperation at the thought of losing her. His consciousness is an exercise in despair, sadness, and bitterness; and this becomes the sign of his life. While Zoraida symbolizes an ambivalence of consciousness and personality, her father remains faithful to his Muslim life and principles.[1]

The *Renegado* is a character similar to Zoraida. He is an ambivalent person: a Christian who adopts the Muslim life, but not so much that he completely forgets his Christian background and becomes a key figure in the escape plan. His ambivalence allows him to penetrate both worlds: the world of the Moors and the world of the Captives. He is difficult to pin down because he has a chameleontic way of blending with the environment he is in. The *Renegado* is also the link between the Captive's wish for freedom and the Muslim world. He will also be the interpreter of the letters the Captive receives from Zoraida.

There are characters that are supernumeraries to the action but the principle ones I have mentioned represent the core-persons in the Captive's experiences.

Fundamental to this episode is history. All beings are subject to time, and history is the frame within which events occur. The tone of this part of the story is direct, with narration limited to general facts.

History is related to us in somewhat of a cold manner, but Cervantes has plotted to have the Captive be in the middle of this history. For readers of fiction, history in its most objective phase is less of interest than is human history. The presence of the fictionalized Captive passes through history as a humanizing force, not a cold, objective one. We see how history is an important force which draws to it persons of all kinds, and Cervantes apparently does not want to write a historical treatise but chooses, through the adventures of the Captive, to signal the place of humankind in history. Therefore, history as human response and endeavor is affirmed. Moreover, there is another feature of history that is important, and this is to show the inner, human content of history by recording all the steps, successes and failures of one or more persons that comprise that history.

The Captive goes to Flanders with the Duke of Alba and becomes an *alférez* [ensign] to Diego de Urbina. This occurs after the League against the Turks. There is the loss of the island of Cyprus. The Captive becomes a friend of don Juan de Austria. The Captive speaks of Lepanto: "Digo, en fin, que yo me hallé en aquella felicísima jornada, ya hecho capitán de

---

[1] See Auerbach, "For us Zoraida's behavior toward her father becomes a moral problem which we cannot help pondering; but Cervantes tells the story without giving a hint of his thoughts on the subject" (119).

infantería, a cuyo honroso cargo me subió mi buena suerte, más que mis merecimientos; y aquel día, que fué para la crisitiandad tan dichoso, porque en él se desengañó el mundo y todas las naciones del error en que estaban, creyendo que los turcos eran invencibles por la mar, en aquel día, digo, donde quedó el orgullo y soberbia otomana quebrantada, entre tantos venturosos como allí hubo (porqué más ventura tuvieron los cristianos que allí murieron que los que vivos y vencedores quedaron), yo sólo fui el desdichado; pues, en cambio de que pudiera esperar, si fuera en los romanos siglos, alguna naval corona, me vi aquella noche que siguió a tan famoso día con cadenas a los pies y esposas a las manos" (I, XXXIX, 195a).

This paean is one of the human and historical foundations of *Don Quijote*, and will be echoed later in the introduction of the second part when Cervantes responds to the charges of Avellaneda that Cervantes was old and crippled. The victory of Lepanto was one of the greatest moments of Spanish history and Cervantes, as transferred to the Captive, is proud to have been involved in it. It is a consciousness of pride and accomplishment on Cervantes's part.

The Captive is brought to Constantinople and in 1572 he is at the oars in Navarino. He did not have the opportunity to trap the Turkish armada and he credits heaven as having decreed punishment for the sins of Christianity and therefore was punished.

In the same year, don Alvaro de Bazán captures "La Presa," and Don Juan de Austria was a captain in Túnez. The same year Venice abandons the League, and two years later the loss of La Goleta takes place. This part ends with praise of the Emperor Charles V. Don Pedro de Aguilar, who was in prison, fled. He is an author, that is, a poet-soldier and his brother recites two poems while at the inn.

The Captive describes the return to Constantinople and the mining of La Goleta. He notes the death of Uchalí. Uchalí is another *Renegado*, a Calabrian turned Moor who will be remembered as having treated the captives well. He goes on to become the king of Algiers and a general. The Captive becomes a slave of Hazán Agá, a *Renegado veneciano*. The Captive goes to Algiers. He describes how there are two kinds of captive Christians: "de rescate y de almacén o concejo" [the king's as well as those belonging to private individuals and also what they call those of the *almacén*, which is to say the slaves of the municipality]. The next scene deals with Agi Morato who is the father of Zoraida and the development of the love and courtship motif.

If memory recalls experience lived, then history is the fabric in which experience is played out. Behind it all is another facet of consciousness—time. If one accepts the cynic's description of time: one damn thing after another, one sees that Cervantes was very perceptive about time. Time is the very warp and woof of experience. The Captive experience is a study in historical or heuristic time. Its history deals with events approximately in 1572. We advance to 1573 and 1574. Within this matrix of heuristic time we have examples of what is modernly called *durée*.[2] The Captive suffers through fifteen long days between contacts with Zoraida. In I, XLII, 42, fifteen days pass while the *Renegado* is buying the boat. The Captive trusts him to buy the boat. No indication is given as to the possibility that he might take the money and run, leaving the Captive and Zoraida behind. Zoraida's father is tied up and bound for two hours, which in terms of *le temps humain* could have been two days of terror and fear. Her father jumps in the water, is saved, and then there is a two-hour wait. Later after the father's plaint there is a further three-hour wait; the French ship which attacks them takes place at midday. They spend six days in Vélez Málaga.

Cervantes's perception is to develop human time within the blank of historical time. This process has been expertly developed by Claudio Guillén with reference to the third chapter of the *Lazarillo* when Lazarillo's hunger causes him to feel the painful slowness of the passage of time. Once Cervantes has established the Captive's presence in the prison of Algiers, he then proceeds to adapt human time to the enterprise of escape, when there are perils and dangers.[3]

To be conscious of time is to be conscious of one's mortality, and Cervantes understands this very well and reserves it as a background to all the action of *Don Quijote*.

It has been said that language forms one of the basic levels of consciousness. In keeping with Cervantes's wish to "humanize" experience within the bounds of language and to record the complexity of the human condition, he submits language to a process of ambivalence. The account of

---

[2] For further examples of *durée* see *infra*. Sieber also touches on this theme. Avalle also discusses *durée* (*Forma*, 185)
[3] Claudio Guillén's pathfinding article on *durée* in the *Lazarillo de Tormes* is a good example of the application of time-studies in literature, as is Hans Meyerhoff's *Time in Literature*.

the story is in Spanish but since a great part of the Captive's adventures occurs in Moorish lands, we observe the use of Arabic in the text (see below).[4]

The love note which Zoraida writes to the Captive is in Arabic, and he is urged to find someone to translate it for him.[5] For students of Cervantes and *Don Quijote*, there is throughout the book the search for an objective truth, a quest, and to judge from Cervantes's handling of it, it will end in frustration and failure. The fact is that throughout the work we see that there are no objective rational truths, and here in the Captive's experiences language becomes yet another chess piece in dealing with the theme. In the Captive's account, the treatment is ironic and coyly tempting. We do not know if the Turncoat who will translate the letter can do it well or not or that he might distort the message to serve his own needs and purposes. She sends other notes (in Arabic) to further her wish to marry the Captive, and these must go through the thorny process of translation and interpretation.

Cervantes turns to this question in several instances during the Captive episode. Arabic words are used in names. The female protagonist is Zoraida/María, thereby reinforcing the vision of the ambivalence that prefaces the work. The Virgin Mary is referred to as Lela Marién who is also referred to us as Nuestra Señora, la Virgen María. Cervantes cloaks his characters linguistically in a dual world. Characters move about amidst the signposts of different languages and signifiers which straddle the often blurred lines that comprise knowledge. Uchalí is known as Uchalí Fartax, el renegado tiñoso'; *jumá*, means 'Friday'; there are three types of Moors in Spain: *"tagarinos,"* the Moors of Aragón; *"mudéjares,"* from Granada; the *"mudéjares"* in Fez are called *"elches."* The double use of similar or equal terms are examples of tolerance (e.g., reference is made to *Alá* and to *Dios*, that is, the Christian God); characters who are different and speak different languages are put on the same plane: Lela Marién and Nuestra Señora la Virgen María; "Támxixi significa ¿Váste?" [do you go?], and "Amexi,

---

[4] Paul Julian Smith notes, "This stress on material specificity is particularly true of language. Much has been written on Cervantes's insertion of (sometimes inaccurate) Arabic words and phrases in his Castilian text. These serve to some extent as 'reality effects': It is their very superfluidity to the development of the narrative that lends them the appearance of direct testimony to the real" (*Quixotic Desire*, 232).

[5] For more precise information on Zoraida the reader should consult Márquez Villanueva's *Personajes*, 77-140 and on Ricote, 229-335.

Cristiano" means "Vete, Cristiano," [go away Christian]; reference to Mahoma and Alá in Zoraida's father's lament; Cava Rumia, "la mala mujer cristiana'; the use of the word *gilecuelco*, which means the 'caftan of the Captive'. (I, XL, 211b)

The Captive speaks to Zoraida's father in a kind of dialect or *patois* that captives learn, which displays the delicate balance between enunciation and meaning.[6]

In sum, in creating this aventure of the Captive, which is filled with historical and personal contemporaneity, Cervantes is appealing to the reading public, some of whom had undergone experiences similar to those that Cervantes's Captive underwent; who might also recall what it was like to be in a situation in which you could not understand or be understood.

There are a number of other consciousness devices that we see at work in the Captive episode. We have mentioned the importance of memory. Memory is what allows us to encapsulate our experiences. By means of memory we make our connections to the past through our positioning in the present. Memory not only affirms our existence in the past but also our presentness, our "in-the-world-at-the-momentness." It is a sure anchor in reality because the present is measured up to the past, and this "in-the-momentness" is also the affirmation of one's being in a place (Spain or Algiers) at a critical time politically (the reigns of Charles V and Philip II). Not only are we creatures and subjects of philosophical speculation and discourse, we are also products of a history and politics. The Captive would not have a particularly interesting dimension were his existential experience not tied to a politics. It is the experience of a Spaniard that is a part of the expansion of the political ambitions of the Habsburgs. While the experience of captivity could have happened in the Middle Ages, it is the link the author, Cervantes, has with the historical events he describes. It is Cervantes's articulation of his life experiences filtered through a fictional character whom he creates to function fictionally in his place in the world.

---

[6] Authorities of Arabic note that this is not the best Arabic, which should not surprise readers of Cervantes. Cervantes's only preoccupation is in spinning a good yarn. The Arabic does not have to be perfect, because people that will be reading this part of *Don Quijote* probably do not know Arabic. It sounds more like the foreign language that soldiers going to other parts of the world learn, a kind of G.I. argot. See also Antonio Medina Molera's book, *Don Quijote e Islam*, as well as María Garcés's work.

Yet, a feature of selfness and consciousness is the question of existential choice. All the sons will choose a way of life. The Captive, modeling himself perhaps on the early experiences of his father's life, chooses the life of soldiering. It is a choice made freely in a particular existential way; it is one which he extols but in which he suffers as a Captive and runs the risk of losing his life when he attempts to escape. Choice is the key to living: in the case of the Captive as it is for Don Quijote himself, choice is an affirmation of selfhood, and in the existential paradigm one must accept all the consequences of choice as part of life's experiences. Allied to this question is a further point. There is a moment where the Captive does not want to tell his father about his experiences, who surely must view them as a failure, with him having been taken a captive and having gone through a series of humiliating experiences. His reluctance to inform his father emphasizes the often crushing human dimensions of his living. Consciousness is an awareness not only of one's "in-the-momentness" but the *how* of one's condition.

One of the most important pinions of the Captive's experience is that of freedom, *libertad*. This theme of course is strongly underscored in the Marcela episode and the parody of the question of freedom in the galley slaves episode.

The wish to return to Spain is accentuated when the Captive observes that while most are left free, he is captured, thereby heightening living with this aspect of existence. The Captive will ultimately obtain his wish for freedom when the escape is successfully carried out. There is an important detail which we must observe in this episode and as it appears in several of Cervantes's *Exemplary Novels*: the detail of money, gold, jewels, and other priceable items.

Part of the configuration of consciousness deals with those things which link us to reality, and here in the Captive experience it is a social and political experience. The 16th and 17th centuries are filled with pecuniary concerns. Gold and silver from the Indies, money to be repaid by Spain to Italian and Swiss bankers, precious cargo aboard the Spanish and Portuguese ships that ply their trade from the Indies, in the Mediterranean basin, and from Portuguese India. Freud would say that money, its handling and treatment, is a link with reality. Keeping this in mind, one can see just how strong a presence money has in this episode. The Captive's father realizes that he could easily lose his patrimony foolishly and so, with a strong wish to leave something to his sons, decides to give it to them before he dies, highlighting his common sense and generosity, and equally his sons' generous response to their father's kind act by each giving a part of their inheritance back to their father lest he be left impecunious.

The wealth of North Africa is evoked through mention of Agi Morato's life. He is a rich man, and his daughter will eventually inherit his wealth. But there are certain ironies to be observed. His daughter, Zoraida, clearly rejects her life as the daughter of a rich Moor in favor of Christianity and the Christian world. But she cleverly prepares a hedge against her loss of a dowry and other wealth.

Earlier she is described as wearing gold, pearls and other jewelry. In anticipation of the escape she brings with her a box full of valuable jewels and other monies. This will allow her and the Captive to establish themselves financially once they reach Spain. But ironically, this will not happen. A French ship from Rochelle overtakes the boat with the Captive, Zoraida, the *Renegado* and others, and in the midst of the attack, the jewel box is thrown overboard and is lost forever. One might repeat the phrase from *La Celestina,* "nuestro gozo en el pozo." I believe that this detail must be examined in the light of liberty, freedom of choice, consciousness, and irony.

Zoraida exerts her wish for freedom from her Arabic background by "marrying" verbally, of course, a Christian captive. There are two parts to this choice. In the first, she is willing to give everything up by choosing the Christian life. Again, within an existential and phenomenological perspective she is gambling with her choice. As it turns out, she will lose a very precious part of her life—her wealth. An old Italian saying is that one cannot have two paradises. She has lost the money but she still has freedom, and it has not been without some sacrifice and cost. The second phase of her choice deals with her father. Zoraida's choice to be a Christian means the rejection and abandonment of her family and her culture. It was possible that Cervantes was faced with highlighting her departure as a change of Gods, so to speak, and he could have had a smooth transition from one life to another. But he adds a human dimension that to me is crucial to his handling of this episode. It is true that since she was a child she wanted to be a Christian, and it is true that she falls in love with a handsome (one assumes) Christian who will be the means of achieving this end. But Cervantes shows that her choice is not one-sided; that is, he shows the full effects her choice has on her father in the scene on the boat in which daughter and father display their deepest emotions. The Captive states that after her father was fished out of the water, Zoraida cries bitter tears over her father: "hacía sobre él un tierno y doloroso llanto" (I, XLI, 209a). When her father regains his composure he says accusingly to her and her friends, "—¿Por qué pensáis, cristianos, que esta mala hembra huelga de que me deis libertad? ¿Pensáis que es por piedad que me tiene? No, por cierto, sino que lo hace por el estorbo que le dará mi presencia cuando quiera poner en ejecución sus malos deseos. Ni penséis que la ha movido a mudar religión entender ella que la vuestra a la nuestra se aventaja, sino el saber que en vuestra tierra se usa la deshonestidad más libremente que en la nuestra.

"Y volviéndose a Zoraida teniéndole yo y otro cristiano de entrambos brazos asido, porque algún desatino no hiciese, le dijo:

"¡Oh infame moza y mal aconsejada muchacha! ¿Adónde vas, ciega y desatinada, en poder destos perros, naturales enemigos nuestros? Maldita sea la hora en que yo te engendré, y malditos sean los regalos y deleites en que te he criado.

"Pero viendo yo que llevaba término de no acabar tan presto, di priesa a ponelle en tierra, y desde allí, a voces, prosiguió en sus maldiciones y lamentos, rogando a Mahoma rogase a Alá que nos destruyese, confundiese y acabase; y cuando, por habernos hecho a la vela, no podimos oír sus palabras, vimos sus obras, que eran arrancarse las barbas, mesarse los cabellos y arrastrarse por el suelo; mas una vez esforzó la voz de tal manera, que podimos entender qué decía:

"—¡Vuelve, amada hija, vuelve a tierra, que todo te lo perdono! Entrega a esos hombres ese dinero que ya es suyo, y vuelve a consolar a este triste padre tuyo, que en esta desierta arena dejará la vida, si tú le dejas!

"Todo lo cual escuchaba Zoraida, y todo lo sentía y lloraba, y no supo decirle ni respondelle palabra, sino:

"—Plega a Alá, padre mío, que Lela Marién, que ha sido la causa de que yo sea cristiana, ella te consuele en tu tristeza. Alá sabe bien que no pude hacer otra cosa de la que he hecho, y que estos cristianos no deben nada a mi voluntad, pues aunque quisiera no venir con ellos y quedarme en mi casa, me fuera imposible, según la priesa que me daba mi alma a poner por obra esta que a mi me parece tan buena, como tú, padre amado, la juzgas por mala" (I, XLI, 209b-210a).

In effect, Cervantes shows the reader that if Zoraida obtained her much sought-after freedom, she left behind her injured and grieving father in its wake. The emotions which rack the father are profound and reach the deepest confines of his consciousness.

This episode, which I consider of absolutely prime importance in the adventure of the Captive completes the picture of consciousness in *Don Quijote,* and gives us an excellent picture of the theme of consciousness in *Don Quijote.* How can we bring together all the threads we have isolated in the quest of the understanding of the Captive episode? Cervantes, firstly, shows us that reality is a commingling of diverse things, nothing is unifaceted, and this is why reality is presented to us in ambivalent terms. Secondly, life is seen as a mixture of positive things (love, most importantly) and negative ones (dread, disaster, sadness, tragedy).

What we see in the design of consciousness is the acknowledgment that life is a chancy experience. There are no guarantees or predetermined results, an intertextual inheritance from *La Celestina,* I suspect. It is a crapshoot, but there is always room for a positive result.

We look to *Don Quijote* for many things. But to me it remains the supreme example of the vital rendition of life in all of its human configurations. There are very few other works that reveal such an x-ray of life as does *Don Quijote,* and consciousness is one of the best means of understanding this facet of the work.

4
The Unending Quest for Truth and Objective Reality in *Don Quijote*

FROM THE BEGINNING OF the work, Cervantes teases the reader with ambiguities, especially when the reader tends to want to sink his/her teeth into facts.[1] Fact-seeking is an aspect of the rational world. But as we have seen, the mood and milieu of the work belong to the realm of "la razón de la sinrazón." The ambiguity begins with the character's name: "Quieren decir que tenía el sobrenombre de Quijada, o Quesada, que en esto hay alguna diferencia en los autores que deste caso escriben: aunque por conjeturas verisímiles se deja entender que se llamaba Quejana." (I, I, 19a).[2] A great deal has been said about Don Quijote's name but I do not recall anyone pointing out that he will be known in the work as a "nickname," an *apodo*. Then what is his real name? That is the part of the search for truth-undertaking. We simply do not know and will not know until the end when he takes the name of Alonso Quijano, el Bueno. Don Quijote's identity is involved in a number of possibilities, which makes the quest for precision and fact impossible. This too is a part of the search-for-truth game. This game consists largely in setting up a labyrinth that the reader must go through and at the end one is not sure that one will ascertain what the truth is about this or that idea. Basically, Cervantes has created a character that does not belong to his own time and space and is a literary character that

---

[1] For a development of this theme, the interested reader should consult Manuel Durán's book, as well as the observations of Milan Kundera. Of basic importance to this theme is Ortega y Gasset's *Meditaciones* as well as Riley's *Life and Literature*.
[2] See the definition of the word "sobrenombre" in the *Diccionario general ilustrada*: "nombre que se añade a veces al apellido para distinguir a dos personas que tienen el mismo: *Plinio el viejo* para distinguirlo del joven."

has been made to wander in and out of another literary environment.

The confusion over his name is followed by his food regime which turns out to be common everyday food, but even there one sees that Cervantes has created further ambiguities: some food is known in some places by one name and another in other places. We have before us a true labyrinthine novelistic situation.

Since the narrator speaks about the importance of the truth, it begs our attention when we note that once again from the beginning there is a further confusion by referring to different authors: "Autores hay que dicen que la primera aventura que le vino fue la del Puerto Lápice" (I, II, 22b). If the foundation of the book is the understanding of consciousness in human affairs, as I believe it is, the second most important theme is the search for objective truth. But the reader starts out on a slippery slope by being unable to authenticate the main character and the confusion about there being different authors, each one, presumably with his/her own point of view, and even the precise area that he harks from.

In Don Quijote's experience at the inn, the people there are taken by the language he uses, which is the language of the fifteenth century. When Don Quijote says, "—Acorredme, señora mía, en esta primera afrenta que a este vuestro avasallado pecho se le ofrece: no me desfallezca en este primero trance vuestro favor y amparo" (I, III, 26a). Such language also creates a boundary between the central character and the other characters, as well as the reader(s). One can suppose that this difference is a distancing device to keep the reader off balance, as well as to accentuate the difference between Don Quijote and others in diction.

The experience with Andrés and Haldudo also give us an ironic sense of the truth. In its refracted dimension there is a truth for Don Quijote, which is that he is fulfilling his duty of a knight-errant; there is also the truth of Andrés and Haldudo: once Don Quijote leaves the scene, Haldudo beats the boy severely. These two positions are later resolved when Don Quijote meets Andrés who later urges Don Quijote never to intervene in his favor ever again. If this episode, with its Hegelian equation signifies anything with regard to the truth, it may be that each person can live with the impression of having done the right thing without realizing that there may be another view of the same event(s). Whether they are ever resolved is something else. What is important, at least, for the sense and meaning of the novel, is that there are temporary truths rather than absolute ones, and in the end there are no absolute truths. This meshes well with my view that

Cervantes has created a novel in which everything is in constant flux.[3]

The writing of a novel signifies many things. One of these is that the author is a progenitor, a father of everything and everyone in the novel.[4] There is a powerful messianic temptation on the part of the author. In I, VI, at the book-burning incident the "inquisitors" come across "*La Galatea*, de Miguel de Cervantes—dijo el Barbero—Muchos años ha que es grande amigo mío ese Cervantes, y sé que es más versado en desdichas que en versos. Su libro tiene algo de buena invención; propone algo, y no concluye nada: es menester esperar la segunda parte que promete; quizá con la enmienda alcanzará del todo la misericordia que ahora se le niega; y entretanto que esto se ve, tenedle recluso en vuestra posada" (I, VI, 36b). One can imagine with what puckishness and self-satisfaction Cervantes writes these words. But Cervantes becomes the judge of Cervantes in this first example of authorial self-consciousness, the *mis en abîme* for which *Don Quijote* is credited with starting in modern literature. One of the problems of autobiography (i.e., authorial self-consciousness) is that the author, as any reader of *Lazarillo de Tormes* can say, can create his own life, *regardless* of the truth. Lázaro presents his father as one of the faithful, his wife as an honorable woman. It is within the power of the author to toy with truth and reality. In terms of *Don Quijote*, with its stated purpose of writing nothing but the truth, the reader is left wondering if Cervantes is giving himself short shrift by looking upon himself as stated above, especially the negative parts, or is it simply a case of false modesty? At any rate, the degree of truth that this conveys may be very variable, and in a world that claims and defines things through the filter of truth, one has reason to question any such games that authors can play, in much the same way as anything an author conjures up may or may not have any link with truth and reality.

Don Quijote's promise to give Sancho an island to govern is also part of the discourse of truth, and it is done to contrast and compare aspects of Don Quijote's own *proyecto vital*, but an island is more tangible than doing acts in the name of a non-existent person (Dulcinea). Just as Sancho hungers after an island, Don Quijote hungers for completion of his mission. Don

---

[3] The basis for this is to be found in the phrase Don Quijote utters when he crashes into the windmills, everything being in "continua mudanza."
[4] In this regard Castro says "En algún caso, el héroe mismo cervantino es, por decir así, quien se tira de los pies. Cervantes hace entonces como el prestigitador que descubre su ardid" (*Pensamiento*, 39).

Quijote's mission is wrapped as we have seen in irony. Being governor of an island is just as elusive for Sancho as Don Quijote's mission is for him. While it is obvious that Sancho has none of the requirements to be a governor, still he is attracted to the idea. It is all a joke, and no attention is paid to the question of ability. Another similarity is that the governorship and the island both do not exist, except as a joke.

As we can see, Cervantes continues throughout the narrative to show that in spite of small differences most people can be attracted to things that do not exist. When one multiplies Sancho and Don Quijote by an infinite number of possibilities, we are in the greater world at large. Apparently, Cervantes has a strong belief in the ability of people "to build castles in the air," no matter how intangible these wishes are. Therefore, the place of truth within that scheme is that much of what is done in jest (Sancho) and seriousness (Don Quijote) is illusory. When revealed publicly it can show how stupid or crazy that person is who has odd strivings that are subject to the denigration of others, and that they are as alive for the individual person as any other striving a person can have. In other words, there are no truths. Truth is relative to individuals but in the maelstrom of multiple strivings one can see that the individual is faced with the grim possibility that we are all crazy and striving after dubious aims. The continuous commentary in the book about Don Quijote's *proyecto vital* and Sancho's wish for an island kingdom shows that Cervantes is constantly testing his theory that we, the readers, and the other characters are really no better than Sancho with his strivings and Don Quijote with his. Basically, there are no objective truths. Related to the matter of Sancho's wish for the island is the experience with the windmills (I, VIII).

Since I have commented on this episode elsewhere in this study, I shall be brief. The basis of the episode also deals with the question of truth. Truth is like consciousness. If people are constantly subjected to minute changes in life, then what does that tell us about truth? Is there such a thing as "a little bit of truth"? Beneath the cover of humor is the usual Cervantine wisdom about life. If the rules of the game are constantly in flux, how can one play? How can one be sure of what they are seeking? No matter how important or meaningful the goal is, so many different variables exist so as to deconstruct the very meaning and value of the quest. Cervantes created an ambience in which there is much activity, but which remains contained within this ambiance. Quite aside from some editorial commentary about values, the windmills' episode is more than a problem of perspectivism. It becomes a problem of critical reality and truth. All the perspectivism occurs within the head of Don Quijote and does not ever step out of his inner fantasy world. What is important is the activity that results from putting his fantasy into play, and that is usually humoristic and sometimes cruel. While the windmills episode is largely the basis of the Don Quijotesque quest, its content, the active requirements of the search are strongly tied to the question of truth and reality. Whatever truth there is in Don Quijote's truth, and since there are multiple truths about the same object, one can conclude that in the presence of some truths and potential truths, there can be no truth as such, especially when one concentrates on the phrase "continuas mudanzas" (I, VII, 40a).

When Don Quijote battles the Basque gentleman in what can be read as an authentic fight, the manuscript ends abruptly. The narrator takes control of the text. The matter of the battle with the Basque and the experiences that precede it are credible. The fact that Don Quijote gets beaten makes the narrative all the more credible, and the question of truth will be tested again. Cervantes's puckishness enters into the text as he has the narrator describe how another manuscript was accidentally found which independently picks up exactly where the earlier one ended. It is not necessary to comment here except to say that such luck is the subject of literature and not life. Cervantes probably was thinking of the kind of incredible experiences of the books of chivalry. Indeed, if this is what Cervantes is doing, he is submitting the adventures of some books to a strict examination of what happens in life.[5] The coincidence of finding another manuscript precisely at the right moment where the first one ended causes the reader to smile because such a thing is nearly impossible. But since Cervantes is in the business of examining things from multiple perspectives, the reader goes along with him, sensing the impossibility of such a thing happening. Cervantes has a number of purposes with this escapade. He shows that Don Quijote is not a coward but someone ready to do battle. He also calls attention to the continuity of the narrative by creating a pause to it. The

---

[5] See Castro, "El agente humano maneja la literatura desde y para sus finalidades expresivas, y partiendo de la posición que ocupa en su propia vida. Cuando la literatura hace sólo con previa literatura, entonces vale muy poco, o nada" (*Conflictiva*, 41). See also Avalle, "Lo que el hombre imagina, sueña o piensa, ¿es verdad? Y al no poder ser verdad empírica, entonces ¿*qué tipo* de verdad será" [Emph. his] (*Forma*, 180).

authenticity of the fight is to show that Don Quijote is ready to fight for his ideas; that is not the thinking of a crazy man. It appears to be a definite touch of reality in the midst of a thoroughly unreal situation. Don Quijote's determination to fight the battle is a note of truth conceded to him. But the substance of the gimmick (finding another manuscript that picks up where the previous one ended), is thoroughly incredible.

Further comments on the truth question of the manuscript deals with the fact that the author of the second manuscript is an Arab, Cide Hamete Benegeli, and Arabs, we are reminded, are liars. This item deliberately puts the whole literary enterprise within the confines of absurdity. The adventures of Don Quijote would be a waste of time. However, we concede to Cervantes the privilege of including this item (the mendacity of Arabs) in the work. No one will give serious credence to it. Once it is stated, it is quickly forgotten. However, for the critic, it becomes an important datum for the question of truth. Does the fact that a conventionally-lying Arab denies the value of the book? Or is Cervantes indicating that no kind of literature, including his own, can be trusted? He shows in a number of ways that certain kinds of literature (picaresque romances, the pastoral, etc.) cannot be used as a gauge to what life's experience is. Is Don Quijote just another false character and life? Or, does Cervantes mean by lying that some things will be understood as being fabrications? Be that what it may, the belief that Arabs are liars taints the novel and positions it toward a negative and devaluating situation. Ultimately, in spite of any caveats about the mixture of fact and fancy, the story is read as a "truthful" fiction, and probably has more to do with the problem of history and poetry. *Don Quijote* as we know it has more to do with poetry, i.e., fiction. It may use the word "truth" in opposition to history, which is based on fact, but *Don Quijote* is pure invention, even when Cervantes is redoing known genres. To have suggested that the manuscript of the adventures of Don Quijote are the product of lies would be to misunderstand the work, that I can only look upon it as a passing gesture of Cervantes, even though he uses Don Quijote to signify serious things. What can be read into the supposed mendacity of Arabs is that one must as a policy not believe everything one reads; that authors are prone to making additions and alterations, thereby proving my belief that there is no such thing as absolute anything.

There are other examples of perspectivism: seeing an inn as a castle; mistaking sheep for armies. The mechanics of the galley slaves incident is the same as that of Andrés, with the same ironic truths at the end of each episode.

When the reader comes across the chapters dealing with Cardenio, the search for perspectivism and truth is taken up again, as does the letter to Dulcinea touch upon other issues relating to truth. She must get someone to transcribe the letter, a detail which will later surface in the episode of the Captive. Will there be intact a "true" message if the letter passes through different hands? The suggestion is that it may not be like the original; each hand can add, change, or delete at will, supplying credible reasons for the changes. The fact that the perspectivism is aimed at the idea that what exists are partial viewpoints, not absolute ones. Even if you add them together, the nature of humankind is such that you cannot get one point of view. Cervantes must be suggesting that each perspective is equal to another, but he does not do that. He is simply suggesting that there are multiple renditions of truth and reality, like a single light that is refracted into many minute strands.

In terms of truth, the complicated situation of the loves between Luscinda/Cardenio, Dorotea/Fernando are also commentaries on truth. Each couple challenges accepted notions of human action and reaction. It is untrue that Luscinda marries Fernando. Cervantes has Cardenio leave before he sees the dénouement. Cardenio accepts the visual steps in the marriage process as true, but as in other episodes, a character bases an opinion on an incomplete understanding of facts (i.e., truths), so just like Cardenio, one reacts correspondingly in an "untruthful" way.

In the case of Dorotea and Fernando, there is a further treatment and extension of the truth polemic. Dorotea's claims on being married to Fernando are based on some tenuous claims "in reality." She saw to it that Fernando swore before the icon of the Virgin that he would marry her after they made love together, and her claim that Fernando cannot be married to Luscinda is based on a flimsy claim. The Council of Trent abolished verbal marriage but Cervantes gives us an example of such things and bolsters it by giving it weight in the development, in spite of the doctrinal differences introduced by Trent. What Cervantes has prevail is a form of custom, i.e., saying something that has a popular tradition and saying it in front of a religious icon is invested with the quality of truth, in spite of the abolishment in Cervantes's time of such a custom. Which is the true marriage? one asks.

5
Cervantes's Don Quijote: Now You See it and Now You Don't

RECENTLY THERE WAS A survey of one hundred writers, and they were asked to list the best novels of all time, and on one hundred lists there appeared the name of Cervantes's *Don Quijote*. There must be a reason as to why there should be such unanimity regarding this work.

As Hispanists, we are trained to refer to *Don Quijote* as the best and most important work in the history of the Spanish language. Other cultures saw *Don Quijote* as a funny book; that is, belonging to the class of books, whose humor could touch everyone. There is, to be sure, a division between Hispanic critics and non-Hispanic ones. The former accept the primacy of *Don Quijote*, without necessarily understanding its genius; and the others have pigeon-holed the book in a series of clichés that might even spare the effort of reading the book; after all, it runs over a thousand pages in most editions. What are some of these clichés? The book presents the conflict between the real and the ideal with Don Quijote himself representing the thread of idealism running through the book, and Sancho representing the real. Another cliché is that the work is a satire of the romances of chivalry. To be sure, Don Quijote possesses all of these clichés in some measure, but the foundation of the work deals with the search for truth and the understanding of the conflictive nature of life. It is my opinion that Cervantes wrote his book so that it would be an encyclopedia of experience in life, all built around the mad Don Quijote and his fat and sassy squire, Sancho. Some critics, namely, Anthony Close, have even suggested it is merely a funny book that tickled the fancy of readers, and while it does not lack a seriousness of purpose, its main thrust is to make people laugh (see Russell *infra,* Chap. VII).

I have a totally different point of view. For me, Don Quijote is the greatest work of literature that depicts the conflictive aspects of life; not all laughs and not all tears, but something in between.

To develop my point I shall be analyzing several crucial episodes which I hope will allow us the luxury of having a key with which to unlock the secrets of the work.

The story is quite simple: a man of the lower nobility lives with his niece and the lady of the house, an *ama*. He has an ideal life, that is, seen from a particular perspective, since he shows no interest beyond eating, sleeping, going to mass and hunting. The only thing he does out of this routine is read the romances of chivalry. He loves the romances of chivalry, especially the language in which they are written with phrases like "la razón de la sinrazón que a mi razón se hace." Essentially, he is interested in the "reason of non-reason." This is the key that he is giving us with which we are to navigate around Don Quijote's literary world. This is a particularly astonishing notion because what rules philosophically in the Western world at that time is rationalism, the rationalism of Descartes, of Baruch Spinoza and others. Leaving us with this key, we shall have to accept many things, including some of those that do not correspond to rational life and thinking.

Don Quijote's reading habits concerning the romances of chivalry get out of hand, and the country nobleman loses his sanity. We know little or nothing about his life before he takes leave of his senses. He adopts the name Don Quijote of the Mancha in imitation of perhaps the greatest of the knight-errant heroes, Amadís of Gaul. Don Quijote develops a code of activity which involves assisting damsels in distress and the needy. When you examine his code of activity, you see that it is not something insignificant. It would test the mettle of a very brave man, yet the narrator always depicts Don Quijote's heroic deeds in a web of ridiculousness.

In order to carry out his *proyecto vital*, he needs the accouterments of a knight-errant: a horse, which turns out to be an anti-horse. In the attic he finds an old, rusty helmet whose strength and efficiency he tests by delivering a blow to it, and the helmet is broken in many pieces. He fixes it again a second time, and as he raises his sword to test it again, he hesitates and gives up the test. How do we understand that reluctance? Cervantes leaves us with the question about why Don Quijote does not try again. I believe that he is suggesting that not everything in reality needs to be tested; that some things are best left alone, so why test it? Anyone who sees a helmet will assume that it is sturdy. Here we see an example of visual reality, in favor of the subject. These two beginning keys will show the reader that what lies ahead will be very tricky indeed.

Still another episode, probably the most popular, is one that has coined an expression, "to tilt at windmills," will also tell us something about the experiences we are going to read about.

Don Quijote and Sancho are going about the plains of Montiel when Don Quijote is seized with an apparition. He sees monsters of the kind that routinely appear in the romances of chivalry, in which monsters, dragons and similar kinds of animals appeared and always in a negative light. Don Quijote decides to attack them and Sancho tells him that these are not monsters. Nevertheless, Don Quijote attacks the windmill/monster and is hit by one of the wings of the windmill. Don Quijote says, "—Calla, amigo Sancho—respondió Don Quijote—; que las cosas de la guerra, más que otras, están sujetas a continua mudanza; cuanto más que yo pienso, y es así verdad, que aquel sabio Frestón que me robó el aposento y los libros ha vuelto estos gigantes en molinos, por quitarme la gloria de su vencimiento; tales la enemistad que me tiene; más al cabo al cabo, han de poder poco sus malas artes contra la bondad de mi espada" (I, VIII, 40a,b). The important phrase "continua mudanza" refers to the subtle changes that occur in the contact with reality. Of course, one must rise above the literalness of the episode as it is narrated to understand what Cervantes is doing. Through a psychological quirk Don Quijote interprets reality through this *proyecto vital*, a lifetime project or lifetime commitment. That is to say that there is no reality outside of what one absolutely needs to see. But as is obvious, one man's lifetime project may not be that of another; hence the difference in the interpretation of reality by more than one person. At its simplest level, Don Quijote needs to see the windmills as monsters because otherwise he would not have a reason of being for his own existence. One can see Cervantes's reasoning. What kind of a world or existence would it be if everyone responded to his/her own lifetime project? It would be chaotic. But this is one of the keys to understanding what life's experience can be like. Not what it is like, but what it can be like. A good example of the consequences of carrying out one's lifetime commitment is to be seen in the experience following that of the windmills, the chapter dealing with the "gallardo vizcaíno" (chap. 9). Once again, Don Quijote's mind is receptive to certain external stimuli, which in turn cause him to react in a bizarre manner. After mistaking some friars for enchanters and the occupants of a carriage as princesses who are being held against their will, Don Quijote attacks the coach in order to rescue the supposedly kidnaped and enchanted damsels and enters into battle with a Basque gentleman. If the reader thinks that

Don Quijote's antics are just fun and games, he/she should be disabused of such a notion when, in pursuit of his ideal of assisting lost damsels, he receives an almost mortal blow on the shoulder, showing an important facet of pursuing one's lifetime ideal: that it is potentially very harmful. In this key and interesting chapter, Cervantes defines some of the limits of action that a knight-errant, of Don Quijote type, must undergo. It is not only an example of how a knight-errant behaves but also the pain he must suffer in the name of his lifetime commitment. The degree of one's commitment is measured in the length of tenure in one's commitment and for Don Quijote that commitment must be for a lifetime.

Naturally, the adoption of such a project has numerous risks. We have seen that one of them is to suffer physical blows as we just described. Another one deals with yet another aspect of the knight-errant's life. It should be understood that with Don Quijote's adoption of the mode of the fifteenth century, he is essentially alienated in his own time (even though no specific time is listed, the adventures of the Captive would place the action of the novel in the time of the battle of Lepanto and thereafter). Dressed as a fifteenth-century knight who has adopted a particular mode of dress and being, he becomes a joke in his own time. Another risk one runs when assuming this guise is that Don Quijote becomes a comic figure and this is best shown by his experience at the inn. There he is looked upon as a character and treated as a joke. The joking is not malicious (as it is in the second part at the palace of the Duke and Duchess). Here Cervantes practices the gentle art of irony. All look upon Don Quijote as a madman and agree to go along with the ritual of his being dubbed a knight. The subtlety of Cervantes's game is to show that when the innkeeper and his staff go along with the request of the mad Don Quijote, seen from an objective distance the perpetrators of the joke are no less mad than Don Quijote is. Again, the question is raised, how do we know who is mad and who is not, and how do we know if the reality we are witnessing is not a joke or a show that is being carried out, and how can we tell the difference? It certainly puts a special light on reality—is it or isn't it? Cervantes does not leave us with the answer to this and other questions. The reader must try to ferret out the truth but in doing so, also knows that one is never sure about the answer, because one person's answer is someone else's poison.

A unique episode of *Don Quijote* that touches upon the subject deals with an object—the helmet of Mambrino. Don Quijote sees a barber in the distance walking with an object on his head. Typically, following the dictates of his imagination he believes that it is the helmet of the knight-errant Mambrino. We have seen and we shall see how in viewing reality, Don Quijote will always see and interpret reality in terms of his lifetime commitment. For Don Quijote it is the golden helmet of Mambrino, and for Sancho it is nothing but a barber's basin, thereby confirming the idea that each person sees what that person needs to see. Sancho has no such elevated commitments.

Don Quijote makes off with the barber's basin and Sancho with the barber's pack saddle, which he rationalizes as the legitimate spoils of war, adopting for the moment his master's proclivity to move around in a warlike environment. By chance they come upon the barber again, who claims the basin as well as his pack saddle. There is a tug of war over whether the basin is a barber's basin or the golden helmet of Mambrino and whether the pack saddle is a pack saddle or a harness. Into the discussion comes the local barber who cites his experience in soldierly affairs that the object is certainly a helmet. He stands as a barber and a man of war and says, "—Señor barbero, o quien sois, sabed que yo también soy de vuestro oficio, y tengo más ha de veinte años carta de examen, y conozco muy bien de todos los instrumentos de la barbería, sin que le falte uno; y ni más ni menos fuí un tiempo en mi mocedad soldado, y sé también qué es yelmo, y qué es morrión, y celada de encaje, y otras cosas tocantes a la milicia, digo, a los géneros de armas de los soldados; y digo, salvo mejor parecer, remitiéndome siempre al mejor entendimiento, que esta pieza que está aquí adelante y que este buen señor tiene en las manos no sólo no es bacía de barbero, pero está tan lejos de serlo como está lejos lo blanco de lo negro y la verdad de la mentira" (226a), and to make matters even more confusing he adds the coda of "también digo que éste, aunque es yelmo, no es yelmo entero" (*ibid.*).

At this point one can reduce the essence of this object to a difference of opinion between the first barber and Don Quijote. But in order for the opinion of the second barber to be decisive, the matter is opened to those present who vote that it is indeed a helmet. Again, as in earlier episodes, Cervantes gives the reader an example deceptively simple but one which has great meaning when seen on a higher level, in spite of the fact that the people present decide to turn the matter into a joke and vote for the object being a helmet. Normally, one believes that matter is not easily misunderstood. A door is a door, a table a table, and so on. But when one sees the process as a symbolic one, one can easily see what pitfalls lay ahead, especially in a human context. Can you imagine what life would be like if everything were held up to a vote? That the very essence of matter could be seen as debatable rather than essentially fixed? That Cervantes has used this lighthearted but loaded episode to suggest that the notion of life as a fixed set of values or components is simply false. Life is a slippery slope that can confound, even deny, some of its basic assumptions, and it can all be decided by a vote of fools.

There is a series of episodes that enter very strongly into the consideration of the nature of reality and how reality is or is supposed to be perceived. The first of these is the interpolated novella of "El curioso impertinente". In my life and career as a student of Spanish literature, I recall that with one exception, whenever we came to this story, the instructor said, quite wrongly it turns out, "since this tale has nothing to do with the novel, we shall skip it." The fact is that when one examines the nature of this tale, one sees that it is fundamentally involved with the whole enterprise of the book, and is a basic part of the discourse on truth and reality.

The story is quite simple, and is of Italian origin, takes place in Florence, and belongs in part to the tradition of the two friends. Anselmo and Lotario are close friends, and at one point Anselmo marries Camila, a wonderful catch, who comes from a good family and is looked upon as a very fine and virtuous woman. Once they marry, the relationship between Anselmo and Lotario is lessened, and Anselmo and Camila set up house, with Lotario visiting discreetly.

At a certain point early in this marriage, Anselmo becomes obsessed with his wife's perfection. Is she as perfect a wife as he thinks? It reaches a critical point when Anselmo asks Lotario to assist him in this quest of ascertaining his wife's perfection, and to do this, he asks Lotario to test Camila's virtue. There is a certain amount of arguing about the feasibility of a friend doing this. Lotario is skeptical about Anselmo's request, and offers good reasons to abandon such a request. What Anselmo is asking is that his friend besmirch the honor of Camila. Lotario is well aware of the implications of loss of honor and urges Anselmo to abandon his strange, obsessive quest. But Anselmo is consumed with this wish to test his wife. Lotario tells him, "Mira, pues, ¡oh Anselmo!, al peligro que te pones en querer turbar el sosiego en que tu buena esposa vive: mira por cuán vana e impertinente curiosidad quieres revolver los humores que ahora están sosegados en el pecho de tu casta esposa" (I, XXXIII,164a). But to no avail. As a way out, Lotario agrees, but only in appearances. At first, Camila will pretend to fend off Lotario but then he realizes just how beautiful and perfect Camila really is. Lotario is beginning to fall in love with Camila, and he lets her know how he feels about her. She rebuffs him but he is too involved passionately to withdraw. Camila writes a note to her husband asking him to return to Florence because she does not know what to do regarding Lotario's attentions. On Anselmo's return Lotario continues with his attentions and desires with Camila, who tries to defend her honor as best she can. Unfortunately, she cannot defend herself and the text resounds with "Rindióse Camila; Camila se rindió" (168b). Essentially, Anselmo's question has been answered, but he won't know this because the lovers begin a series of melodramatic adventures in order to conceal the truth of the betrayal of Anselmo, and to allow the lovers to take advantage of Anselmo's erroneous confidence.

The lovers plot a melodramatic scene in which Camila will insist upon her virtue (thereby satisfying her husband's belief, such as it is, in her perfection and virtue) and in which Lotario's wish to help a friend in this bizarre experiment is verified. Camila, with the help of her servant Leonela prepare a scene in which, Anselmo, hiding behind a curtain, will witness the feigned virtue of his wife and the pretended efforts of his friend. Camila challenges Lotario and asks what if anything had she done to encourage him in his attempts at her virtue. Claiming vengeance on him she rushes toward him with a dagger and as he tries to disarm she stabs herself lightly in her shoulder and falls into a faint. "Estaban Leonela y Lotario suspensos y atónitos de tal suceso, y todavía dudaban de la verdad de aquel hecho viendo a Camila tendida en tierra y bañada en su sangre" (I, XXXIV, 175b). This part of the melodrama needs some comment. Piero Camporesi, in a number of works, speaks of the importance that blood held in society and what it means in terms of the critical sense of this episode. For one thing, blood tends to put a seal of certitude on any act. Blood, going back to the example of Jesus being beaten and crucified holds a very special value. Above all, the presence of blood in this highly contrived situation becomes the convincing touch for Anselmo. The text reads, "Atentísimo había estado Anselmo a escuchar y a ver representar la tragedia de la muerte de su honra; la cual con tan extraños y eficaces afectos la representaron los personajes della, que pareció que se habían transformado en la misma verdad de lo que fingían. Deseaba mucho la noche, y el tener lugar para salir de su casa, y ir a verse con su buen amigo Lotario congratulándose con él de la margarita preciosa que había hallado en el desengaño de la bondad de su esposa" (*ibid.*, 176ab). The concluding lines of the novella explain the results perfectly, "Con esto quedó Anselmo el hombre más sabrosamente engañado que pudo haber en el mundo" (*ibid.*, 176b).

What has Cervantes done here? He shows how appearances can be deceiving; how reality can be adulterated, and foolish individuals like Anselmo can be tricked so easily, thanks to the ingenuity of some bad people and the verifying force of blood. As we gaze at the reality we have before our eyes, how can we be sure of the truth of what we see? The answer is, we can never be completely sure of what we see, and this is the complicating factor of life, and lies at the foundation of the understanding of *Don Quijote*. I should like to shift to two other episodes that have some similar characteristics as the novella of "El curioso impertinente." I refer to the marriage of the rich Camacho (II, XX- XXI).

The projected marriage takes place in an idyllic pastoral setting. The chapter begins with a passage by Cervantes of the redolent of the poetry of Luis de Góngora's *Soledades*. In this episode, besides the beautiful setting, there is an abundance of food and wine, much to the pleasure of Sancho Panza. The description of the place of the marriage ceremony is particularly visual, and we shall see that this becomes just as important to this episode as it was for "El curioso impertinente." The stress of the episode depends upon visual effects and their corroboration through visual perception, including an accent on the chromatic features, since, as we shall see, color becomes fundamental to the dénouement of the story.

The marriage is between the wealthy Camacho and the beautiful Quiteria. In the middle of this bountiful and happy scene comes the young Basilio, also known as "El gallardo Basilio." He arrives on the scene and will become the specter at the feast. His arrival creates a momentary tension, since the outsider Basilio could easily represent a potential case of honor. Quiteria is, after all, about to be married to Camacho, and Basilio's arrival is particularly noted as he arrived tired and breathless. Basilio is also carrying a cane, which has a steel tip, and as he faces Quiteria he takes the cane, and places it on the ground and impales himself on it. The bleeding Basilio says, "—Bien sabes, desconocida Quiteria, que conforme a la santa ley que profesamos, que viviendo yo, tú no puedes tomar esposo: y juntamente no ignoras que por esperar yo que el tiempo y mi diligencia mejorasen los bienes de mi fortuna, no he querido dejar de guarder el decoro que a tu honra convenia; pero tú, echando a las espaldas todas las obligaciones que debes a mi buen deseo, quieres hacer señor de lo que es mío a otro, cuyas riquezas le sirven no sólo de mi buena fortuna, sino de bonísima ventura" (II, XXI, 343a).

Once again, blood becomes the verifying ingredient to this happening. On its face the Basilio episode is seemingly tragic, with a case of suicide over a lost love—an example of Cervantes's treatment of the love romance. The sympathy of some of the spectators clearly is leaning toward Basilio, especially Don Quijote. Basilio's last wish is for Quiteria to marry him in a deathbed marriage, and his wish is made more attractive by the fact that once Basilio dies, then Quiteria can still marry the wealthy Camacho. In his dying breaths Basilio uses a rhetoric and the diction of love: "—¡Oh Quiteria, que has venido a ser piadosa a tiempo cuanto tu piedad ha de server de cuchillo que me acabe de quitar la vida, pues ya no tengo fuerzas para llevar la gloria que me das en escogerme por tuyo, ni para suspender el dolor que tan apriesa me va cubriendo los ojos con la espantosa sombra de la muerte! Lo que te suplico es ¡oh fatal estrella mía! que la mano que me pides y quieres darme no sea por cumplimiento, ni para engañarme de nuevo, sino que confieses y digas que sin hacer fuerza a tu voluntad, me la entregas y me la das como a tu legítimo esposo; pues no es razón que en un trance como éste me engañes, ni uses de fingimientos con quien tantas verdades ha tratado contigo" (*ibid.*, 344a).

The other part of this love situation is Camacho, who, according to the customs regarding an affair of offended honor supposedly calls for his killing Basilio and even Quiteria.

This atmosphere of tension, fear and apprehension is broken by Sancho who is obviously the agent of practicality. He breaks the tension when he says after hearing Basilio speak, "—Para estar tan herido este mancebo—dijo a este punto Sancho Panza—, mucho habla; háganle que se deje de requiebros, y que atienda a su alma, que, a mi parecer, más la tiene en la lengua que en los dientes" (*ibid.*, 344b).[1] Sancho's intervention here represents a brusque invasion into the world of sentimentality that is prevailing since Basilio impaled himself. Behind Sancho one senses yet again the manipulation by Cervantes. No one witnessing the impalement scene questions the realism and the truthfulness of the happenings. The

---

[1] See Redondo for his comments regarding Sancho's perspicacity in the light of Basilio's prolixity (386).

episode grows in a step-by-step process. Once again, the convincing agent is the blood spilled, and is the same kind of blood that is spilled in the many honor plays of Lope de Vega, against whom certain facets of this episode are aimed. But here in this episode Cervantes reverses the probative value of blood.

As the spectators look upon the moribund Basilio, he leaps up athletically and to the claims of others that it is a miracle (they say, "—¡Milagro, milagro!) "Pero Basilio replicó: '—¡No milagro, milagro, sino industria, industria'" (*ibid.*, 344b). This sudden change of affairs goes beyond the limits of narration and depends greatly upon the surprise element which his ingenuity has created. Basilio's solution is as much a sham as it is inventive; it is an act of magic that wins over the spectators (except Sancho, of course) in accepting it as truth. Quite different from "El curioso impertinente" where one sees the Renaissance topos of "deceiving with the truth" here the spectators (and readers) are deceived by falseness, even if it gives the episode a serio-comic cast.[2]

Camacho is the victim of this gambit and he ends up watching the supposed suicide of Basilio and his subsequent marriage to Quiteria. The text reads, "Todo lo oía Camacho, y todo le tenía suspenso y confuso, sin saber qué hacer ni qué decir; pero las voces de los amigos de Basilio fueron tantas, pidiéndole que consintiese que Quiteria le diese la mano de esposa, porque su alma no se perdiese, partiendo desesperado desta vida, que le movieron, y aun forzaron, a decir que si Quiteria quería dársela, que él se contentaba, pues todo era dilatar por un momento el cumplimiento de sus deseos" (*ibid.*, 343b). There is a moment when swords are unsheathed and the reader prepares him/herself for the conventional violent resolution of a dishonor. But there is a change of attitude, "La esposa no dio muestras de pesarle de la burla; antes, oyendo decir que aquel casamiento, por haber sido engañoso, no habia de ser valedero, dijo que ella le confirmaba de nuevo; de lo cual coligieron todos que de consentimiento y sabiduria de los dos se habia trazado aquel caso; de lo que quedó Camacho y sus valedores tan corridos, que remitieron su venganza a las manos, y desenvainando muchas espadas, arremetieron a Basilio, en cuyo favor en un instante se desenvainaron casi otras tantas; y tomando la delantera a caballo Don Quijote, con la lanza sobre el brazo y bien cubierto de su escudo, se hacía

---

[2] Also see Redondo for his perceptive view of the "teatralidad" of this episode (385) as well as my essay "La teatralidad en la prosa de *Don Quijote.*"

dar lugar de todos" (*ibid.*, 344b). A most unusual way of settling differences.

The ingenuity of Basilio turns Camacho into a booby, who, on top of everything still ends up paying for the opulent wedding feast. He does not act in a way like a man whose honor is soiled, that is, at the ready for violence. In a way reminiscent of Mambrino's helmet, people rally to Basilio's side, asking Camacho to step aside and let him marry Quiteria, who happily and willingly accepts him as a husband. It was blood that added the clinching argument to Basilio's gambit. Just as in the case of "El curioso impertinente," the spectators believed what they saw. What kind of life, we ask, is it where everything you see cannot be completely believed?

I save for last in this series of events, the tragic history of Claudia Jerónima and Vicente Torrellas, which involves another situation punctuated by the shedding of blood (II, LX). In this episode Claudia Jerónima becomes enamored of Vicente, and he promises marriage to her, a situation which, barring some unforeseen changes, is looked upon as permanent as marriage, and with honor implications. The text reads, "yo soy Claudia Jerónima, hija de Simón Forte, tu singular amigo y enemigo particular de Clauquel Torrellas que asimismo lo es tuyo, para ser uno de los de tu contrario bando; y ya sabes que este Torrellas tiene un hijo que don Vicente Torrellas se llama, o, a lo menos, se llamaba no ha dos horas. Este, pues, por abreviar el cuento de mi desventura, te diré en breves palabras la que me ha causado. Vióme, requebróme, escuchéle, enamoréme a hurto de mi padre; porque no hay mujer, por retirada que esté y recatada que sea, a quien no le sobre tiempo para poner en ejecución y efecto sus atropellados deseos. Finalmente él me prometió de ser mi esposo, y yo le dí la palabra de ser suya, sin que en obras pasásemeos adelante" (485a). Later she learns that Vicente was going to be betrothed to a different woman that morning. She mounts a horse and catches up with Vicente and without any frills she shoots him, and she says, "le debí de encerrar más de dos balas en el cuerpo abriéndole puertas por donde envuelta en su sangre saliese mi honra" (485ab). Now she hopes that the bandit Roque Guinart can help her flee. Roque says, "—Ven, señora, y vamos a ver si es muerto tu enemigo; que después veremos lo que más te importare" (*ibid.*, 485b). The text continues, "Llegaron al lugar donde lo encontró Claudia, y no hallaron en él sino recién derramada sangre" (*ibid.*, 485b). When they reach the party that is transporting the bleeding Vicente: "Hallaron a don Vicente en los brazos de sus criados, a quien con cansada y debilitada voz rogaba que le dejasen allí morir, por que el dolor de las heridas no consentía que más adelante pasase" (*ibid.,* 485b-486a). Claudia reaches for Vicente's hand, and he says, "—Bien veo, hermosa y engañada señora, que tú has sido la que me has muerto, pena no merecida, ni debida a mis deseos, con los cuales, ni con mis obras, jamas quise ni supe ofenderte" (*ibid.,* 486a). It happened that she was falsely informed about Vicente. He was not going to be betrothed to another woman. As he lay dying, Vicente says, "No, por cierto—respondió don Vicente—mi mala fortuna te debió de llevar estas nuevas, para que, celosa, me quitases la vida; la cual pues la dejo en tus manos y en tus brazos, tengo mi suerte por venturosa. Y para asegurarte desta verdad aprieta la mano y recíbeme por esposo, si quisieres; que no tengo otra mayor satisfacción que darte del agravio que piensas que de mí has recibido" (*ibid.,* 486a). Does this plot sound similar? Think of Basilio who lies in his blood asking Quiteria to join him in a deathbed marriage. The text resumes, "Apretóle la mano Claudia, y apretósela a ella el corazón, de manera que sobre la sangre y pecho de don Vicente se quedó desmayada, y a él le tomó un mortal parasismo" (*ibid.,* 486a).

The reader of *Don Quijote,* by how accustomed to the tricks of prestidigitation, sits tensely awaiting a last minute change; perhaps to see Don Vicente leap up from his deathbed and cry that since Claudia was fooled by someone else's jealousy or malice, and especially since Vicente forgave her, they could marry, but alas, that does not happen. Vicente's death takes place and is permanent. And so Cervantes tricks the reader once again. He teases us right up to the last minute until the reader finally gives up another time, but this time in the opposite direction. If Cervantes were a baseball pitcher, he would tease the batter until he deceived him completely and throws the pitch that the batter never expected. Cervantes keeps us on tenterhooks as we await yet another slight of hand. We can surmise that for every happy ending there must be an unhappy one. The reader or the individual who sits and hopes and prays for a certain outcome may be granted his wish, but on the other hand it may not be granted. Miguel de Unamuno, the twentieth-century Spanish writer, novelist, poet, essayist, said that life resisted any and every attempt to control it, to dominate it, to predict with certainty its outcomes. This process of life charting its own course, regardless of the wishes and hopes of people, is what happened in these three episodes that involved blood; two are successful and one is not. At every step of the way Cervantes tricks those that await easy answers. Now you see it and now you don't.

I save for last a pair of experiences that show once again what kind of game Cervantes plays with the concept of reality and truth, that is, if there are such things.

In chapters twenty two and twenty three of the second part, we read of Don Quijote's experience in the descent to the cave of Montesinos.[3] The scene is set as if it were from a vampire film. Crows and bats emerge from this cave and Don Quijote wishes to descend into it, ignoring the advice of others of not trying to enter into something he knows nothing of—shades of the repairing of the helmet he makes at the beginning of the work and the curiosity of Anselmo. In spite of the well-meaning pleas of others, Don Quijote has a rope tied around his waist and is let down into the cave. As time passes, Don Quijote calls for more rope and more rope is given to him. A half hour later Don Quijote is pulled up and is found in a sleepy and drowsy state. Don Quijote explains that while he was down there he fell into a deep sleep and when he woke he saw a beautiful landscape, and then he relates how he encountered characters from the Carolingian ballad tradition. Don Quijote gives a very detailed description of all he saw, a true praise of the power of the imagination. As Don Quijote is narrating all this, the Cousin [*el primo*] a character in this moment of Don Quijote's adventures, begins to question some parts of his story. He finds it a bit difficult to swallow. How could he see so much in so little time? As far as Sancho is concerned, the time it took to descend and stay down in the cave was an hour at the most. Don Quijote disagrees; he insists that he was down there three days. Naturally Sancho titters at that. Don Quijote also says that he saw Dulcinea, the lady of his dreams, along with two country lasses, which

---

[3] For a useful critical overview of the episode of the Cave of Montesinos, see Sullivan's chapter, p. 31 *et seq*. Also see Wardropper's fundamental article "The Pertinence of the Curious Impertinent," *PMLA*, 1957, pp. 587-600. Avalle/Riley say, "Lo que Don Quijote ha soñado en el fondo de la cueva es, ni más ni menos, que el sentido de la vida" (59). See also Sullivan's interesting remark: "Throughout this study [Sullivan's book], I have systematically linked the Cave of Montesinos episode to the theme of pain. This is because I believe that the vein of cruelty and torment that readers since at least the eighteenth century have sensed running through the action of Part II, comes to the surface in grotesque guise in the text of the dream" (155). Sullivan also analyzes the episode as a dream (126). Sullivan notes the salting of Durandarte's heart and mention of Belerma's having ceased to menstruate as an example of modern science (43-44). Of course, Madariaga's *Introducción al Don Quijote* is a genesis of his question.

really makes Sancho laugh because Sancho invented a tale involving Dulcinea and the two country girls. Recall what I said about "la razón de la sinrazón," the reason of unreason at the beginning. I recall something that that master of prestidigitation, the Argentine writer, Jorge Luis Borges once related. At the beginning of his short story, "El milagro secreto" he cites a passage from the Koran II, 261: "Y Dios lo hizo morir durante cien años y luego lo animó y le dijo: —¿Cuánto tiempo has estado aquí? —Un día o parte de un día—respondió." Can we believe Don Quijote if Sancho and the Cousin calculated Don Quijote's descent according to chronological time and Don Quijote's calculation of it in terms of *durée*.[4] The matter is then dropped, but its spirit is picked up again in the episode of Sancho's flight on Clavileño (II, XLI).

Don Quijote and Sancho have regularly been subjected to pranks and practical jokes and to cruel humor, and this episode is one of them. A large wooden horse is built, and Sancho is told that he will ride the wooden horse to the skies, no doubt in imitation of Ariosto's *Orlando Furioso*. Fires are lit around the horse, and by means of bellows smoke is created while Sancho sits atop the horse, his eyes covered with a cloth. Sancho is made to think that he will travel through the various levels of the sky. At the supposed end of his flight, Sancho is told that it is finished and he is back on terra firma. Then he relates what he saw. He informs the people present that while he was up in the sky, he lifted the cloth that covered his eyes so he could get a good look at the sky. From his height, he tells us, he saw the world as a tiny mustard seed; men looked like hazelnuts. Then he dismounted lightly from his wooden horse and saw seven kids (goats) each of different colors. All those present are now tittering about Sancho's ingenuousness, his ignorance of what really happened. Quite satisfied with himself Sancho turns to Don Quijote who tells him, "—Sancho, pues vos queréis que se os crea lo que habéis visto en el cielo, yo quiero que vos me creáis a mí lo que vi en la cueva de Montesinos. Y no os digo más" (II, XLI, 417b).

---

[4] My view is that the game of time that is played here is the difference between Don Quijote's *durée* and Sancho and the Cousin's heuristic time. Redondo says, "En ese mundo, el tiempo es muy diferente del tiempo ordinario y profano, es un tiempo fuera del tiempo: por ello, nuestro héroe piensa haberse quedado tres días en la cuenta, mientras que le afirma que su estancia en ella ha durado poco más de una hora" (413). See also Sieber and Avalle, *Forma*, 184-185.

We examine reality again. We have seen that you cannot trust what you see and now we see that you cannot trust what you hear. We see that reality can be a product of the imagination, hardly what you would call facts or anything factual. The lesson of these episodes, which the reader comes to see as pure invention, CAN BE admitted into our consciousness and that in later stages may turn to fact, especially since there is only one witness in each.

Cervantes's object, I believe, is to give a wide view of human activity, very much in the manner of Boccaccio's *Decameron*. Concerning love, there is happy love: Lucinda and Cardenio (at the end). But there must also be tragic love; otherwise readers would be left with a mistaken or false impression of life's processes. This is why Cervantes puts under his philosophical microscope all the current narratives of his time: the picaresque romance, the Moorish tale, the romances of chivalry, the Greek romance, the Italianate novella. Cervantes rejects these forms of narration as purveyors of the sense of existence because they give a stilted or false view of life's experiences. He opts instead for a middle-aged man who undergoes a mid-life crisis, "man-o-pause," as some call it, who embarks on a career that most regard as sheer craziness and in the development of his experiences, often turns out to be saner than most people.

In all, we have seen how Cervantes charts the adventure of life in ironic tones. Living life becomes a dangerous proposition. If *Don Quijote* is an example of the search for reality and truth, which it is ostensibly, we must at the end of the book come to the conclusion that there is no such thing as objective reality and certainly there is no such thing as objective truth. It is very romantic to say that Don Quijote lives on, even though he dies at the end.

6
Cervantes and Consciousness: "Yo sé quién soy," El caballero de los leones, and Ricote el Morisco

AT THE END OF the first sally, Don Quijote fights with a peasant after Don Quijote recites ballads from the chivalric tradition. After hearing Don Quijote, the peasant helps him and says, "—Señor Quijana, — que así se debía llamar cuando él tenía juicio y no había pasado de hidalgo sosegado a caballero andante—, ¿quién ha puesto a vuestra merced de esta suerte? and "—Mire vuestra merced, señor, pecador de mí, que yo no soy Don Rodrigo de Narváez, ni el marqués de Mantua, sino Pedro Alonso, su vecino; ni vuestra merced es Valdovinos, ni Abindarráez, sino el honrado hidalgo del señor Quijana" (I, V, 31b-32a).

Don Quijote's answer is meaningful because he argues his identity. "—Yo sé quién soy—respondió Don Quijote—, y sé que puedo ser, no sólo los que he dicho, sino todos los Doce Pares de Francia y aun todos los nueve de la Fama, pues a todas las hazañas que ellos todos juntos y cada uno por sí hicieron se aventajarán las mías" (32a). What is he telling us? Is he really crazy or is he merely acting, putting on a show of madness? If the latter were true, we would have to revise many of our ideas on Don Quijote.[1] While he is being a knight-errant, Don Quijote functions on different levels. Since the episode happens at the end of the first sally, would Cervantes be giving us a clue to the composition of his work? One could fall into the temptation of thinking that there is no one Don Quijote but several ones. There is Don Quijote of "carne y hueso" and another one which is the sum

---

[1] The interested reader should consult Van Doren's *Don Quijote's Profession*, on this point.

of bookish influences,[2] including the one of being a literary character placed in the middle of a fictitious yet "real" literary world that Cervantes is creating. Don Quijote would like to silence the farmer who is seeing things solely from his own point of view. Don Quijote sees them from a multitude of points of view since he is a polyfacetic character who acts according to the particular character he is playing. In this episode, Don Quijote carries out the role of a character from the world of ballads; therefore it is perfectly permissible for him to talk in the manner of a knight-errant.

When Don Quijote defends himself one supposes that he has a good picture of who he is. His identity is formed in his mind. What is important about what Don Quijote says is the verb "puedo." With his identity securely fixed in his mind, Don Quijote is alerting the farmer and the rest of the people that he, Don Quijote, knows exactly what he is doing. One could think that when Don Quijote says this, he is feigning the role of knight-errant as if he were an actor. This represents a tempting hypothesis but not a correct one. The basis of the conduct of Don Quijote consists in this consciousness of knowing who he is. Is it possible to be a knight-errant and not be aware of what he does? Psychiatrists say that a madman does not know that he is insane. If one asks, "but, am I going mad?" He is sane.

The uniqueness of character of Don Quijote is that Cervantes commits the daring act of creating a character, Don Quijote, who is *a literary character* and Cervantes takes this literary character from another era and places him in the present time of the novel. This is an interesting invention. To put it another way, Don Quijote de la Mancha belongs to another entity and his author will have him live among persons of a different (in this case, later) time and space; that accounts for the strange reaction of people when they meet this man dressed as a knight from the fifteenth century, a figure completely outside of his own era as well as the time of others. Cervantes creates a literary world which is one entity and into that entity Cervantes drops a literary figure from another time. In this way, one could account for and see the peculiar invention of *Don Quijote* and its greatness and uniqueness.

When one sees *Don Quijote* in this manner I believe that many doubts and questions regarding the conduct of Don Quijote will disappear.

The already much commented upon *proyecto vital* of Don Quijote

---

[2] See both Avalle Arce, Riley and Gilman on the literary connections between *Don Quijote* and such literary traditions as the books of chivalry.

depends upon the intellectual and physical capacities that Don Quijote possesses. Were it not for this freedom of choice, Sr. Quijana, as he is described by his neighbor Pedro Alonso, he could not have become a knight-errant. "Yo sé quién soy," indicates that Don Quijote arrogates to himself the right to conceive of himself as a knight-errant in life and in literature.

One of the great finds of Cervantes is to have created a character who is not one-sided. In this way, Don Quijote becomes a "man for all seasons," a find of literary creativity. When we think about literary characters, we think of them in their wholeness, but like the good literary baroque writer that he is, Cervantes does not create for us a solidly whole character, but rather various characters at the same time. Such an explanation would answer those who think that Don Quijote is mentally sound and is kidding his fellow characters and readers.

I underscore this episode because consciousness signifies a *"toma de conciencia"* of a character who knows who he is and what he is made of. The above-mentioned episode shows that Don Quijote already knows that he is a knight-errant (in his imagination and in the only reality that he knows of himself).

In the first test of his new career in this lifetime project he learns such an enterprise is not going to be a gentle pastime and fun. The personal exertion which his lifetime project consists of is already part and parcel of his person; which is like saying that Don Quijote knows himself, knows who he is and therefore represents an excellent example of consciousness. Such consciousness also consists of the space to which he belongs. It will not deal with far-off lands like those of the chivalric novel. It is his own Spain of the time of the beginning of the sixteenth century to the seventeenth century. The historical point of reference can be measured by the adventures of the Captive, but Don Quijote belongs rather to the end of the fifteenth century, because after the Reconquest many nobles and *segundones* were left free to carry out their lives in a politically safe time but an economically difficult one. When Don Quijote discusses the Golden Age, he laments that the present time has nothing to commend it, that the present time has lost its capacity for greatness even in human relations.

To know oneself in his/her own time and space indicates the capacity of placing himself into the flow of time. The only difference is that Don Quijote moves in a time different from that of his contemporaries, and there lies the work's dynamism: the conflict between the individual and his neighbors who have different value systems, because they belong to different times.

So that when Don Quijote says, "Yo sé quién soy," he is speaking wisely about who he is, and the reader should not understand anything else but the affirmation of a person that has articulated his presence in the world in a specific time and place.

The episode of the lions says and explains much more than what appears. Normally, one tends to interpret this episode within a humoristic frame. Let us review what we have here: Don Quijote is in the presence of the man in the green kaftan (II, XVII). The man in the green kaftan is yet another bit of trickery by Cervantes (one among many others that Cervantes offers to his readers, I should add). The trick here is to measure the progress that Don Quijote has made since the time in the first part when Don Quijote becomes a knight-errant to the present. The man in the green kaftan can be compared to Sr. Quijana at the beginning of the book—devoted to reading books, a leisurely life, attends mass, etc. But Don Quijote no longer is the man he was at the beginning. He has undergone many experiences—some sad, some comical, some tragic and some satisfying.

At the moment with the man in the green kaftan, Don Quijote is already a veteran of sorts in the matter of chivalric affairs. The man in the green kaftan is not driven by the same ideals as Don Quijote. He is a docile sort, generally unbothered by things, except his preoccupation that his son wants to be a poet. Cervantes forces this comparison on the reader because he does not want the reader to forget all that has gone into making Don Quijote who he is.

One must note that the lions belong to the lion keeper. They are his property, and his property is converted into terms of lucre, money being the best barometer of reality. Let us examine how the lion keeper looks after his property and how Don Quijote is ready to destroy the lion keeper's goods. At that moment, Don Quijote does not have any property; that was left behind. His encounter with the lions must also be seen as a challenge to the lion keeper as a possessor of property, even though they are animals. The lion keeper says, "—El carro es mío; lo que van en él son dos bravos leones enjaulados, que el general de Orán envía a la corte, presentados a su Majestad; las banderas son del Rey nuestro señor, en señal que aquí va cosa suya" (II, XVII, 326a). When Don Quijote asks the lion keeper, "—¿Y, son grandes los leones?" (*ibid.*), he is not revealing signs of fear but rather curiosity, as if he were to prepare a strategy. Also, when Don Quijote hears that they are huge, his true feelings emerge. His answer is, "¿Leoncitos a mí? ¿A mí leoncitos, y a tales horas? Pues, ¡por Dios que han de ver esos señores que acá los envían si soy hombre que se espanta de leones!" (*ibid.*). The use of the diminutives to describe the lions is part of Don Quijote's strategy. He wants to reduce the size of the lions to that of kittens because Don Quijote sees himself as strong and brave. There is an interchange—a reduction of the lions and an increase of Don Quijote's posture to gigantic proportions. All of this possesses dramatic and theatrical aspects (as do many of the episodes of *Don Quijote*). One must take into consideration the idea of identity that we began with. The vision Don Quijote has of himself is all-exclusive. We can confirm this when we see that the people around Don Quijote in this episode flee because they know what a lion is capable of doing. But Don Quijote does not belong to the same sphere of perceptions as they; he lives by and for himself. Don Quijote is capable of convincing the lion keeper to open the door in spite of the latter's reservations. This episode is a perfect mirror of the fact that Cervantes has refracted reality and each character lives within the sphere of his/her own world. Sancho pleads with the lion keeper not to open the door, "—Señor caballero, los caballeros andantes han de acometer las aventuras que prometen esperanza de salir bien dellas, y no aquellas que de en todo la quitan; porque la valentía que se entra en la jurisdicción de la temeridad, más tiene de locura que de fortaleza" (326b). Don Quijote always refers to the world of knights-errant and not to the supposed reality of others. Everything that happens is always in ambivalent terms of the reality outside of Don Quijote and that inside him.

As part of the question of identity of "Yo sé quién soy," Don Quijote in the blindness or obstinacy of a madman cannot understand why people doubt him. His answer is, "¡Oh hombre de poca fe!" (II, XVII, 326b), the same way when he orders people in a coach to swear that Dulcinea is the most beautiful woman in the world. The Basque gentleman suspects that Don Quijote is mad and he answers partly in a logical way and in another way as to tease someone who may be mad: How can he make such a vow if he has never seen her?

Some people call Don Quijote crazy, but that is too easy an out—to call him crazy is the answer of reason, while Don Quijote's behavior responds to "la razón de la sinrazón," as was explained in the first chapter of *Don Quijote*. It is very obvious that Cervantes is creating a fictional world that responds to reason on the one hand and to the imagination on the other.

It is worth studying how Cervantes constructs this episode. It consists of the affirmation of caution of the lion keeper and Don Quijote's rash aggressiveness who wants to battle the lions. They represent pauses full of tension. The lion keeper goes out of his way to declare that he is not responsible for what is going to happen if he opens the door of the cage, including the death of Don Quijote. One must read this passage carefully: "—Séanme testigos cuantos aquí están cómo contra mi voluntad y fuerza abro las jaulas y suelto los leones, y de que protesto a este señor que todo el cual y mal y en daño que estas bestias hicieren corra y vaya por su cuenta, con más mis salarios y derechos. Vuestras mercedes, señores, se pongan en cobro antes que abra; que yo seguro estoy que no me han de hacer daño" (II, XVII, 326b-327a).

The last act of Don Quijote before opening the cage is to decide if he is going to fight on horseback or standing, then, "arrojó la lanza y embrazó el escudo, y desenvainando la espada, paso ante paso, con maravilloso denuedo y corazón valiente, se fue a poner delante del carro, encomendándose a Dios de todo corazón, y luego a su señora Dulcinea" (II, XVII, 327b). Don Quijote is prepared to fight, and this represents the apex of tension.

Don Quijote is not so mad that he cannot see and take measure of the lion's size. He guesses what his strength is: "el león, el cual pareció de grandeza extraordinaria y de espantable y fea catadura" (II, *ibid.*, 327b). The narrator says, "Lo primero que hizo [el león] fue revolverse en la jaula, donde venía echado, y tender la garra, y desperezarse todo; abrió luego la boca y bostezó muy despacio, y con casi dos palmos de lengua que sacó fuera se despolvoreó los ojos y se lavó el rostro" (*ibid.*, 327b-328a.). This is the anti-action of a total rejection of Don Quijote. Here Cervantes plays with the reader, creating on the one hand, an immense sense of size and proportion, pointing to the statement that the lion had "dos palmos de lengua." These details seem to aim at satire and the subversion of the true seriousness of what is going on. This is the last pause before the forthcoming battle. But suddenly the tension is broken by the lion's unwillingness to engage Don Quijote in battle: "volvió las espaldas y enseñó sus traseras partes a Don Quijote" (328a), symbolically castrating (in Freudian terms) Don Quijote. The lion categorically refuses to fight him. The reference to "traseras partes" seems to belong to the subtextual deconstruction of Don Quijote's mission by the author(s) and narrator(s). Perhaps Don Quijote's greatest enemies are the authors and narrators themselves. Recall the sarcasm of the narrator when he refers to Don Quijote in his first sally as "nuestro flameante aventurero" (I, II, 22a), especially since Don Quijote is dressed in a bizarre and not-completely chivalric manner; it is here that he is a totally anti-heroic figure. It is the authors and narrators that deny Don Quijote his greatest victory. Had Don Quijote won and slayed the lion, the world of Don Quijote would have been confirmed as the "true" life; and contrarywise, had the lion eaten Don Quijote, this would have represented another "truth." But since Cervantes does not believe that there is *a truth* or exclusive truths, he does not allow either of the contenders to win.

I have attempted to show here that aspects of Don Quijote's identity exist in a special world without contact with reality. By not having been eaten alive by the lion, Cervantes is showing his love or predilection for his character. Apparently, we can deduce that an unsound man with ideas totally in conflict with the perception of reality of others deserves to live. Cervantes has certified this by allowing both parties to live. Beneath the humoristic veil of the episode there lie some very provocative questions.

The case of Ricote the Moor has been the object of much discussion. Cervantes is not so aesthetically oriented that he does not have opinions regarding political, social and economic situations. In the second part, chapter 63, we witness an episode with various Cervantine themes: the anagnorisis of Ana Félix with her father, the thorny problem of perspective and the question of the injustice done to the Moriscos through the use of the figure of Ricote. These themes have an intimate relation with the question of consciousness in *Don Quijote*. The episode begins with a familiar disguise of the *edad conflictiva*, especially the theater—the disguise of the woman. Cervantes makes use of this topos in one of his exemplary novels, "Dos doncellas". In *Don Quijote,* the Viceroy sees a proud and beautiful person and he asks, "—Dime, arráez, ¿eres turco de nación, o moro o renegado?" (*ibid.,* 498b-499a). The answer he receives is, "—Ni soy turco de nación, o moro, o renegado." The viceroy continues, "—Pues ¿qué eres?" to which he answers, "Mujer cristiana" (II, LXIII, 499a). An important aspect of consciousness is autobiography.[3] To know what or who one is marks the beginning of consciousness. It demonstrates knowledge of the self. The

---

[3] Autobiography enlists thoughts and feelings about oneself and this comprises consciousness.

woman related her life: "nací yo, deMoriscos padres engendrada," and to add to the confusion of perspectives, she says, "En la corriente de su desventura fui yo por dos tíos míos llevada a Berbería, sin que me aprovechase decir que era cristiana, como, en efecto, lo soy, y no de las fingidas ni aparentes, sino de las verdaderas y católicas" (*ibid.*). Cervantes treats these themes in a varied way in the story of the Captive; this episode seems to be a twin of the theme of the foreign Christian woman. She further says, "Tuve una madre cristiana y un padre discreto y cristiano, ni más ni menos; mamé la Fe católica en la leche; criéme con buenas costumbres; ni en la lengua ni en ellas jamás, a mi parecer, di señales de ser morisca" (*ibid.*, 499a). The *disfraz* is one of Cervantes's favorite topoi, and its use seems to belong in part to Cervantes's wish to keep the reader confused. We have already discussed the importance of the absence of truth or truths or of anything objective. When you see someone at times it is not possible to discern who or what that person is or where he or she is from. In the case of Ana Félix we do not know positively what her gender is, Cervantes continues his usual game: confound the reader and the character(s) in a labyrinthine way. The case of Ana Félix is somewhat different from that of the other characters. Ana Félix's and her father's experiences tied to historical circumstances—the persecution of theMoriscos. In another essay I tried to show that the treatment of gypsies in "La gitanilla" is due to Cervantes's sensibility toward the presence of minority groups in Spain (in that case of "La gitanilla" this should also be read as "conversos," of which Cervantes probably was one),[4] and which is also dealt with in "La española inglesa" and the persecution of Catholics in Elizabethan England. Cervantes does not change this sensitivity. Following my suspicions as expressed in the chapter on gypsies, I would hazard the guess that theMorisco question is something Cervantes obviously is sensitive to.

Ana Félix's situation is particularly tender because she displays her Catholic origin with pride, but in real historical life, theMoriscos were badly treated. It is the tenderness of this situation that Cervantes utilizes because he wishes to attract attention to her situation (just as he did in "La gitanilla"). Readers respond positively to Ana Félix's situation. As an

---

[4] The subject of Cervantes's possible converso background is a very complicated one, which I can only treat in passing within the perspectives of the current book. However, I would urge the interested reader to consult Gilman and Johnson for a detailed and intelligent treatment of this matter.

example of gypsies, Preciosilla wins over the readers as well as the other characters in the story. Cervantes's purpose is to show not only a difficult situation in which the much hated gypsies lived, but also to depict them as people unworthy of the various punishments inflicted upon them. Cervantes's reaction is one of benevolent comprehension and of revulsion toward some of the methods used by the authorities to punish them. Ana Félix's situation should incite the reader's ire. Cervantes continues with this problem in the second part of the episode, the one related to her father, Ricote.

We saw already how Cervantes utilizes the topos of the improbable anagnorisis. But in the episode of the Captive, at the end, Cervantes surprises his readers and his characters when we see that the Captive accidentally meets his long lost brother.

The episode consists of a verticality of thought and significant and universal characters and a wide horizontality, so that there will be space where improbable things can take place. A good example of this is the figure of Ginés de Pasamonte, whose presence in the novel is very important, whence the modernity of the first modern novel. This detail of *Don Quijote* is something that did not pass unnoticed by Galdós, who adopts many of Cervantes's techniques in *Don Quijote*.

The second part of the Ana Félix episode treats in greater depth the motif of anagnorisis. Ana ends the story of her life, and there is described "un anciano peregrino que entró en la galera cuando entró el Virrey" (*ibid.*, 500b). This man looks around and says, "—¡Oh Ana Félix, desdichada hija mía! Yo soy tu padre Ricote, que volvía a buscarte, por no poder vivir sin ti, que eres mi alma" (*ibid.*). For those that may see this dénouement as saccharine sentimentality, one can say that Cervantes created it because it was a part of the narrative discourse of his time—the sentimental romance. But in the sentimental romance, certain emotions and sentimentality fall to improbable depths. What Cervantes does is give it a more human face. Any reader can see that the separation between father and daughter is very painful, but Cervantes does not exaggerate it to improbably melodramatic dimensions. Cervantes must have been thinking of the exile of Jews and Moriscos who insisted on preserving their cultural and religious heritage in spite of the edicts promulgated against them. Ricote's joy knows no human limits. Syrupy gestures that one sees in the sentimental romances such as *Cárcel de amor* do not have any human validity, torn away from some political or moral code.

If *Don Quijote* is a book about books, a book that critiques other books, Cervantes can imitate them at will within a parodic or satirical tradition. Cervantes's skill is to utilize such materials but not to fall into the kind of boredom of the original forms that Cervantes insists on criticizing and satirizing.

An aspect of the encounter between father and daughter underscores Ricote's history. The motif for Ricote's flight from Spain is exemplified by Ricote when he says, "Yo salí de mi patria a buscar en reinos estraños quien nos albergase y recogiese, y habiéndole hallado en Alemania, volví en este hábito de peregrino, en compañía de otros alemanes, a buscar a mi hija y a desenterrar muchas riquezas que dejé escondidas" (*ibid.,* 500b). Ricote's narration encapsulates the history of Spain with respect to the treatment afforded to Jews and Moors. The Spanish "establishment" did not permit a religious life to those outside the traditional Christian church. Religious and social minorities were forced to convert to the Christian faith or leave the country; to submit to the humiliation of having to adopt other religious and spiritual practices outside of their ways of life and do like Ricote, hide their wealth and to return some day to reclaim it.

What is particularly interesting is that the feelings of Cervantes in this case go beyond and against a powerful edict, like the case of the gypsies ("La gitanilla") or the misfortunes of English and Scottish Catholics ("La española inglesa"). Masquerading the problem behind other groups is a defensive posture by Cervantes. But here, in a time when Moriscos suffered at the hands of the government, Cervantes presents this unfortunate situation of Ricote and Ana Félix, without defenses or stratagems of hiding his own feelings; he passes these on to the characters who reveal these openly. The reader feels and can see Cervantes's true feelings, which, as we know, like those of Galdós, loved his characters without making distinctions of religion or social class.

It is of note that the episode of Ana Félix and her father resemble that of the Captive and Zoraida, only that here Zoraida's father is an Algerian Muslim and Ricote is a Spaniard of Muslim religious heritage. So typically of Cervantes, one can even see how he always gives us different views of something: Zoraida's father is anguished over his daughter leaving her country and her religion. Ana Félix is reconciled with her father who is joyful over their reunion, while Zoraida's father is physically and psychologically destroyed.

My purpose has been to show three examples of *Don Quijote* through the concept of consciousness of human beings who understand themselves in their own time and place. These examples display Cervantes's great human perception and compassion. They reveal, moreover, Cervantes's ability to take literary forms, some of which are *passées* and inject them with new life. This is a great part of Cervantes's creation of the modern novel.[5]

---

[5] See Márquez Villanueva' s perceptive notes on Ricote, *Personajes*.

7
Cervantes and the "Funny Book" Syndrome

CONSCIOUSNESS CAN EXPRESS ITSELF in many ways, and humor is one of them. In 1969, P.E. Russell published an interesting, provoking, yet flawed article, an article which had the effect of influencing a good number of critics.[1] In this article Russell focuses on "the element of boisterous laughter," (312) and the various episodes that subject Don Quijote to tricks and which produce laughter. Basic to Russell's point of view is the belief that Cervantes's intention was "To produce laughter of this kind" (312). Furthermore he states that Europe received *Don Quijote* as "a brilliantly successful funny book" (312). Anticipating, I believe, some adverse response, Russell protects himself and his hypothesis by stating that seeing this masterpiece as a 'funny book' does not undermine the seriousness of purpose of the work or its 'profundity as a work of art' " (313).[2]

Neo-Aristotelian criticism, he avers, "had failed to develop any theory of high comedy capable of embracing the sort of comic book [Cervantes] had written in *Don Quijote*" (314). Russell cites both Quintilian and Cicero, and continuing in his task, Russell states that "between 1612 and the end of the eighteenth century…their authors [translators of *Don Quijote*] regarded this book as anything except a brilliantly funny book" (316). For Saint-Evremont "the book was a 'funny book,' and Don Quijote himself as a beguiling comic portrait of a madman" (317). Even Tomé Pinheiro da Vega

---

[1] " 'Don Quijote' as a Funny Book," *MLR*, 64 (1969): 312-326. See also Anthony Close, *Cervantes and the Comic Mind of his Age*. Oxford: UP, 2000.
[2] See p. 313 for his reference to some people who viewed some of the humor of *Don Quijote* as being out of place in a book as important as *Don Quijote*. It is this "older, pre-romantic view of the book's meaning" that Russell wishes to correct.

saw Don Quijote as "a figure of fun," and King Philip III thought of Cervantes's masterpiece as a funny book (318). In his concluding remarks Russell reiterates his viewpoint that *Don Quijote* is a funny book and turns to the time of Cervantes for its understanding of "laughter, folly and madness" (319). Cervantes's ideas of laughter and the comic is no different from that of his contemporaries.[3]

Russell accepts the fact that a work "of literature may have an independent life which their authors could not foretell and that writers of all ages have sometimes spoken as prophets and seers" (325). Russell rejects Sismondi's notion that *Don Quijote* is "the saddest book ever written" (325), and yet stresses again his contention that Cervantes meant to write a funny book and that readers of his time read it as a funny book.

Russell's theory found a fertile field among other British Hispanists, notably Anthony Close, who in an early book commented on the hilarity of *Don Quijote* and later in a lengthy and learned book repeats Russell's argument.

Close brings to his task a great deal of knowledge and erudition but like Russell, he sees *Don Quijote* as a static work, one that is petrified in its time. Therefore, it is unmoveable as far as critical intent is concerned, and fails to see that each generation views a work through its own time and ideas, not that this changes how people in the seventeenth century may have read the work. What one can see is how the meaning and essence of a concept like humor can be seen differently in other times, thanks to added knowledge about the concept which Cervantes and his contemporaries had not known but which is latent in the work.

Close begins by denying the image of Cervantes as a person "critical of the political regime and, by extension, social system and ideology, of the Spain in which it was his lot to live" (30). In the course of his work on Cervantes he uses the example of *Lazarillo de Tormes* and other picaresque works (also, in his view "funny books"). Throughout his review of picaresque narratives words like 'comic' and 'funny', abound).

Another part of Close's theory is the effectiveness of comic fiction (47). Cervantes presumably has two sources: "*burlas* and the depiction of mannerisms of character and speech" (49). Close cites passages which depict "pandemonium at the inn" (50-51). Cervantes supposedly has taken aspects of contemporary humor and "made it an emblem of a familiar

---

[3] See also p. 324 for more statements by Russell of his thesis.

predicament of conscience" (55). Whatever does not fit into Close's view becomes "untypical" of Cervantes's comic fiction.[4] Even language is supposed to reflect the comic vision: "Don Quijote's vocabulary, by virtue of its bizarreness and familiarity, plays up the comic effect in untranslatably imaginative ways, which both overdo and undermine grandiloquence" (67).

Close also profiles examples of burlesque and farce. For Cervantes, his comic creations are "complementary to romance, rather than antithetical to it" (70).

For Close, "Cervantes saw his comic prose fiction as subject to the canonical poetics, and made a deliberate effort to bring it into line with that jurisdiction" (70). Moreover, "For Cervantes, the skillful and effective telling of a comic story is an end in itself and an art in its own right, requiring the highest qualities of taste, intelligence, wit" (70). Close also points to Cervantes's clever ability in handling comic characters and situations (71).

In conclusion to his chapter Close states "In sum, Cervantes's critical attitude to the comic genres of his age, his sense of their coarseness and vulgarity, acts as a conscious and active spur to his modifications of motifs taken from them" (72).

The genius of Cervantes, presumably, is to have presented "it [the humor of *Don Quijote*] from a central perspective which is, however comical, basically enlightened or honourable" (74).

In reviewing the Classical sources of comedy, Close notes how Cervantes is to be identified with Classical comedy through "merriment, unpretentious style, and educative purpose" (75). He observes how Classical comedy contributes to Cervantes's treatments of humor, farce and comedy. He also notes the links with other peninsular theatrical concepts such as decorum (118) and of chronicle (130).

In a later chapter, Close observes the comic mentality so common of the era that exists between "genteel viewpoint and risible object" (250 *et seq.*). He points to López Pinciano and his ideas on style and the comic and how wit can be blended, creating the links between risibility and the social element. Humor also is seen as a safety valve for people on a high(er) social level. The link between the comic and the courtly viewpoint is noted in Tirso's *Cigarrales de Toledo*.

Close also notes other aspects of the comic in "the age's comic

---

[4] "The censorious, partly sombre tone of the *Coloquio de los perros* makes it untypical of some important aspects of Cervantes's comic fiction" (59).

mentality: blasphemy, delight in derisive taunting, personification of these forms of humor in stereotyped rogues, the intensification of 'ugliness' and, in particular, the tension between all this and the courtly viewpoint which contemplates it" (270).[5]

He repeats his perception of Cervantes's poetics of the comic in which he opposed didacticism, "lawlessness... of the *comedia*; the coarseness of the *novela* tradition" (277).

He believes that Cervantes differed from his contemporaries in that "he recognized the need for synthesis and rationalization, whereas they, around 1600, tended to shun both things. His radical conception of the synthesis puts him several decades ahead of his time" (327). Cervantes also refines the kind of burlas one finds in contemporary literature, which remain ludic. Cervantes's humor, Close notes, relates him to Renaissance Humanism rather than to any literary influence (332).[6] In some ways although Cervantes conflicts with the degree of Alemán's didactic, novelistic mission, he does retain some identification with Mateo Alemán's presentation. In effect, according to Close "Cervantes's great originality lies in his ability to synthesize opposites that his contemporaries tended to treat as separate and irreconcilable" (335).

As I see Close's position, he believes in an immanent power of comedy in Cervantes's works but Close does not take into consideration that a work of art does not live solely in the view people had of it in the past. If this were the case, we would not need critics like Close or myself, and we would all be mouthing the ideas of don Marcelino Menéndez Pelayo. Each generation applies newer ideologies and criticism of literature in order to get a fresher view of it.

In spite of the authority and the erudition of Close's book, it fails, as does Russell's article, to understand that the literary work of art can transcend the bounds of its own creation. This is what happens to *Don Quijote* which is a compendium, an encyclopedia, of life and life's experiences, of which humor is a basic part.

Close speaks of linkages between Cervantes's view and that of others.

---

[5] With respect to practical jokes Close is impatient with modern critics who fail "to ask whether they [practical jokes] are 'cruel' in relation to the traditions and practices of which they are a natural extension" (272).
[6] For reasons unknown to me, Close ignores the obvious debt Cervantes has to Boccaccio. See my *Cervantes's Novelas ejemplares: Between History and Creativity*.

Cervantes is involved with giving as complete an understanding of what the basic aspects of life are, its positives as well as its negatives. Humor, like love, has many faces, and the eclectic mind of Cervantes displays itself in an intergeneric manner.

In response to Russell and Close, I can say that *Don Quijote* (and *Lazarillo de Tormes* as well) are *not* a part of the "funny book syndrome," no matter how hilarious things may seem in the book. Humor and comic action are pieces of a larger mosaic, and the statements to the effect that contemporaries regarded the work as a "funny book" do not mitigate the view of current readers who may have a strongly different point of view.

Those that do not think that *Don Quijote* is a funny book, but rather one where humor had a basic part, but that the ultimate effects are not humorous, are widespread, in spite of the positive reaction of those that see *Don Quijote* as an entertaining book.[7]

My purpose is to show where and how *Don Quijote* is not a funny book, although it contains many parts where the humor and comic action represent a first level toward a more serious one. The final chapter of the work frames the *desengaño* aspect of the work, where the frivolity and humor pale at the final resolution of the novel. I intend to disprove that *Don Quijote* is by definition "a funny book," or that it belongs to the "funny book" syndrome. To do this I shall be examining some features and aspects of the humor of *Don Quijote* and I shall analyze certain parts and aspects of the work through the modern, psychological view of humor, its origins and its effects. I shall also be reflecting on some aspects of the nature of *Don Quijote*, and how humor figures in its composition.

One of the best examples in support of my position has been proposed by Howard Mancing in his influential book.[8] Mancing points out that Pero Pérez and others are really Don Quijote's enemies. They are "the real enchanters in his chivalric world who use and abuse him for self-aggrandizement and for entertainment" (2). Don Quijote is also subjected to

---

[7] The number of people that agree in one way or another with Close's and Russell's point of view are legion, but also those that do not agree with it are probably the same number. I do not list critics of either side because listing them in this way does not serve any particular purpose, other than to show that the question is divided.
[8] Howard Mancing, *The Chivalric World of Don Quijote, Style, Structure and Narrative Technique*. Columbia, Mo.: University of Missouri Press, 1982.

"humiliation and ridicule" (*ibid.,* 3). Moreover, Cervantes places in Don Quijote's mouth linguistic archaisms which a reader of another era might find humoristic. I take this to be a form of authorial subversion where the speeches and acts of the central character produce laughter and other comic effects; that Don Quijote's actions are an aspect of humiliation. Mancing says: "The events at the inn are brought to a conclusion with the 'enchantment' of Don Quijote by his friends. After two days and nights of being ignored, laughed at, humiliated, and incapacitated as a knight-errant, this enchantment comes almost as a 'welcome relief'" (100). We are not speaking just of comic acts but rather the application of attitudes and motives that are less than funny.

Another episode which exposes the value content of supposedly comic acts directed against Don Quijote is when Don Quijote is placed in a cage and returned home. This is done in the middle of the day, when exposure to the *qué-dirán* would be at its maximum. As Mancing says, "It would never occur to the priest and the barber to take any precautions to avoid ridicule for Don Quijote" (111). He continues: "With friends like these, Don Quijote has no need of enemy enchanters" (111). He also notes that when Don Quijote returns home and is dutifully put to bed, "Don Quijote is no longer a participant; rather he is a mere object, evoking laughter, pity, or anger" (111).

Mancing quotes Gerald Brenen who "'identifies Don Quijote with Cervantes and sees the book as twice over a tragedy that depicts 'the defeat of the man of noble feelings by the second rate and the vulgar' and simultaneously convinces us the 'defeat was right'" (123).

After reading these observations by Mancing and Brenan, we can hardly subscribe to Russell's and Close's view of the *nature* and *purpose* of humor. Mancing goes on to restate the problem in convincing and succinct terms: "There is no question that *Don Quijote* is an immensely funny book and that the protagonist is the appropriate object of much humor. Nor can we have any quarrel with those who want to determine what the work meant to its contemporary readers. This task is valid and valuable, but ultimately *insufficient* [Emph. mine]. As stated in section 1.2 [of Mancing's book], the first step that must be taken in an attempt to comprehend a literary work from a past age is precisely that of trying to view it again, as clearly as possible, through the eyes of its contemporaries. But to stop at that point is, it seems to me, to deny the reality of our own times" (125).

In commenting on Vladimir Nabokov's lectures on *Don Quijote,* Guy

Davenport attempts to penetrate Nabokov's motives in his analysis and reading of *Don Quijote;* he says, "Here was a state of affairs that Nabokov like to go at *bec et ongle*. He began to find symmetry, of sorts, in the sprawling mess. He begins to suspect that Cervantes is unaware of the book's 'disgusting cruelty' " (xviii).[9] Davenport goes on to say "*Don Quijote* remains a crude old book, full of peculiarly Spanish cruelty, pitiless cruelty that baits an old man who lays like a child into his dotage" (xviii). One could apply Nabokov's opinion of the book to critics like Russell and Close when he says, "I shall have a good deal to say, later, about the brutality of the book and about the curious attitude toward that cruelty on the part of experts and laymen alike, who view it as a kindly humane work" (15). Instead of "kindly humane work" we could substitute "a comic work" of Russell and Close. He goes on to say: "I must apologize for listing these gruesome details—but we need them so as to refute the champions of wholesome fun, of humane titters" (15). Nabokov goes on to say that "When Don Quijote recants at the end of the book, in its saddest scene, it is neither from gratitude to his Christian God, nor is it under divine compulsion—but because it conforms to the moral utilities of his dark day" (18).

Focusing on another episode of the book, Nabokov further advances the non-comic aspect of the book: "And the two curves cross in that saddest of adventures, one of the cruelest in the book, when Sancho enchants Dulcinea, bringing the most noble of knights, for love of the purest illusion, to his knees before the most repulsive of realities: a Dulcinea course, uncouth, and reeking of garlic" (23).

Nabokov says the following: "Scholars who speak of sidesplitting episodes in the book do not reveal any permanent injury to their ribs. That in this book the humor contains, as one critic puts it 'a depth of philosophical insight and genuine humanity, in which qualities it has been excelled by no other writer' seems to me to be a staggering exaggeration" (24). He also touches on the meaning of the *burla*. He says: "Finally... the mystification theme, the cruel burlesque jest (the so-called *burla*), which can be defined as a sharp-petaled Renaissance flower on a hairy medieval stem" (31).

Nabokov devotes a chapter to "Cruelty and Mystification," in which he wishes "to illume a corner of the torture house by means of my little

---

[9] Bowers, Fredson, ed. *Vladimir Nabokov.* Lectures on Don Quijote, with an introduction by Guy Davenport. N.Y.: Harcourt, Brace, Jovanovich, 1983

torchlight, and this is the first thing I shall do today—samples of cheerful physical cruelty in part one" (51). Later he talks about mental cruelties, i.e., various enchantments and enchanters. As for the composition of these episodes, Nabokov says: "The author seems to plan it thus: Come with me, ungentle reader, who enjoys seeing a live dog inflated and kicked around like a soccer football" (51). Keeping in mind Russell's and Close's views on the "funny book syndrome," note how Nabokov reacts to some of Aubrey Bell's views of the "sensitive, keen-witted folks, humorous and humane" (52) Nabokov says: "Humane indeed! What about the hideous cruelty—with or without the author's intent or sanction—which riddles the whole book and befouls its humor?" (*ibid.*). Further he says; "Both parts of *Don Quijote* form a veritable encyclopedia of cruelty. From that viewpoint it is one of the most bitter and barbarous books ever penned. And its cruelty is artistic" (52).

In reviewing some episodes of *Don Quijote*, he notes that an innkeeper "allows a haggard madman to stay at his inn just in order to laugh at him" (53), the beating of Andrés by Haldudo; the beating Don Quijote receives at the hands of a mule driver; how Sancho is beaten by the "servants of some traveling monks" (53); a beating Rocinante receives at the hands of carriers. Nabokov says "What a riot, what a panic!" (53). He also reviews other painful experiences like that of Sancho Panza in chapter 15; Don Quijote's loss of an ear; a bevvy of punches. He sarcastically adds, noting Sancho Panza's blanketing, how some people "amuse themselves at Sancho's expense by tossing him in a blanket as men do with dogs at Shrovetide—a casual allusion to humane and humorous customs" (54).

Speaking of the second part, Nabokov repeats his sarcastic remark, viewing the second part as "our humane, humorous book" (56). "Compared to the fun in the first part, the mirth-provoking cruelty of the second part reaches a higher and more diabolic level in regard to the mental forms it takes and sinks to a new low of incredible crudity in its physical aspect" (56-57). As for the episode with the cats (II, XLVI), he refers to the so-called sidesplitting but in reality atrocious and brutal and fundamentally foolish episode of the cats" (69).[10] The accent on Don Quijote's usefulness (only in a context of being manipulated) is stressed when Nabokov observes that in a situation Don Quijote is completely exhausted, and when: "Don Antonio,

---

[10] Nabokov obviously does not see the humor in the work in the same way as do Russell and Close.

seeing no further fun can be squeezed out of the martyr, has his servants carry him off to bed" (73). Nabokov further highlights the non-comical quality of the jests when Don Quijote turns on his tormentors saying " 'Away with you, ministers of Hell! I am not made of brass so that I do not feel such unusual torture as this!' " (74). Apparently the readers that found Don Quijote such a funny book must have overlooked an episode such as this one (and that of the cats) for them (and I include critics like Russell and Close in that group) to have seen the book as funny and comical. Referring to chapter 43 Nabokov studies an episode in which Maritornes plays a prank on Don Quijote. Nabokov says: "This is an excellent scene from an artistic point of view but its cruelty is appalling (147-48). This is the episode of when Don Quijote is made to hang from his wrist.

Without necessarily carrying my own point too far, Nabokov does bring to the question the varying mores and standards between Cervantes's time and our own time. He says: "Cervantes himself, an educated person, finds 'droll' forms of cruelty that are absolutely impossible today in this country [USA] or in England and are, of course, censured by all civilized people in modern times. One suspects that now and then the author himself does not quite realize how disgustingly cruel the priests, barbers, innkeepers, etc. were in relation to Don Quijote" (157).

As Russell and Close speak of the hilarity that is the response of readers of the 17th century, one is forced to wonder where and what the sensibilities of such people were. For people as religious as the seventeenth-century Spaniard must have been, it becomes unthinkable that the treatment accorded Don Quijote would be laughed at so coldly.

Perhaps one way the public of the time of *Don Quijote* regarded it was the same way people regard slapstick comedy today. No one takes slapstick comedy seriously. Pratfalls, slipping on banana peels, falling from tall buildings; no one believes that there will be a realistic consequence to these situations. On the other hand, is *Don Quijote* to be placed in the same category of the Marx Brothers or Abbott and Costello? There is an undoubtable dimension of the work that can be simply called "serious," in spite of the comical experiences that Don Quijote has. Duffield (as quoted by Bowers) says the following: " 'It is therefore of the greatest interest to us to be assured that Cervantes knew what he was about when he began to make his map of the human mind. He was perhaps the first to navigate its darkest region, to tell us of the quality of this terrible darkness, and to show how it could be shined upon with the healing blessedness of light. There is as much pleasure to be obtained in proving this statement as in following the adventures of Don Quijote in his native land' " [editor's comment] (9). The image of the "map of the human mind" is a very apt and useful one. No one thinks in such terms about farce and slapstick. It is for this reason that Russell and Close are far off the mark.

There is another aspect to the thinking of Russell and Close. To insist on the literary work of art as frozen in its own time and place is too narrow an approach and a misapplication of the principle of historicism. When M. Bataillon saw the *Lazarillo de Tormes* as a "livre pour faire rire," he had obviously forgotten the advice that Lázaro gives in the prologue to the effect that those who would accept the work on its first level of acceptation were free to do so, but for those who wish to delve deeper there was more to be gotten.[11] Russell and Close have remained on the superficia of the text and have not delved *behind* the comical events to see what is to be found there.

Having laid out the terrain of this question—the "funny book syndrome" versus the deep and comprehensive book, it becomes my purpose to show what Mancing had alluded to above: that even in the presence of obviously comic material, *Don Quijote*, when seen in its totality, is indeed a serious book with a serious purpose and not merely a "livre pour faire rire."

My task, therefore, is to do a survey of some of the comical and funny episodes and experiences of *Don Quijote* in an effort to understand their place in the *whole* work.

It would do well to review *Don Quijote* with the purpose of defining what exactly is meant by the humor of *Don Quijote.*

No doubt the reader and the critic are faced with the very subjective nature of this task. What one person finds funny another may not laugh at. But I believe that a dissection of the subject could be made by using a general classification, in which case the subject of humor can be seen over a large number of possibilities, always governed of course by customs of a given culture and society at a given time. The task may be more difficult

---

[11] Morel-Fatio, A. transl. *La vie de Lazarillo de Tormes (La vida de Lazarillo de Tormes).* Introduction by M. Bataillon. Paris: Aubier, 1958. See also Joseph H. Silverman's cogent response to Bataillon's notion that *Lazarillo* was a "funny book": *RPh*, 15(1961): 88-94.

than it seems, but there are certain experiences in the book that can strike one as obvious at some level of humor. The purpose of this exercise is to see if Don Quijote or the *Lazarillo* belong to the funny book syndrome.

Like so much of Cervantes's work, it cannot rightly be defined in a strict manner. Cervantes's works often defy an easy classification but I believe a close examination of the examples of humor would not support Randall's and Close's view of *Don Quijote* as belonging to the "funny book syndrome."

It would be foolhardy to say that there is no humor in *Don Quijote*. But to say that the book belongs to the "funny book syndrome" is just as erroneous. There are episodes in it that would negate this concept, but more important the meaning and value of the work when seen in a comprehensive whole would reject a classification such as the "funny book syndrome." Seen in its totality, *Don Quijote* contains humor of different kinds but the dénouement would deny it the title of a "funny book."

Another consideration that must be dealt with and which forms the basis of Close's book is the standard of humor during the author's time, and the fact that Don Quijote, like the *Lazarillo*, has been seen as a "livre facétieux" by various critics. Close makes a cutoff point between contemporary critics (of Cervantes's time and shortly after) and Romantic critics. These latter ones accepted the sad or tragic contours of *Don Quijote*, and would then be regarded, as Close does, as "Romantic" readers.[12] Close's method is too easy and too simple. That some contemporary critics of Cervantes saw *Don Quijote* as a funny book only means that one sector of readership holds this as true; but this does not mean that such a point of view is universal; it is not incised in stone.

At the same time, one would have to ask why *Don Quijote* is read and appreciated century after century (quite apart from the question of its purported humor). It is because it has something to say to each generation. It does contain elements of common value to more than one era but at the same time there is an *evolution* of values and this evolution may account for why one generation appreciates a work and another one rejects it. A modern generation, perhaps a more enlightened one to be sure will see a canonical work through the lens of new ideas and new sensibilities. Close would put precedence of Cervantes's contemporaries over that of more

---

[12] *The Romantic Approach to Don Quijote: A Critical History of the Romantic Tradition in Don Quijote Criticism.* Cambridge: UP, 1978

modern readers. Humor is in some ways constant, but in other ways is subject to change. There is nothing stodgier than an old joke or one that is out of style. Literature speaks many tongues, and its humor is variable. What for Close is humorous may not be so for others.

To repeat, I accept the presence of humor in *Don Quijote*, but I deny that this makes the work a "funny book."[13]

One of the first aspects of humor in the book is the appearance of Don Quijote. From the very first we read "Frisaba la edad de nuestro hidalgo con los cincuenta años: era de complexión recia, seco de carnes, enjuto de rostro, gran madrugador y amigo de la caza" (I, I,19a).[14] Throughout the work the appearance of Don Quijote will be the cause of wonderment and of trouble. But there are aspects of his appearance which are also of a humorous nature. The above quote begins with a certain absurdity of the character, of being out of touch with his time. Don Quijote adopts a "new" way of life that is discordant with the mores of his peers. He is looked upon in a certain humorous fashion because of his appearance and his particular use of language.[15] If his appearance at the beginning of the work provokes humor, at the beginning of the second part it has a similar function and affect:

"Visitáronle, en fin, y halláronle sentado en la cama, vestida una almilla de bayeta verde, con un bonete colorado toledano, y estaba tan seco y amojamado, que no parecía sino hecho de carne momia" (II, I, 269a). In both cases his appearance defies any contact with what one would normally expect in this regard.

At the beginning of the second part Cervantes has the readers get a perspective of what his appearance was when he was returned home in a cage. Don Quijote's ama does this when she speaks to Sansón Carrasco. She says: "La vez primera nos le volvieron atravesado sobre un jumento, molido a palos. La segunda vino en un carro de bueyes, metido y encerrado en una jaula, adonde él se daba a entender que estaba encantado" (II, VI, 290a).

These perceptions of Don Quijote, even in cases where some cruelty is involved, elicits no doubt some benign humorous reaction.

---

[13] Ambiguity and double-entendres are rife in *Don Quijote*, and they also are a basis of humor. Humor belongs to the icon of Janus, one side is sadness and the other is the smile.

[14] See Redondo who focuses on Don Quijote's appearance and sees him as a "ser cuaresmal" (206, 207).

[15] See below for other observations on the use of language and humorous results.

When Don Quijote and Sansón Carrasco decide to do battle, their squires retire to a safe spot to avoid any combat themselves. Neither Sancho Panza nor Don Quijote knows that the opponent knight is Sansón Carrasco and his squire, since both wear masks, and in this case Tomé Cecial, Sansón's squire, has a disguise with a very big nose. Quite apart from the nature of their conversation, the picture of Tomé Cecial is smile-provoking, and has something to do with theatrical effects. The mask, as in the Commedia dell'arte, is done not to deceive, as Sansón and Tomé Cecial think they are doing, but to put their figures in a humoristic frame.[16]

An excellent example of the reaction of others caused by Don Quijote's appearance can be seen when he goes to Don Diego Miranda's house: "Desta última razón de don Quijote tomó barruntos el caminante de que don Quijote debía ser algún mentecato, y aguardaba que con otras lo confirmase" (II, XVI, 322b). It is Don Quijote's appearance, subtly juxtaposed with don Diego's, plus his strange manner of being, and the decidedly strange mission he is on that brings don Diego's doubts on him. Later Don Diego will retract his suspicions about Don Quijote's sanity. His first reaction to Don Quijote is, "Detuvo la rienda el caminante, admirándose de la apostura y rostro de Don Quijote, el cual iba sin celada, que la llevaba Sancho como maleta en el arzón delantero de la albarda del rucio" (II, XVI, 321b), later Don Diego observes: "Lo que juzgó de Don Quijote de la Mancha el de lo Verde fué que semejante manera ni parecer de hombre no le había visto jamás: admiróle la longura de su cuello, la grandeza de su cuerpo, la flaqueza y amarillez de su rostro, sus armas, su ademán y compostura: figura y retrato no visto por luengos tiempos atrás en aquella tierra" (II, XVI, 321b). The verb "admirar," used in this context can easily belong to 'surprise' 'to evoke laughter'. This same reaction is to be seen shortly after at the beginning of the chapter dealing with the wedding of Camacho. When some students and *labradores* meet Don Quijote, they have the same reaction as Don Diego: "y así estudiantes como labradores cayeron en la misma admiración en que caían todos aquellos que la vez primera veían a Don Quijote" (II, XIX, 334a). Once again, Don Quijote's appearance is a matter for surprise, if not the benign humor that they are dealing with someone who is not quite balanced.

We see another example of Don Quijote's person at the home of Don Diego during the party and where the narrator informs us of Don Quijote's

---

[16] The uses of disguise will be further explored below.

person, i.e., his appearance: "Estas dieron tanta priesa en sacar a danzar a Don Quijote, que le molieron, no sólo el cuerpo, pero el ánima. Era cosa de ver la figura de Don Quijote largo, tendido, flaco, amarillo, estrecho en el vestido, desairado y, sobre todo, no nada ligero" (II, LXII, 493a). From the very beginning his appearance is a matter of jest and his appearance, together with his strange manner of speech, renders him a strange object to others, and this strangeness leads to humor or practical jokes, some of which are in the poorest taste for any century.

One of the common ploys when dealing with a suspected madman is to go along pretending all is well. However, there is a boomerang effect to this in *Don Quijote*. When someone "goes along" with the madman and adopts that person's quirks, he/she inadvertently becomes as mad as the supposed madman. In fact, an early episode begins on several notes of humor beginning with Don Quijote's appearance. His perceptions or misperceptions set the stage for humorous happenings. He sees the prostitutes at the door of the inn as ladies and the inn a castle. So different is he that the "distraídas mozas" seem to him to be elegant ladies": "Mirábanle las mozas y andaban con los ojos buscándole el rostro, que la mala visera le encubría, mas como se oyeron llamar doncellas, cosa tan fuera de su profesión, no pudieron tener la risa" (I, II, 23a). Moreover, we are told, "El lenguaje, no entendido de las señoras, y el mal talle de nuestro caballero acrecentaba en ellas la risa" (*ibid.*). Don Quijote's appearance even catches the attention of the inn-keeper: "viendo aquella figura contrahecha, armada de armas tan desiguales como eran la brida, lanza, adarga y coselete" (*ibid.*). The innkeeper joins the madcap affair by adopting some of Don Quijote's language: "Si vuestra merced, señor caballero, busca posada, amén del lecho (porque en esta venta no hay ninguno), todo lo demás se hallará en ella en mucha abundancia" (I, II, 23a,b).

The subsequent dubbing of Don Quijote as a knight is full of contained humor. The innkeeper, not one to let an occasion for fun to go by, focuses on the event. The narrator says, "El ventero, que, como está dicho, era un poco socarrón y ya tenía algunos barruntos de la falta de juicio de su huésped, acabó de creerlo, cuando acabó de oírle semejantes razones, y por tener que reír aquella noche, determinó de seguirle el humor" (I, VI, 25a). The participation of the "damas" continues the thread of the make-believe dubbing. "Hecho esto, mandó a una de aquellas damas que le ciñese la espada, la cual lo hizo con mucha desenvoltura y discreción; porque no fue menester poca para no reventar de risa a cada punto de las ceremonias" (I, II, 27a).

All of this is done with much staging but by acceding, the characters themselves become "mad" as it were, and from a further perspective, the whole inn seems like an insane asylum. The ultimate change and irony is that the innkeeper does not charge Don Quijote for his stay: "El ventero, por verle ya fuera de la venta, con no menos retóricas, aunque con más breves palabras, respondió a las suyas y, sin pedirle la costa de la posada, le dejó ir a la buena hora" (I, II, 27b).

This technique, which shall be repeated in different ways throughout *Don Quijote,* is a part of depicting a mildly humorous situation with touches of irony punctuating the events.

There are several characters that contribute to the air of humor and comic action. The innkeeper whom we have just studied throughout the episode takes the role of comic provocateur. It is especially useful to note that from the beginning of the episode, there are small points which punctuate the happenings like the dubbing itself: "en mitad de la leyenda alzó la mano y dióle sobre el cuello un buen golpe, y tras él, con su mesma espada, un gentil espaldarazo, siempre murmurando entre dientes, como que rezaba" (I, III, 27a). The innkeeper becomes an unforgettable character because he imitates a serious ritual with comic overtones and for his change of spirit in not charging Don Quijote for his lodging.

The case of Andrés the shepherd who is being beaten by his master, Haldudo, is a good case in point because the three characters are indelibly brought together in this episode which contains various levels of humor.

Don Quijote's vision does not allow the episode to be seen in toto; in fact, the episode is structured oddly. Haldudo and Andrés perceive the same thing, i.e., Andrés is being punished for his theft or for the loss of the sheep through carelessness. They can both see the problem equally clearly, but Don Quijote does not see the full picture. He can only see what his mental condition will allow him to see. In this divergence consists the humor, although the beating that Andrés receives is not funny at all. The obvious physical aspect of the episode is later crowded out by Don Quijote's fantasy that he has complied with one of his functions as a knight-errant, with Don Quijote going off happily as Haldudo goes back to beating Andrés. The light humor which marked Don Quijote's perception comes to an end. The episode will be further developed and finished when Don

Quijote again meets Andrés later in the work and he destroys Don Quijote's belief that he had in fact carried out a good deed.

There is a certain amount of humor created toward deliberately implausible things or happenings. It is also a matter of some humor for the reader to hear Sancho Panza talk about the promised island: "Decíale, entre otras cosas, Don Quijote que se dispusiese a ir con él de buena gana, porque tal vez le podía suceder aventura, que ganase, en quítame esas pajas, alguna ínsula, y le dejase a él por gobernador della" (I, VII, 38b). The humor derives from the discordant juxtaposition of governing by a bumpkin. Moreover, the word *gobernador* in the mouth of such a fellow who is considered to have "poca sal en la mollera," becomes funnier. All the incidents related to his assumption of office in Barataria are an important function of the comic in *Don Quijote*.

Of further comic value is the conversation between Don Quijote and Sancho concerning the fasting habits of knights. It comes as a mild shock to Sancho to hear his master say, "hágote saber, Sancho, que es honra de los caballeros andantes no comer en un mes, y, ya que coman, sea de aquello que hallaren más a mano" (I, X, 48b). A similar effect is achieved when Don Quijote insists that knights do not carry money around with them. Don Quijote's answer after some commentary by Sancho is that "—No digo yo, Sancho—replicó Don Quijote—, que sea forzoso a los caballeros andantes no comer otra cosa sino esas frutas que dices; sino que su más ordinario sustento debía de ser dellas, y de algunas hierbas que hallaban por los campos, que ellos conocían, y yo también conozco" (*ibid.*). This of course does not bode well with Sancho who has higher thoughts and ambitions with regard to satisfying the demands of his stomach.

Well into the first part the reader becomes accustomed to the fact that Don Quijote will undergo considerable difficulties in achieving his goal as a knight-errant. Some of these episodes are humorous, but lest the reader not get the picture of Don Quijote that Cervantes has prepared for him/her, he transfers to his steed the same examples. This process of literary refraction is common throughout *Don Quijote* but to extend it to animals is unexpected. Rocinante undergoes the problems of equine libido and is rejected roundly by the mares. Then the carriers attack him: "viendo los harrieros la fuerza que a sus yeguas se le hacía, acudieron con estacas, y tanto palos le dieron, que le derribaron mal parado en el suelo" (I, XV, 64a). This episode is fairly clear. Cervantes gives us another look at Don Quijote and his knightly endeavor but through his steed.

The principal feminine focus of *Don Quijote* is Dulcinea, although she does not appear except in the imagination and fantasy of Don Quijote. However, other women have an important place in the work, and I think of Maritornes, who has a close suggested tie with Dulcinea, even if only as a complete opposite of her.

The episode I refer to is the one dealing with Don Quijote when Maritornes goes to a tryst with a carrier. She walks into Don Quijote's arms, who thinks that she is the daughter of the innkeeper. Maritornes is caught in Don Quijote's arms and the carrier rains down blows on him. This episode is clearly of a farcical nature, and like all farce, it involves physical aspects. Don Quijote, who is deeply involved in a fantasy about this supposed princess receives a beating at the hands of the carrier.

Another character who is very much involved in episodes of a physical nature is Sancho who is victimized by being blanketed: "y allí, puesto Sancho en mitad de la manta, comenzaron a levantarle en alto, y a holgarse con él, como perro por carnestolendas" (I, XVII, 74b).

There are of course other characters that do things that can be considered humorous, but the above is just an example of how Cervantes creates different kinds of humor through characterization.

A form of humor that appears in the book is the use and manipulation of implausible things. Perhaps the best example of this deals with the game the author/narrator plays with the manuscripts of the work: "Pero está el daño de todo esto [the battle with the Biscayan] que en este punto y término deja pendiente el autor desta historia esta batalla, disculpándose que no halló más escrito destas hazañas de don Quijote, de las que deja referidas. Bien es verdad que el segundo autor desta obra no quiso creer que tan curiosa historia estuviese entregada a las leyes del olvido, ni que hubiesen sido tan poco curiosos los ingenios de la Mancha, que no tuviesen en sus archivos o en sus escritorios algunos papeles que deste famoso caballero tratasen; y así, con esta imaginación, no se desesperó de hallar el fin desta apacible historia, el cual, siéndole el cielo favorable, le halló del modo que se contará en la segunda parte" (I, VIII, 43b).

In the beginning of the following chapter the narrator writes about how he accidentally came across the continuation of the battle with the Vizcaíno. It is the work of a "morisco aljamiado": "Estaba en el primero cartapacio pintada muy al natural la batalla de don Quijote con el Vizcaíno, puestos en la mesma postura que la historia cuenta, levantadas las espadas" (I, Ix, 45a).

It is this kind of outlandish coincidence that could not have been done except within the view of humor or satire. It is the kind of benign humor that Cervantes delights in, not farce, but not-too-subtle but happily arranged and composed happenings. This is also a part of Cervantes's commitment to tongue-in-cheek humor.

There is another good example of this kind of humor that Cervantes indulges in and that is to be found in the Cautivo episode. Zoraida wrote in Arabic with a cross. There are some epistles that follow this pattern of highly implausible things. Zoraida decides to use a novel method of communication; she uses a long stick of cane to which is attached the letter. "Acaeció, pues, que un día, estando en un terrado de nuestra prisión con otros tres compañeros, haciendo pruebas de saltar con las cadenas, por entretener el tiempo, estando solos, porque todos los demás cristianos habían salido a trabajar, alcé acaso los ojos y vi que por aquellas cerradas ventanillas que he dicho parecía una caña, y al remate della puesto un lienzo atado, y la caña se estaba blandeando y moviéndose casi como si hiciera señas que llegásemos a tomarla" (I, XL, 199a).

Cervantes injects into this episode the elements of these implausible happenings. The prisoners are under careful watch, and so the possibility of being caught at the game is very high if seen in a realistic sense, but realism and practicality are not one of Cervantes's necessary ingredients in this part of the Captive episode. Following the dictum of satire as "treating serious things humorously or treating silly things seriously," Cervantes adds these touches to the story because he knows that such touches are a delight to the readers, as Cervantes indulges in his own brand of satirical humor with respect to the happenings of the romance of chivalry or the Greek romance.

All critics are in agreement over the interpretation of *Don Quijote* as a work of great irony. The late Joseph H. Silverman, in his lectures, once defined irony as taking a tortuous path to its object. To be sure, there are several fundamental episodes that co-involve humor. The message of these episodes, if, indeed there is a message to be drawn, is tightly allied with the major theme of *Don Quijote*.[17]

The chapters dealing with the *baciyelmo* provide such ironic humor. The treatment begins benignly: "De allí a poco, descubrió don Quijote un

---

[17] Don Américo flatly denies that there is any "message" in *Don Quijote*.

hombre a caballo, que traía en la cabeza una cosa que relumbra como si fuera de oro, y aún él apenas le hubo visto, cuando se volvió a Sancho y le dijo...." (I, XXI, 91a).

The reader by now becomes accustomed to Don Quijote's (mis)perceptions. Sancho does not think it is the Yelmo de Mambrino. We have here one of the fundamental themes of the book—perception of the individual and its possibility being questioned or denied by other perceptions. In Chapter 45, part I, the problem of whether it is a barber's basin or Mambrino's helmet reappears. Once again supporters of the Yelmo face the supporters of the barber's basin. The consternation of the put-upon barber is best expressed when he says: "—¡Válame Dios!—dijo a esta sazón el barbero burlado—. ¿Que es posible que tanta gente honrada diga que ésta no es bacía sino yelmo? Cosa parece ésta que puede poner en esta admiración a toda una Universidad, por discreta que sea. Basta: si es que esta bacía es yelmo, también debe de ser esta albarda jaez de caballo, como este señor ha dicho" (I, XLV, 226b).

In Cervantes's view of the world nothing "is," things are subjected to relative perceptions. Basically, if you think it is a barber's basin, so be it. It is not the final decision that is important for the author and the narrator(s), but the tongue-in-cheek humor that emanates from the discussion. It is this kind of humor that Cervantes is expressing, one that is subtle, not audacious or raucous in the tradition of Roman comedy, for example.

A similar form of humor in this same vein is the episode of the puppet show. Cloaked in the commonplaces of the chivalric tradition, the play deals with the freeing of Melisendra by Gaiferos. The puppet master presents a little drama together with music and effects. Don Quijote succumbs to the action of the mini-drama and ends up destroying the pageant, puppets and all.

As in other episodes, the humor derives from Don Quijote's confusion between play and reality. We see a visual spectacle worthy of a comedy, especially with the destruction of the tableau. No subtlety here. The visual object of seeing someone, dressed in the same manner of the characters of the play breaks the barrier between the conventional spectator and the play is humor-provoking. The irony, of which humor is a sub-set, consists of the subtle connection between play and reality; for Don Quijote one is equal to the other. The humor is to be seen when Don Quijote says: "Viendo y oyendo, pues, tanta morisma y tanto estruendo don Quijote, parecióle ser bien dar ayuda a los que huían, y levantándose en pie, en voz alta dijo:

—No consentiré yo que en mis días y en mi presencia se le haga superchería a tan famoso caballero y a tan atrevido enamorado como don Gaiferos. ¡Deteneos, malnacida canalla; no le sigáis ni persigáis; si no, conmigo sois en la batalla!" (I, XXVI, 364b). It is this misperception, this confusion of levels that creates the humor.

The episode recalls Don Quijote's innocent misapprehension of the chained convicts who go to the galleys against their will. The humor derives from Don Quijote's ignorance of the real status of the convicts, an episode analogous to the Andrés/Haldudo experience. What trips the wire of Don Quijote's fantasy world is the sight of people he believes are being dragged against their will. The play exists between the public outside of the chivalric imagination of Don Quijote and the reader. For the spectator of this episode there is no sense other than that Don Quijote is crazy and to see him functioning on one level of knowledge (the dictates of his *proyecto vital*, opposed by another one is what creates the humor). The comic quality of the episode ends when Don Quijote asks the prisoners to go to the Toboso and to tell Dulcinea that Don Quijote freed these persons in her name. The stoning of Don Quijote and Sancho becomes the comic dénouement of the episode.

Equally, the episode of the lions (II, XVII) provides other aspects of comic relief.[18] But here the author provides the character and readers with a bona fide antagonist, the lion.

At the beginning of the episode there is a tension created by the on-lookers who are afraid that Don Quijote will be devoured by the lion, and there is every reason to believe that this could be so. When the lion cage is opened and everyone scatters for protection, Don Quijote is standing in a one-on-one situation with a truly dangerous animal. But the tension is dissipated when the lion fails to take Don Quijote's challenge. The lion's reluctance signified by the turning of his hind parts on Don Quijote is what creates the humor and the persons that climbed up trees to be out of the reach of the lion are equally humorous. The subversion of Don Quijote's valor is what causes the humor. What was initially a very dangerous and potentially catastrophic situation ends with the laughter of the reader. There are several other categories of humor that can be noted. There are the conclusions where Fernando swears he will marry Dorotea, yet not

---

[18] It should be noted that Thomas Mann thought that the episode of the lions is "the climax of Don Quixote's "exploits' " (Lowry Nelson, Jr. 62).

knowing there is at work a greater moral and religious law. Fernando does not know that he is stepping deeper and deeper into marriage. The skeptical reader smiles, probably well-informed of the changes in Counter Reformation rules concerning verbal marriage. Fernando's promise, although not made in good faith, will boomerang upon him later.

All of the chapters dealing with Dulcinea's letter are based upon a number of misconceptions. Sancho forgets the letter and he must invent excuses. The nature of the excuses constitutes a vivid example of humor since the reader and Sancho know the truth.

Two of perhaps the best known episodes of *Don Quijote* are those of the Cave of Montesinos and the flight of Clavileño. In the former Don Quijote tests the credulousness of others by insisting that he had been down in the cave for several days instead of the hour that Sancho calculates. On the one hand Cervantes suggests the comparison of heuristic time with *durée*, but Cervantes uses his character to create a humorous situation. Even Sancho gives a laugh of disbelief when Don Quijote says he has been in the cave for several days. Don Quijote is asking people to believe him in the same way he wanted people to swear that Dulcinea is the most beautiful woman in the world, even though they have not seen her. What he saw in the cave is supposed to be endorsed also as true. The reader, however, is as skeptical as Sancho and others there present. The reader knows that Don Quijote is probably teasing, and the readers' attention shifts to the description of the tale. Cervantes is attempting a major coup here. In order to show that Cervantes is in fact joshing, he has Don Quijote add a detail which clearly gives away the invention. Don Quijote says that the heart of Durandarte has been salted so that it would not smell and be preserved (see II, XXIII, 351a). The incongruence of salting the heart and the general environment of a chivalric ballad is brutal. One salts pork, fish, or other foods, but salting the heart of Durandarte surely belongs to the world of humor and kidding, not the seriousness of the chivalric novel. But the meaning and consequence of the episode is not final; that is to be found in the Clavileño episode.

Sancho essentially repeats the antics of Don Quijote with respect to the question of belief. Don Quijote tested the faith of others by inventing an outlandish tale; Sancho Panza does the same. Both of them had witnesses to verify their claims. The witnesses must find Sancho's account of what he saw in the skies quite humorous, and it is a credit to Sancho's powers of the imagination, as it is for Don Quijote and his description. Cervantes puts the process of faith in its proper relative context: "—Sancho, pues vos queréis que se os crea lo que habéis visto en el cielo, yo quiero que vos me creáis a mí lo que vi en la cueva de Montesinos. Y no os digo más" (II, XLII, 417b).

Both episodes are filled with humor-provoking ingredients, in spite of the very serious questions which their actions provoke.

When Don Quijote is defeated in various battles, many times he uses different excuses. In the windmills episode there are *encantadores* that have changed the substance of things. This is done in several instances, as well as when Don Quijote outrightly lies as when he says he fought ten giants (I, 5).

A rather low-level form of humor occurs when there are disguises. The funniest of which is when Tomé Cecial assumes the role of squire to Sansón Carrasco. Sancho is entranced by the disguise of Cecial, especially the nose: "cuando la primera que se ofreció a los ojos de Sancho Panza fue la nariz del escudero del Bosque, que era tan grande que casi le hacía sombra a todo el cuerpo" (II, XIV, 316a). The mask is very reminiscent of those used in the *Commedia dell'Arte*. No one can react other than with a smile.

The Priest and the Barber also assume disguises. At first, the priest dresses as a woman but then realizes that such a thing is an offense to religious and priestly decorum but the idea that he and the Barber would dress in a different fashion merely belongs to the template of "dressing up," just as Don Quijote "dresses up" as a chivalric figure, which leads the reader to think that "dress up" is contagious.

Dorotea uses disguises twice, the first when she sets out in search of Fernando and when she assumes the role of the Princess Micomicona. Even Ginés tries the disguise of a "gypsy" (I, XXX). These examples all function within a perspective of some humor, no matter how farcical or subtle they may be.

An excellent example of slapstick is when Don Quijote is in the battle in the inn (I, XVI). Here the humor reaches grotesquely comic proportions when Don Quijote mistakes Maritornes for an angelic character and embraces her, speaking in chivalric language. Later in I, XXXV, the melodramatic episode of trying to convince Lotario by putting on a drama of his own, steps into the area of farce, especially with the use of blood as a falsely certifying detail to his farce. The farcical aspects appear when Don Quijote slashes at the wine skins, thinking it is the head of a dragon. Even the second battle in the inn where the government officials come to arrest Don Quijote for freeing the prisoners is humorous (I, XXII). To complete this picture in the second part the adventure of the *rebuznadores* is not only farcical but it practically enters the area of surrealism.

Cowardice has been used by writers and dramatists for comic effects, and Cervantes is no different. Both Don Quijote and Sancho Panza tremble before the carts of death and the dead body, eliciting fear and worry. This achieves its humor due to the fact that Don Quijote has pretensions to courage. This inconsistency between valor and cowardice devaluate the characters, rendering them silly and comical.

An additional area of humor in *Don Quijote* is the use of language. From the very first, when Don Quijote adopts his lifetime project he is essentially stepping back in time to an age long gone but whose language could not necessarily stop evolving. The temporal span of Don Quijote's activity is placed in the late Middle Ages and therefore his speech reflects that time. In I,I, Don Quijote pronounces the all-important phrase of "La razón de la sinrazón." It was this kind of language that he loved to read in the romances of chivalry and consequently will use himself in his adventures. It is precisely this incongruence between the speech patterns and vocabulary of the Middle Ages and Don Quijote's own use of such speech that easily creates some humor and occasional silliness. Later at the first inn he speaks: "—Dichosa edad y siglo dichoso aquel donde saldrán a luz las famosas hazañas mías, dignas de entallarse en bronce, esculpirse en mármoles y pintarse en tablas, para memorias en lo futuro. ¡Oh tú, sabio encantador, quienquiera que seas, a quien ha de tocar el ser coronista desta peregrina historia" (I, II, 22a). This kind of speech immediately puts people on their guard and after some thinking a person realizes that he/she is dealing with a strange person. From then on, Don Quijote is not taken seriously; in fact, he is looked upon as a crazy individual, and it gives him very little credibility and mostly a lot of derision.

When facing the Toledan merchants Don Quijote, in a spirit of challenge, deals with them in the language of the chivalric romance: "—¡Non fuyáis, gente cobarde; gente cautiva, atended; que no por culpa mía, sino de mi caballo, estoy aquí tendido!" (II, IV, 30b). Arriving at home, the *labrador* says: "—Abran vuestras mercedes al señor Valdovinos y al señor Marqués de Mantua, que viene mal ferido, y al señor moro Abindarráez, que trae cautivo el valeroso Rodrigo de Narváez, alcalde de Antequera" (I, V, 32b). Thereby showing how Don Quijote's antics are contagious and others like the Labrador will ape him. Later in the same episode, Don Quijote would say: "—Ténganse todos; que vengo malferido, por la culpa de mi caballo. Llévenme a mi lecho, y llámase, si fuere posible, a la Sabia Urganda, que cure y cate de mis feridas" (*ibid.*).

In the coincidentally-found second manuscript of the work which continues the interrupted fight, Don Quijote addresses the ladies: "—Por cierto, fermosas señoras, yo soy muy contento de hacer lo que me pedís; mas ha de ser con una condición y concierto" (I, IX, 46b).

During the episode of the Yelmo de Mambrino Don Quijote gives a long disquisition within which he uses several older forms such as "fermosas," "fablar" and "furto." From the point of view of the "conventional" speech use, this use of antiquated language makes Don Quijote look and sound foolish and belongs to a Janus-like double face of comedy and tragedy.

Don Quijote's *carta de amor* to Dulcinea represents a significant part of the plot, and it is bound up with silliness. The question of the letter is a parallel action to the essence of the "truthfulness" of the very book. It will pass through various hands and authors. Don Quijote asks Sancho to see to it that the letter gets transcribed by a literate individual, but the humor of the matter derives from the fact that Dulcinea is illiterate: "Dulcinea no sabe escribir ni leer, y en toda su vida ha visto letra mía ni carta mía" (I, XXV, 117a).

Even Sancho uses Don Quijote's language, and becomes "Don Quijotesque" when he addresses Dorotea, now the Princess Micomicona: "—Dichosa buscada y dichoso hallazgo—dijo a esta sazón Sancho Panza—, y más si mi amo es tan venturoso, que desfaga ese agravio y enderece ese tuerto, matando a ese hideputa dese gigante" (I, XXV, 141a). The principle of incongruity applies here where someone like Sancho would use a diction alien to his station, flouting thereby one of the fundamental tenets of Renaissance literary theory, decorum.

An important source of humor is based on the changes in the *loco-cuerdo* axis. The episode dealing with both the Toledan merchants and the Viscayan, are examples of that humor.[19]

In the former, the Vizcaíno confronts Don Quijote who sins on the mad side of the equation when he insists all swear to Dulcinea's supreme beauty. The Vizcaíno responds, and this leads to a singular physical battle between

---

[19] There is an interesting feature of the humor that is the fact that the Vizcaíno is speaking Castilian and not so well, either. "[The Vizcaíno] se fué para Don Quijote y, asiéndole de la lanza, le dijo, en mala lengua castellana y peor vizcaína, desta manera" (I, VIII, 42b).

them. Here the *cuerdo* part takes over and the narrator describes one of the fiercest battles that Don Quijote has. There is no interference by the "malos encantadores" in this episode. In fact, most of these episodes like the windmills, the galley slaves, the lion, all fall into this category of the *loco-cuerdo* theme, and each one of them provides the readers with pleasant humor.

There is another form of humor that can be called, for better or worse, "slight and subtle humor." These are episodes and events that offer interesting insights into the character. For instance, the *celada de encaje* that Don Quijote repairs and reconstructs and then leaves it untested brings a smile to our face, if only because it provokes our curiosity and makes us think more about what is happening. The reader knows that the *celada* will not stand up to a second strong blow.

The whole story of Barataria is filled with humorous episodes, from the concept of someone like Sancho Panza receiving it as a reward for his services to putting Sancho on a bare subsistence diet; the false battle; the chapters relating to Dulcinea's letter including the attempt to pass off the three country women as Dulcinea and her attendants.

Cervantes decides to use the figure of Sansón Carrasco as the Caballero del Bosque. The use of masks and Sansón's adoption of Don Quijote's role bring a smile to our face as well as the parallel action of the squires. All of these make for entertaining reading.

The dynamic of disappointment is operative in the episode of the lions, where the valor of Don Quijote is destroyed by the indolent lion. The twin episodes of the Cave of Montesinos also provide moments of mirth as when Don Quijote and Sancho relate what they saw in their respective experiences.

More than just mirth occurs when Don Quijote destroys the puppet tableau, and reality and imagination conflict. We smile over the fact that Sancho is supposed to give himself 3,300 lashes. Many of the episodes at the castle of the Duke and Duchess entertain us, in spite of some of them being cruel. Don Quijote's second set of advice to Sancho Panza as governor is amusing, especially since they come in the wake of his serious advice. Sancho's decisions as a judge are as witty as they are wise. How the Duke sets up a situation in which Don Quijote is to defend the honor of Doña Rodriguez's daughter; the turnabout in the story of Basilio at Camacho's wedding. All these episodes exist on a lower level of humor and are a part of the first level of consciousness of the work.

There is a category that forms a part of the mosaic that is the cruel jokes that are perpetrated on him and/or Sancho. Within the purview of carnival Sancho's blanketing may be seen as acceptable, but for the modern person such an act has a cruel, bonejarring basis to it. While this may have been the gusto of the time, it does not make it any less cruel. As was said earlier there is a discharge of extra energy through laughter and this is probably one of the kinds of humor that Freud saw.[20]

There are several other forms of "humor" that stand in direct contrast and opposition to the type of humor that I have been discussing above. It is cruelty of the basest kind, without explanation for its cruelty. An example of this is to be found in I, XLIII, where Don Quijote is hung by the hand: "Parecióle a Maritornes que sin duda Don Quijote daría la mano que le habían pedido y, proponiendo en su pensamiento lo que había de hacer, se bajó del agujero y se fue a la caballeriza, donde tomó el cabestro del jumento de Sancho Panza, y con mucha presteza se volvió a su agujero, a tiempo que Don Quijote se había puesto de pies sobre la silla de Rocinante, por alcanzar a la ventana enrejada donde se imaginaba estar la ferida doncella" (I, XLIII, 219b). "Ahora lo veremos—dijo Maritornes; y haciendo una lazada corrediza al cabestro, se la echó a la muñeca, y bajándose del agujero ató lo que quedaba al cerrojo de la puerta del pajar, muy fuertemente. Don Quijote, que sintió la aspereza del cordel en su muñeca…" (I, XLIII, 220a). But later the narrator gives a better description of how Don Quijote feels. "Estaba, pues, como se ha dicho, de pie sobre Rocinante, metido todo el brazo por el agujero, y atado de la muñeca, y al cerrojo de la puerta, con grandísimo temor y cuidado que si Rocinante se desviaba a un cabo o a otro, había de quedar colgado del brazo" (I, 43, 220a). The cruelty of this practical joke needs no extra explanation. Moreover, the narrator does not describe it as funny although the "risibility factor" of the age might see it as something worthy of Buster Keaton or worse. The narrator uses words like "temor" and "cuidado" that would have no place in a "funny" account of the story. Later the text reads "cuando se desviaron los juntos pies de don Quijote, y resbalando de la silla, dieran con él en el suelo, a no quedar colgado del brazo; cosa que le causó tanto dolor que creyó, o que la muñeca le cortaban, o que el brazo se le arrancaba;" (I, XLIII, 221b). Once again, what we have here is pain and terror on the part of Don Quijote. There is no

---

[20] For interesting and significant psychological observations on humor see Martin Grotjahn, a Freudian psychoanalyst: *Beyond Laughter*. New York: Blakiston, 1957.

way one can see this as a funny episode, except as some kind of personal perversion. Cervantes does not intend for it to be so; he intends for it to belong to the design of cruelty that some inflict upon others. Within this view, humor would exist only in the perspective of others, not on that of the victim of the *burla*.

There is still the episode which would fall into the category of a cruel joke and that is the episode of the cats. "Aquí llegaba don Quijote de su canto, a quien estaban escuchando el Duque y la Duquesa, Altisidora y casi toda la gente del castillo, cuando de improviso, desde encima de un corredor que sobre la reja de don Quijote a plomo caía, descolgaron un cordel donde venían más de cien cencerros asidos, y luego tras ellos derramaron un gran saco de gatos, que asimismo traían cencerros atados a las colas. Fué tan grande el ruido de los cencerros y el mayor de los gatos, que aunque los Duques habían sido inventores de la burla, todavía les sobresaltó, y, temeroso don Quijote, quedó pasmado" (II, XLVI, 431b). Don Quijote is taken by surprise, he unsheathes his sword and begins swinging it at the cats: "aunque uno, viéndose tan acosado de las cuchilladas de don Quijote, le saltó al rostro y le asió de las narices con las uñas y los dientes, por cuyo dolor don Quijote comenzó a dar los mayores gritos que pudo" (II, XLVI, 432a). For once, the Duke and Duchess, in whose castle Don Quijote finds himself, "le [Don Quijote] dejaron sosegar, y se fueron, *pesarosos del mal suceso de la burla; que no creyeron que tan pesada y costosa le saliera a don Quijote aquella aventura que le costó cinco días de encerramiento y de cama*" [Emph. mine] (II, XLVII, 432b). The text makes it explicitly clear that Don Quijote is subjected to a terrible experience, fueled by bad judgment and hostility. There is nothing funny about these two episodes which I use to show that the term "funny book" misses the point of the book by a wide margin.

The level of hostility that is to be seen in the treatment of Don Quijote can only be called pathos. I refer to his return home at the end of the first part. The Priest and the Barber entice Don Quijote into a cage, which is demeaning enough. But there is a detail in timing. They return to town "adonde entraron en la mitad del día, que acertó a ser domingo, y la gente toda en la plaza, por mitad de la cual atravesó el carro de Don Quijote" (I, LII, 256a). The text also adds "Cosa de lástima fué oír los gritos que las dos buenas señoras alzaron, las bofetadas que se dieron" (I, LII, 256a).

The characters of the inner text are just as shocked as the readers outside the text should be. Symbolically, Don Quijote is reduced to an animal status. These are all in the text, and their consequences are not looked upon happily o something over which to rejoice.

The final point to be made in qualifying (but not totally rejecting Russell's and Close's hypothesis) deals with a variety of episodes in the text, beginning with the story of Grisóstomo and Marcela, and the suicide of Grisóstomo. While critics agree upon the substance of the "Curioso impertinente" as a use of the Italianate tale, it also involves several "unfunny" things—the end of what seems like a perfectly good marriage and the death of Anselmo and the retirement of Camila to a convent (as well as the death in battle of Lotario). There is no way of looking upon these as funny.

In the story of Leandra and Vicente de la Roca we find out "Vicente de la Roca la había engañado, y debajo de su palabra de ser su esposo la persuadió que dejase la casa de su padre" (I, LI, 251b). Or the tragic story of Claudia Jerónima, who takes the law into her own hands and kills her supposed violator. After she shoots Vicente Torrellas, unlike Basilio who leaps up in glory and joy having convinced Quiteria to marry him, Leandra's story has no such dénouement: "Volvió de su desmayo Claudia, pero no de su parasismo don Vicente, porque se le acabó la vida" (I, LX, 486a).

The strategies of Don Quijote's defeat at the hands of Sansón Carrasco belong to a two-part plan. The first where Sansón challenges Don Quijote, but is legitimately beaten by him, is certainly humorous, brought about largely by our expectation that the younger man will prevail. However, Don Quijote surprises us all and together with his *simpatía*, he earns our respect and affection. There is certainly something humorous about Don Quijote's victory, but his demise is something else. Here the turnabout (Sansón's victory over Don Quijote) produces no humor but rather a tragic and sad sense. It signifies the end of Don Quijote's *simpatía* as well as his *proyecto vital*. This has all the earmarks of a tragedy rather than a funny account. Moreover, Don Quijote's death by melancholia and depression do not make for the close of a funny book.

Taken in toto, the book contains a few examples of farce, many examples of humorous incidents, but a sad and tragic finale.

It is, I insist, an error to see *Don Quijote* as belonging to the funny book syndrome. The humor of the book belongs to the author's wish to present life in a complete perspective; it is not a completely funny book, because I have shown episodes that are tragic, nor is it fully a tragic book because there are numerous comical examples. Cervantes, I sense, wishes to give his reader the idea that a life fully lived has examples of everything.

Don Quijote's death puts the final seal not of a funny book, but of a sad one. The reader should return to *Lazarillo de Tormes*'s prologue, alluded to above, which suggests the double-faceted structure of the work: "pues podría ser que alguno que las lea halle algo que le agrade y a los que no ahondaren tanto los deleyte" (91). The key words here are "no ahondaren tanto," signifying that there are several levels. In *Don Quijote*, the superficial level presents humor in its many facets, but the substructure and subtext are very serious indeed, and I am not talking about the kind of seriousness that a great book purports to have. I am talking about emotions, sentiments and feelings that are not funny at all. This substantial reading demands a deeper view of the text, and for this the reader and critic must stand back and see the work in its totality. *Don Quijote* is not a funny book, but one that touches on all aspects of life

8
Cervantes, Lepanto, and the Concept of Wounding, Pain and Suffering

IT IS FAIR TO SAY that the mention of the word "Lepanto" conjures up more associations with Cervantes than with the actual historical event that took place on October 7, 1571. At the same time the word "Lepanto" meant more to Cervantes than anything in his lifetime, including *Don Quijote*. For him, it meant participation in the greatest military naval event of the early modern period. It is also in Lepanto that Cervantes sustained wounds to his chest, arm and hand that were lifetime reminders of his participation in that battle. Indeed, the wound to his left hand and arm meant the permanent dysfunction of the arm.

According to Robert Cowley and Geoffrey Parker, Lepanto involved approximately 160,000 men and 400 galleys.[1] Difficulties with the Ottoman Empire began in 1570. The following year Spain and Venice formed an alliance with the Papacy to create a fleet to relieve Cyprus of the Ottoman power. Early in 1571 the Christian Alliance located the Ottoman presence in the Gulf of Lepanto and engaged them on October 7 whereby they destroyed and captured 200 of the 230 galleys and their supplies, as well as approximately 30,000 men (*ibid.*, 262b). According to Cowley and Parker, this debilitating step did not totally destroy Ottoman sea power, but that in 1572 the Turks could move 200 galleys to their fleet.

One reads of the anecdote of when Philip II received the news of the results of Lepanto while he was in his chapel. Supposedly *El Rey Prudente* told the messenger "Pull yourself together...Wait until I have finished here

---

[1] Cowley, Robert and Geoffrey Parker, eds. *The Reader's Companion to Military History*. Boston: Houghton Mifflin, 1996.

and then we shall see."[2] These anecdotes are often seen as the king's lack of interest in the military affair. Rather, his estimate of the importance of the battle and his opinion thereof is better seen in his final approval of Titian's "Spain's Coming to the Aid of Religion," details of which the king approved through his own court painter Alonso Sánchez Coello (Parker, *Philip II*, 111). The best part of the painting endeavor is to see what Philip understood his role to be: which is the support of the secular state in favor of religion, an attitude present in Lepanto as it was in other military situations (including the fiasco of the Armada off the British coast in 1588).

There are numerous accounts of Cervantes's participation in the battle. Although feverish from illness, he came on deck and participated actively in the fight, during which time he received two wounds in the chest and serious wounding in the left hand and arm (for descriptions of this see Bordoy Cerda, Navarro Ledesma and Astrana Marín, among others). Some accounts are dramatic creations of the event, probably embellished by admiration and passion for Cervantes, but the facts are clear: Cervantes did receive serious wounds and spent a period of time after the battle in Messina recuperating from these wounds.

Navarro Ledesma describes the post-battle state of the wound as being "gangrened" (62). A certain amount of polemic has dealt with whether Cervantes had lost his arm (see Bordoy Cerda who states that he lost the *use* of the arm, but not the arm itself).

What interests us is that there is a rather relative silence by Cervantes on the subject, or rather, not as much is said of this beyond two instances (the prologue of the *Novelas ejemplares* ["Llámase comúnmente Miguel de Cervantes Saavedra. Fue soldado muchos años, y cinco y medio cautivo, donde aprendió a tener paciencia en las adverdsidades. Perdió en la batalla naval de Lepanto la mano izquierda de un arcabuzazo, herida que, aunque parece fea, él la tiene por hermosa, por haberla cobrado en la más memorable y alta ocasión que vieron los pasados siglos, ni esperan ver los venideros, militando debajo de las vencedoras banderas del hijo del rayo de la guerra, Carlo Quinto, de felice memoria"[3]] and the prologue of the Second Part of *Don Quijote*, where Cervantes defends himself from the attacks of the

---

[2] Parker, Geoffrey. *Philip II*. Boston: Little, Brown, 1978. See also *The Grand Strategy of Philip II*. New Haven: Yale University Press, 1998; p. 19 for another version of Philip's reaction.

[3] Sieber, Harry. *Las novelas ejemplares*. 2 Vols. Madrid: Cátedra, 1980. See I, 51.

author of the spurious *Don Quijote*, noting that he did not acquire the wounds in a tavern brawl but in the greatest happening of his time: "Lo que no he podido dejar de sentir es que me note de viejo y de manco, como si hubiera sido en mi mano haber detenido el tiempo, que no pasase por mí, o si mi manquedad hubiera nacido en alguna taberna, sino en la más alta ocasión que vieron los siglos pasados, los presentes, ni esperan ver los venideros."[4] That his wounding and its physical consequences were obvious to others, Bordoy Cerda quotes Lope de Vega's reference to Cervantes as "el estropeado español" (91).[5]

The experience of his wounding must have been traumatic. As Navarro Ledesma points out, we tend to examine matters of health and health care through a modern light.[6] In Messina, survival was a matter of luck: there was a lack of necessary medications, exposure to robbers, lack of resources and charity (Navarro Ledesma, 63). Any number of reasons could have condemned a person to a quick death. The experience from the wounding to the convalescence was fraught with terror and fear. All of which raises a serious question: why the relative silence on Cervantes's part? Lewis B. Puller, a Vietnam Marine veteran and son of the fabled General "Chesty" Puller, writes with regret, emotion and at times with controlled rationality about a similar experience of being severely wounded in Vietnam and the recuperation afterwards until his untimely death by his own hand; but he writes about it, most probably for the cathartic effects it could offer him.[7]

In a brief note, Maldonado de Guevara sees a symbolic link between the "pesadilla" of Lepanto and the episode of the windmills in *Don Quijote*.[8] He says: "Don Quijote, armado, acomete el remolino de los molinos de viento, asimiladas ahora las aspas—oníricamente—a las velas de los barcos en batalla naval. Acometida, riesgo y salvación" (247). Moreover, Maldonado reads into this linking a cathartic purpose: "Me atrevo, pues, a aventurar mi

---

[4] Castro, Américo. *El ingenioso hidalgo Don Quijote de la Mancha*. op. cit. See prologue to Part II, p. 267.
[5] Bordoy Cerda, Miguel. *Mallorca, Lepanto y Cervantes*. Palma de Mallorca: Cort, 1971.
[6] Navarro Ledesma, Francisco. *Cervantes. The Man and the Genius*. N.Y.: Charterhouse, 1973, p. 60.
[7] Puller Jr., Lewis B. *Fortunate Son: The Autobiography of Lewis B. Puller*. N.Y.: Grove Weidenfeld, 1991.
[8] Maldonado de Guevara, Francisco. "La pesadilla de Cervantes: Lepanto," *Anales cervantinos*, 15 (1976): 247-48.

estimación hasta poner en los poderes del artista la pesadilla creadora por la virtud de la creación misma, por su transfiguración en la estatura de una figuración y configuración en el firmamento del arte. Si Cervantes fue víctima de tal pesadilla, tengo por cierto que se libró definitivamente de ella al estampar en el blanco papel la que es la aventura primordial de la gran obra" (248).

Stanislav Zimic associates Lepanto with Cervantes's own *Weltanschauung*.[9] For Zimic, "La batalla de Lepanto se convertiría así también en una representación valiosa de aquella tragicomedia que para él era la vida: exaltación de ideales, comicidad de recursos en el intento de materializarlos, heroismo que se manifiesta hasta lo absurdo, tragedia, ironía, gravedad, comedia, inutilidad del esfuerzo...Fue el acto humano en sí, independiente de la significación ideológica, lo que, en definitiva, debió de impresionar a Cervantes" (175).

For me and for the analysis I wish to make of this aspect of *Don Quijote*, the wounding at Lepanto is a tragic and traumatic beginning in Cervantes's mature life, followed by the experience in Algiers which "rounds out" the initial wounding experience. Given the relative silence of Cervantes about this trauma (and I would urge a reading of Puller's autobiography to show what one does and what one thinks when victimized by a war wound) we must see if he bore his cross silently and why, or if he deliberately encoded this trauma into his works, or if by some experience of sublimation, the feelings and physical experiences become channeled into his writing. As I hope my analysis will show, there is a concern in *Don Quijote* with wounding, a presence of sensitivity about the body, a thoughtfulness and concern about wounding others or the wounding of the self. *Don Quijote* will, as both Zimic and Maldonado suggest, reveal Lepanto and its presence in Cervantes's life.

After Cervantes's recuperation he leaves Sicily for Spain and on the way is captured by Turkish corsairs; he is brought to Algiers and placed in a *bagnio*, a type of prison camp. As in any prison situation, there is largely an experience of loneliness, pain, suffering, both psychological and physical. Algiers is the complementary episode to Cervantes's traumatic experience at Lepanto.

---

[9] Zimic, Stanislas. "Un eco de Lepanto en la ironía cervantina," *Romance Notes*, 12, #1 (1970): 174-176.

Donald P. McCrory, using the Captive's Tale (*DQ*, I, 39-41) fills in the various *lacunae* of both Lepanto and Algiers.[10] He says: "Cervantes added his name to the 25,000 Christian slaves imprisoned in the city. As he walked to the slave market, however, he would have noticed that the port was in full swing; lithographs of the period reveal a thick labyrinth of roads and houses which led to and from several *souks* or markets, a series of public gardens and baths, several mosques and a fascinating array of different dress-styles to be expected in a society where the cultural mix was unusually rich" (21). This is a slghtly exaggerated approach to Cervantes's story in Captivity (although McCrory goes on to reveal other important aspects of the experience, most of which are negative). Other than a pleasant picture of Algerian life, life in the *bagnio* was closer to what the convicted criminal Jack Abbott wrote in his book, *In the Belly of the Beast*.[11]

Cervantes's attitude in prison life is best explained by McCrory when he says: "As he trudged back to Hasan Pasha's royal prison, memories of his enforced flight and exile from Spain, his maimed left hand and deeply scarred chest, his unexpected capture with the subsequent confiscation of coveted letters of recommendation may have stirred deeply within him, giving him grounds for regret, even despair" (31). McCrory says: "La Goleta and the fortress, both mentioned by Rui Pérez, fell to numerically superior Turkish forces and although Lepanto was still green in both armies' memory, the crushing defeat of Tunis demoralized Spain; the effect on Spanish prisoners in the *bagnios* and dungeons of Algiers must have been catastrophic" (26). He further states "The incredible energy he [Cervantes] displays later, when working for the authorities in the south of Spain, indicates how intensely frustrating imprisonment must have been. Moreover his admission that adversity taught him patience suggests that by nature he was prone to be otherwise" (26-27). Very much like the quasi-silence of the traumatic wound his experiences in the *bagnio* are, as McCrory states: "Cervantes says very little of his private inner world in captivity, yet

---

[10] McCrory, Donald P. *Miguel de Cervantes. The Captive's Tale (La historia del cautivo). Don Quijote, Part One, Chapters 39-41*. Westminster (England): Aris and Phillips, 1999. New studies focus on Cervantes's suspicious survival after several attempts at escape; such attempts usually meant death. See P.J. Smith, *Quixotic Desire*, and the recent book by Medina Molera. See also María Antonia Garcés, *Cervantes in Algiers*.
[11] Abbott, Jack Henry. *In the Belly of the Beast: Letters From Prison*. N.Y.: Random House, 1981.

it was an experience he never would forget and one which continued to have meaning for him up until his death" (30).

Perhaps the very best examples of life in the Algerian prison have been penned by Fray Diego de Haedo.[12] Basically, Haedo describes life in the *bagnios* as an example of the greatest cruelties imaginable: torture of many kinds, the deforming of extremities, the cutting off of ears, the slitting of noses (I, 178). He describes some of the most gory and horrendous unburdening of anger by guards. Prisoners are beaten even after dying. Describing the actions of the guards and soldiers, he notes the pleasure they take in doing evil, hanging prisoners, burning them alive, hanging and hooking alive the prisoners, without anyone stepping in to the stop or attenuate the tortures (I, 179). It was all a joke for the Moorish guards. In an almost Gracián-esque way he notes "dexan al momento de ser hombres y se visten de entrañas de tigres y bestias fieras" (I, 179).

In another volume of his *Topografía e historia general de Argel,* Haedo continues describing the tortures. Throughout he describes inhuman tortures, starvation diets, whippings, attacks on galley slaves. When guards become drunk they unburden their anger on their prisoners. The best word to describe the life of the Christian prisoners is martyrdom. Galley slaves are often thrown into the sea. Prisoners are walking skeletons. Sometimes they receive as many as 300 strokes of the lash on their back, abdomen and legs. One particular cruelty was to tie up a prisoner, hang him and jerk the rope about until his arms, legs, nerves and bones are disjointed, and he is left for dead (II, 98-99). Fray Diego says: "Son cosas éstas que parecen increíbles a quien no las vido con el ojo y con experiencia tocó; pero son tan ordinarias y de tan grave tormento, que por eso no nos maravillamos de que se muera tanto número de cristianos cada día en el corso, y que otros, de aborridos y aun desesperados ellos mismos, se den la muerte con sus manos, mas antes cómo sea posible que vuelvan algunos vivos a Argel y no queden todos allá sepultados en la mar" (II, 100). That this world was not foreign or distant from Cervantes is proved by Haedo when he writes "y particularmente maniataron a Miguel de Cervantes, un hidalgo principal de Alcalá de Henares, que fuera el autor deste negocio, y era, por tanto, más culpado [reference to the escape attempt], porque ansí lo mandó el Rey a quien los presentaron luego" (III, 163). The king "retuvo solamente en casa

---

[12] Haedo, Fray Diego de. *Topografía e historia general de Argel*. Vol. 1, Madrid: Sociedad de bibliófilos españoles, 1927; Vol. II, 1929; Vol. III, 1929.

a Miguel Cervantes" (III, 163). In fact, when describing some of Cervantes's experiences in the *bagnio* Navarro Ledesma says "For the third time, Miguel was brought before Hassan Pasha, and the familiar court of bailiffs, soldiers, and executioners. The King ordered a rope placed around his neck and his hands tied behind his back" (III, 120). That is, bodily harm was not foreign to Cervantes. He must have been a witness to some of the tortures exacted on Christian prisoners.[13] Given what we know about life in the bagnio, however, it is a matter of great curiosity that Cervantes was not killed after his several unsuccessful attempted escapes. It is true that he bore letters of recommendation from powerful protectors and was thought to be ransomable at a high price because of that. But how he was not killed is a mystery that critics and historians have not been able to decipher but only leaves the imagination open to numerous founded and, indeed, unfounded hypotheses.

In the face of Cartesian reliance on reason, Blaise Pascal wondered just how "reasonable" or reasoned someone would be if he were placed in a cage and hung from a spire of the cathedral of Notre Dame. Compared to the supposedly iron-clad power of reason, "unreason" pales. Our civilization has taken the function and meaning from the Greeks and made it a fundamental part of our civilization. But Pascal was certainly on the right track when he alluded to the frailty of reason in certain situations. He is talking about embodiment, and in this scheme, a person is as strong as his ability is to control his fears and emotions. He is governed by forces below the surface of his reason. James M. Edie, in his edition of Merleau Ponty, frames the question in the following way: "As Descartes once said profoundly, the soul is not merely in the body like a pilot in his ship; it is wholly intermingled with the body. The body, in turn, is wholly animated, and all the functions contribute to the perception of objects—an activity long considered by philosophy to be pure knowledge" (5). He continues: "We grasp external space through our bodily situation. A 'corporeal or postural schema' gives us at every moment a global, practical, and implicit notion of the relation between our body and things, of our hold on them. A system of possible movements, or 'motor projects,' radiates from us to our environment" (5). For Cervantes, his wounded body is projected outward

---

[13] The tortures of the bagnio are also treated by Sola (142, 147) [Sola, Emilio and José F. De la Peña]. *Cervantes y Berbería (Cervantes, mundo turco-berberisco y servicios secretos en la época de Felipe II]*, and Bordoy Cerda (105).

toward the world.[14] "The phenomenological person," as Lakoff and Johnson note, "who through phenomenological introspection alone can discover everything there is to know about the mind and the nature of experience, is a fiction. Although we can have a theory of a vast, rapidly and automatically operating cognitive unconscious, we have no direct conscious access to its operation and therefore to most of our thought. Phenomenological reflection, though valuable in revealing the structure of experience, must be supplemented by empirical research into the cognitive unconscious"(5). In assessing Cervantes's functioning we must use the term cognitive to refer to what Lakoff and Johnson define as "to describe any mental operations and structures that are involved in language, meaning, perception, conceptual systems, and reason. Because our conceptual systems and our reason arise from our bodies, we will also use the term *cognitive* for aspects of our sensorimotor system that contribute to our abilities to conceptualize and to reason" (12). Therefore, Cervantes's thoughts, works and utterances must be understood as to have passed through the filter, so to speak, of his interior emotive apparatus. Again, Lakoff and Johnson state: "We will suggest, first, that human concepts are not just reflections of an external reality, but that they are crucially shaped by our bodies and brains, especially by our sensorimotor system" (22). Departing from Lakoff and Johnson's approach in part, I shall be examining *Don Quijote* from a perspective that includes all the examples of bodily involvement actions that are likely to mold Cervantes's world view. Lakoff and Johnson examine "2. Concepts of bodily movement represented by verbs like *grasp, pull, lift, tap,* and *punch.* 3. Concepts indicating the structure of actions or events (what linguists call *aspectual concepts*) like *starting, stopping, resuming, continuing, finishing,* including those indicated grammatically as in process (in English *is/are* plus the verb stem plus -ing: *is running*) or completed (has/have plus the verb stem plus -ed: *has lifted*) (39). In the middle of this system one finds spatial relations and how what one views is interwoven by the logic of spatial relations and how our bodily movements can structure concepts (*ibid,* 39). In essence these authors are basing the world

---

[14] See Edie: "For us the body is much more than an instrument or a means; it is our expression in the world, the invisible form of our intentions. Even our most secret affective moments, those most deeply tied to the humoral infrastructure, help to shape our perception of things" (5). *The Primacy of Perception,* James M. Edie, ed. Evanston: Northwestern University Press, 1964.

of concepts and conceptual thinking on inner processes rather than on mere ratiocination. The body stands as an island at the center of such mental and physical activity.

In her important book, Susanne K. Langer treats themes which are very applicable to *Don Quijote*. Symbols, myths, ritual and their symbolization all point to the manner in which Cervantes creates his world.

She points to "the function of *symbolic transformation* [Emph. hers] as a natural activity, a high form of nervous response, characteristic of man among the animals" (xiv), because we can see that experiences which Cervantes undergoes become transposed into characters in a literary setting. I hasten to remind that the traumatic wound and the agonies of incarceration will form the mental structure that creates his literary world. There is a process by which blood metamorphoses into symbol and will appear in various guises in *Don Quijote*. Semioticians will rejoice at the process of symbolization. Langer asserts that "Ritual, like art, is essentially the active termination of a symbolic transformation of experience" (45). Cervantes will assimilate his experiences and funnel them into his art. Experience and psychological necessity are absorbed and then channeled, often without particular targets but operate amorphously so that they appear unexpectedly and emanate from the combination of consciousness and unconsciousness. Langer refers to Freud's contribution to the philosophy of mind "has been the realization that human behavior is not only a food-getting strategy, but is also a language; that every *move* is at the same time a *gesture*. Symbolization is both an end and an instrument" [Emph. hers] (51). Cervantes's discursiveness (cfr. Langer, 81-82) is a verbal construction to express the maelstrom of emotions deriving from key experiences like the wound-trauma and the incarceration.

Edmund Wilson's work, *The Wound and the Bow* is a fundamental study of psychological injury and how it affects the victim.[15] For Wilson, Charles Dickens's early experiences created a trauma that he carried with him all his life. Although his stay at the blacking warehouse was only six months, the experience was enough to incise its mark on his creative intellect. This attitude was forever present in him and he never forgave his mother for putting him there (8). Speaking of one of Dickens's novels, Wilson says: "Dickens has here, under the stimulus of the chartist agitation, tried to give his own emotions an outlet through an historical novel of insurrection" (18)

---

[15] Edmund Wilson, *The Wound and the Bow*. See also "Dickens" The Two Scrooges."

While examining Dickens's *Little Dorrit*, he says "is that the fable is here presented from the point of view of imprisoning states of mind as much as that of oppressive institutions" (47). He closes the book with a disquisition of Philoctetes who is an emblem of the disabled person who bears his wound with great pains, and whereby the malady and the wound become more than stains but cognition-enabling interpretations.[16]

In his book, *The Juice of Life*, Piero Camporesi studies the presence and meaning of blood across certain chronological eras.[17] He studies the presence of blood in self-lacerating flagellations, usually performed as a part of the religious ceremony. He suggests the blood/wine relationship begins perhaps with the crucifixion. Blood assumes many symbols beyond the merely hematological. I associate Cervantes's wound with a 'bloodletting" that could conceivably place in Cervantes's mind a meaning of more than mere loss of blood. When you couple this with the significance of the event in which this happens one can understand why this wound could achieve such significance. Was it perhaps a "God-given" experience? The connotations of blood or blood-letting urge cautious interpretation but should not avoid understanding the action within a cultural construct of blood/wine/religiousness. This wound was a symbol consigning semiotic codes which carried with it cognitive contours over and beyond what an industrial accident might do. There is a big difference between a wound sustained at the Normany beachhead and one obtained at a construction site even though the final consequences may be the same. The victim bears an enormous sign. As David Waterman states in a context dealing with British authors, "The body is marked by power and ideology and becomes as well the primary site of resistance, becoming in fact a text which can be read and interpreted," (introduction, unnumbered pages)[18] and he adds "The body is often inscribed and interpreted by the dominant power on the basis of race, gender, age and so on, using a system of cultural codes (i.e., binary opposition)" (*ibid.*). Both as a participant in Lepanto and a prisoner

---

[16] "And the malady of Philoctetes may have figured his moral defects: the unruly and unscrupulous nature which, even though he seems to have been innocent of charges brought against him, had given them a certain plausibility" (235).
[17] Camporesi, Piero. *The Juice of Life*. The Symbol and Magic Significance of Blood. Forward by Umberto Eco. Translated by Robert R. Barr. N.Y.: Continuum, 1995.
[18] Waterman, David. *Disordered Bodies, Disrupted Borders*. Representations of Resistance in Modern British Literature. Lanham: University Press of America, 1999.

in Algiers, Cervantes's body becomes inscribed with historical distinctions that signify outwardly. There is a circular development between body and history. Waterman says: "A materialist approach to body/text must also involve history, resulting from what [Edith] Scarry and Pierre Macherey call intervention, which assumes that history (and, I would add, power/ideology as well) acts on the text, and that the text also acts on historical reality" (*ibid.,* [see Scarry xxiii, xxv]). Essentially keeping in mind that the wound and the incarceration co-involve political acts: "The body/text becomes a political text as a result of its involvement in social relations of power, placing the subject in different positions and/or oppositions, often depending on how the body is marked in terms of age, race, nationality, socioeconomic class, gender and sexual orientation" (*ibid.*)

Stephen Greenblatt carries the blood symbolism a bit farther than Camporesi[19]. Focusing on blood, he says "The root perception, and it is one that Christians embraced far more than Jews, is that there is a link between mutilation, as a universal emblem of corporeal vulnerability and abjection, and holiness" (223). He says further "Pious men and women in the Middle Ages were not content only to read the sacred book of Christ's wounded body; they longed for Christ to inscribe his truth on their own bodies and in particular on their hearts" (223). He discusses self-mutilation, as does Camporesi, in the name of religious devotion. Like Langer and others, Greenblatt attempts to trace the conversion of thought into reality: "How do 'affections'—passions, ideas, responses, projects—pass from the silent and inaccessible inner reaches of the mind to the world? The obvious passageways, of course, are speech and writing" (231). The body, in whatever state it exists, sends out messages, creates ideologies and affects the observer.

In his interesting book, *The Wounded Body: Remembering the Markings of the Flesh,* Dennis P. Slattery traces the body in the works of several authors.[20] Quoting Mark Selzer's study, *Serial Killers,* Seltzer says that " 'in wound culture, the very notion of sociality is bound to the excitations of the torn and opened body; the torn and exposed individual, as public spectacle' "

---

[19] Greenblatt, Stephen. "Mutilation and Meaning," in *The Body in Parts:* Phantasies of Corporeality in Early Modern Europe., Hillman, David and Carla Mazzio, eds. N.Y.: Routledge, 1997, pp. 221-241.
[20] Slattery, Dennis Patrick. *The Wounded Body. Remembering the Markings of Flesh.* Albany: SUNY Press, 2000.

(7). Slattery comments further: "The wounded body certainly reflects the wound culture that gives it life and a place" (7). And focusing on the notion of the centrality of the wound, Slattery says "At the same time, the body's vulnerability and changeability, its mortalness and susceptibility to wounding 'reminded the audience of the ephemeral nature of the body, human life, and thus more so, the importance of home' " (38). It is the ephemeralness that must have struck Cervantes; the knowledge that his life could have ended if the bullets had penetrated other parts of his body, precipitating his demise.

The question of the social "appearance" of a wounded individual is examined by Jean Starobinski in his study of Valéry and his concept of the three bodies.[21] For the purposes of my paper I refer to his statement: "Our *Second Body* [Emph. his] is the one which others see, and an approximation of which confronts us in the mirror or in portraits. It is the body which has a form and is apprehended by the arts, the body on which materials, ornaments, armor sit, which love sees or wants to see, and yearns to touch. It knows no pain, for it reduces pain to a mere grimace" (399).

Once again returning to the wound as a social marker, Slattery notes "Over time, our bodies are continually marked with experience, from an original birthmark to a scar [cfr. Odysseus], surgical wound, or physical deformity that reveals something crucially significant about our identity, the nature of our actions, and the texture from biography, as Odysseus' boar scar from hunting has just shown us" (51). Therefore, Odysseus becomes an example of difference. Slattery continues: "We will see, for example, that through the wound that he is forced to remember, the shackles put through his ankles shortly after his birth, Oedipus comes to know that he is out of place, and that this is the genesis of his polluting effect on the city and the land. Pollution would seem to have close ties to displacement and to disorder" (54). Cervantes's awareness of his difference may have not only restructured his worldview but done so in a strange way. Slattery says referring to Morris Berman's book (*Coming to Our Senses*) focusing on Rousseau and his reasons for creating his autobiography: "that the self is created not exclusively by the Other but by one's self in a conspiracy. Our own body image is prominent and central to our visual image of our selves" (90). Turning to Melville's Ahab, Slattery says: "Ahab's

---

[21] Starobinski, Jean. *Fragments for a History of the Human Body*, Part II. Feher, Michael and Ramona Naddaff and Nadia Tazi, eds. N.Y.: Zone, 1989.

shattered body is the emblem of this narcissistic rage as well as the source of its seemingly limitless energy. His exterior, visible body wounds mark deeper afflictions that finally surface shortly after he offers the Ecuadorian doubloon as reward to him who sights the white whale" (148-49). If language is to be the final step of the result of physicality, as Langer says (see above), then we could not help but agree with Slattery that "Ahab's language is full of images of wounding to avenge his own deep afflictions. While Queequeg's markings remember cosmic and unitive designs of the psyche, Ahab's markings, dismemberment, and language express a tyranny of chaos in the soul" (150) just as the useless and withered hand of Cervantes was a reminder, for Ahab his "phantom limb feels the original flesh taken by the whale. The phantom limb is an absent but powerful memory of the original wounding" (151).

The appearance of this man, Cervantes, must have been in some measure a strong social statement. This assumes greater meaning when one considers Lope's statement about "el estropeado español" (see above).

In a psychological vein, when one considers a wound, with its pain and bloodletting, one cannot ignore the psychological/psychoanalytical associations with castration. In studying the grotesque in literature, Peter L. Hays acknowledges that the subject is vast. He says: "What I say of crippled figures in this study may appear equally relevant to others who are not lame or castrated: the blind or deaf, those missing hands or arms. But I have limited my work to lame or emasculated characters for several reasons. First, the number of characters in literature who are in some way maimed must be enormous" (7). While my study focuses on the body, it also hopes to understand the author and his crippling and the extent to which it structures his work.

In his perceptive book, *A History of Disability*, Henri-Jacques Stiker surveys the subject of disability in several epochs and his perspective contains a hope to change negative attitudes towards disability.[22] The history of disability coinvolves the history of attitudes, prejudices and biases. It also is connected to values in the societies he studies. For Stiker, the example of Jesus "breaks the connection between disability and individual fault" (33). Jesus becomes, as noted above, an icon of pain, suffering and wounding and has encouraged people to undergo pain; to

---

[22] Stiker, Henri-Jacques. *A History of Disability*. Translated by William Sayers. Ann Arbor: University of Michigan Press, 1999.

endure flagellation and other forms of self-discipline (Cfr. also Camporesi). Attitudes were changed by Jesus's example even though some of these are examples of self-debasement and self-mutilation. Yet while the sense of difference is unacceptable it is reminaful of an earlier time and values; it involves the uncovering of non-reason and irrationality (cfr. 63). It might almost be nostalgic. Earlier attitudes involved the exclusion of "different" people: "The rules of the almshouses, however, at times excluded paralytics (as was often to prove the case) or bedridden persons incapable of working; more frequently, the lame, one-armed and blind were excluded, since their incurable disability did not constitute a sickness in the narrow sense of the word" (79) and one might add, marginalized those people that could not fit into the economy. Cervantes's wounding must have placed limitations upon him, but they were not enough, as biographers have pointed out, to prevent him from having jobs that he was able to carry out. His status as a wounded person was that of the "half-outsider." Yet, we could ask ourselves, could Cervantes's disability have limited his opportunities and options? Could it be yet another reason to deny him permission to emigrate to the New World? These are unanswered questions that stimulate the imagination.

Another feature of Stiker's view, and which has been touched upon lightly above, is the religious link. For the baroque Spaniard, there is no area in which God does not represent a presence. Stiker says: "I have stated that the Gospels dismantle the rule of a strictly religious conception in favor of an ethical one. Let me now continue with my chosen topic. If we had to generalize—and thereby necessarily analyze—this development, I would need to write a very different book" (87). He continues: "God sends us disease and disability as *trials* on the one hand, as *opportunities* [his emphasis in both cases] to exercise our greatest virtue, charity, on the other, and thirdly as the sign of his presence. This does not entail a sacrificial attitude but puts the authenticity of our faith and our customs to the test" (87). Must the injury and subsequent trials and tribulations as God-sent not have passed through Cervantes's mind? Could he have ignored the religious and theological suggestions of why *he* was the victim? Surely, any consideration of Cervantes, his time and his plight, could not ignore such a possibility.

In one of the most important books on pain. Elaine Scarry analyzes many aspects of the question, albeit with a view to understanding pain in the area of politics, torture, and incarceration, themes not far from our own focus.

She notes the existence of pain in a pre-linguistic phase, something one *feels* before speaking, thereby placing its locus *in* the body (4); in fact, she notes that there should be a resistance: "language is not simply one of its incidental or accidental attributes but is essential to what it is" (5). Not only does she treat pain in the body but also "*Psychological* suffering, though often difficult for any one person to express, *does* have referential content, *is* susceptible to verbal objectification, and is so habitually depicted in art that, as Thomas Mann's Settembrini reminds us, there is virtually no piece of literature that is *not* about suffering, no piece of literature that does not stand by ready to assist us" (11). For those that might tend to dismiss our preoccupation with pain and wounding (and its consequences) one must recall that while physical pain may cease, its remnants stay in the mind occasioning phobias and other types of psychological trauma. Inanimate objects become laden with suggestions for the pain it might occasion, e.g., a lance. She convinces us of the ramifications of pain and political consequences (19), which of course are supremely applicable in the case of Cervantes.

I have saved for last perhaps one of the best examples of pain and wounding and one which parallels the experiences of Cervantes and which offers numerous suggestions about Cervantes's handling of his own predicament, and that is the example of Ignatius of Loyola, ably studied by the Jesuit psychoanalyst, W.W. Meissner.[23]

In a battle at Pamplona, Iñigo de Loyola was struck by a French cannonball delivering numerous injuries, "the French artillery put an end to Iñigo de Loyola. Iñigo was never more fully himself...It was in this moment that he was struck down. If the man Iñigo de Loyola survived, the identity of Iñigo was never to be the same" (37). After he was wounded he was operated on, but surgeons felt that the leg needed to be operated on again and the leg reset. "Thirty years later, he recalled this surgery: 'Again he went through this butchery, in which as in all the others that he had suffered he uttered no word, nor gave any sign of pain other than clenching his fists' (Vita2). We must remind ourselves that this was several centuries before the introduction of surgical anesthesia" (44). Meissner informs us that the conversion process, which Loyola underwent, is tied to this signal

---

[23] Meissner, S.J., W.W. *The Psychology of a Saint*. Ignatius of Loyola. New Haven: Yale University Press, 1992.

event in his life, as Lepanto was for Cervantes. The wounding at Pamplona essentially did away with his personality, his ideals and ambitions. Meissner notes how the "narcissistic grandiosity and omnipotence" which characterized his personality was shattered (55). He had developed inwardly the self-image of a "sword-swinging hidalgo" (55). This came to an end when he was severely wounded and left him with a very noticeable limp. Meissner notes that, "Basic to this underlying core of anxiety had to be the threat of castration, intensified by the trauma of psychical injury and broken bones" (55). For Meissner, the process led Ignatius to go from one kind of life (a swashbuckling hero) to another one (religious convert and religious fighter). "The hypothesis we have been following here is that the strong, courageous, and fearless identity the young Iñigo had shaped, in the image of the chivalrous knight who feared no danger and sought glory and conquest on all sides, whether libidinal or aggressive, was formed around a phallic, narcissistic core that left him vulnerable to certain kinds of regressive stress" (77). Essentially Meissner argues that "the physical trauma he suffered at Pamplona and the subsequent convalescence, enforced helplessness, and painful dependence, as well as the intolerable resulting deformity, severely attacked his underlining narcissism, with far reaching consequences" (77).

Here we have the parallel experience of Cervantes. Cervantes even shared with Iñigo the Turkish threat. The kind of vanity that had marked Iñigo's personality now had to acknowledge that he no longer was a physical example of the knight: Meissner says "Actually Iñigo would not have cut a very impressive figure at this time. Aged about forty, he was a former man of arms who had been forced out of service by his war wound, which left him with a deformed leg and a noticeable limp" (143). We could be speaking of Cervantes. Both had to live with lifelong consequences of their wounds, only Cervantes conceals this—it is the great incognito of his life. For Iñigo one could say "no hay mal que por bien no venga": it began the road to conversion and to the development of a new person. For Cervantes, it meant a life of trials and tribulations, the re-forming of his creative consciousness, culminating in his writing of the first modern novel.

We have already discussed the effects of Algiers ("Cervantes says very little of his private inner world in captivity, yet it was an experience he would never forget and one which continued to have meaning for him up until his death," McCrory, 30). One can only imagine the sense of isolation, loneliness and despair in which he lived. McCrory surmises "memories of his enforced flight and exile from Spain, his maimed left hand and deeply scarred chest, his unexpected capture with the subsequent confiscation of coveted letters of recommendation may have stirred deeply within him, giving him grounds for regret, even despair" (31). Whatever his frame of mind, he indulged in bravado that may have been the acts of a desperate man, given what we know about punishment in the *bagnio*, but he was never punished for his sedition and attempts at escape. It seems fairly obvious that the Cautivo episode becomes the "filtered" version of his own biographical experiences in the *bagnio*. This can be seen as a channeling of his experiences along constructive lines and shows the extent to which the Algerian experience of incarceration had been impressed upon him (see also Cervantes's letter to Mateo Vázquez, in which he poetically describes his experiences [Astrana, 542 *et seq.*]. There are other sublimations that occur in the book, which will be discussed below.

From the wound that makes Cervantes a marked man, it would do well to study particular episodes in which the body figures in its tangible physicality.

When we meet Don Quijote he is described to us in terms that highlight his frailty: "Frisaba la edad de nuestro hidalgo con los cincuenta años: era de complexión recia, seco de carnes, enjuto de rostro, gran madrugador y amigo de la caza" (I, I, 19a). Cervantes has rejected a central character that will correspond to Renaissance imagery and portraits of perfection; not a portrait from Castiglione's *Cortigiano* but rather the depiction of an anti-hero whose fragilities will assume an important part in his experience, unlike Amadís de Gaula who represents, in his idealness, the perfect knight-errant. While his "complexión recia" may suggest some strength, his being "seco de carnes" can reveal a less-than-dominant physique and being "enjuto de carnes" creates the image, less of a knight than of an ascetic. All of this seems calculated to reduce the character from the picture of a "caballero andante" to a caricature of one, solely based on the negative characteristics revealed in his description.

When the subject of the insane comes up, as Don Quijote is usually thought to be, one tends to think of the mind as an intangible entity. However, insanity carries with it physical characteristics. If Don Quijote is mad, his appearance, with his spindly body and unhealthy looking face is an example or reflection of something that is not quite right in his mind. Throughout his adventures, attention is drawn to him not only because of his bizarre outfit and armor that is out of date, but also because his face betrays something that is unhealthy. Depictions of Don Quijote, as done by Daumier and others, all show him to be somewhat thin, wild-eyed and bizarre.

Another example of the connection between an infirm mind and the body is the character of Cardenio who goes mad after hearing that the woman he loved supposedly married someone else. We read: "Figurósele que iba desnudo, la barba negra y espesa, los cabellos muchos y rebultados, los pies descalzos y las piernas sin cosa alguna; los muslos cubrían unos calzones, al parecer, de terciopelo leonado, mas tan hechos pedazos, que por muchas partes se le descubrían las carnes" (I, XXIII, 105a). Cardenio's melancholy and depressive spirit lends to the body the appearance of someone distraught. His frustrated love has emptied his body of vitality, and he resembles less a man than a walking scarecrow. At times when his depression overcomes him, his head lowers as his consciousness recedes to some unknown point in the darkness of his mind.

If, as Elaine Scarry says, an inert object can reveal its potential damage to the body, then the subject of the "celada de encaje" is a symbol of the damage a sword or lance could do to the human head. It is in this episode, then that Cervantes has his hero understand precisely the damage that could be done. Don Quijote, after he tests the sureness of the "celada," destroys it with one fell swoop. Don Quijote knows what will happen if he received a blow, but chooses not to test the reality of a lance blow. Nevertheless, we receive an intimation of what the wounding process would be like. The wounding by a lance or any other blunt weapon is the analogue to Cervantes's own wounding. His reluctance to test the helmet may well be his wish that he not have ever been wounded and subjected to that pain, or merely to be reminded of it again.

The episode of Andrés the shepherd and Haldudo introduces us to the motif of beatings. In his mania in interpreting everything he sees as belonging to the world of chivalry and his adopted *proyecto vital*, he assumes that Andrés is a victim. Reminiscences of his experience in Algiers must have come through because Cervantes describes the boy/victim as "desnudo de medio cuerpo arriba" who was crying out because "le estaba dando con una pretina muchos azotes un labrador de buen talle" (I, IV, 28a). Negotiating with the labrador Don Quijote says "que si él rompió el cuero de los zapatos que vos pagasteis, vos le habéis rompido el de su cuerpo" (I, IV, 28b). The image of the wounds from the whipping, "*romper el cuerpo,*" accentuates the physicality of the punishment in the same way that physical punishment was meted out in the *bagnio.*

Further physicality and punishment can be observed when Don Quijote insists the Toledanos swear that Dulcinea is the most beautiful woman in the world. This creates a matrix of humor that tends to diminish Don Quijote's involvement in the episode. But when the Basque refuses, a battle between them is about to begin with Don Quijote suffering bad luck as his horse trips; Don Quijote falls to the ground and is not able to move. A groom finds him on the ground and proceeds to beat him with the remnants of a lance: "le molió como cibera… Dábanle voces sus amos que no le diese tanto y que le dejase; pero estaba ya el mozo picado y no quiso dejar el juego…y acudiendo por los demás trozos de la lanza, los acabó de dejar sobre el miserable caído, que, con toda aquella tempestad de palos que sobre él [llo]vía, no cerraba la boca, amenazando al cielo y a la tierra, y a los malandrines, que tal le parecían" (I, IV, 30b).

The experience with the windmills which is probably the most anthologized part of the work, depicts the Don hallucinating and attacking the windmills thinking they are giants. The force of the wind turns the arms which then come down on him knocking him and his horse to the ground, both of whom suffer in the process, which is followed by a battle with the Vizcaíno, which, because the Vizcaíno had turned his wrist, prevents Don Quijote from being outrightly killed. He merely suffers a terrible blow which affects one side of him and he loses part of an ear "que todo ello con espantosa ruina vino al suelo, dejándole muy maltrecho" (I, IX, 45b). His opponent receives a similar blow: "comenzó a echar sangre por las narices, y por la boca, y por los oidos, y a dar muestras de caer de la mula abajo" (I, IX, 46a). Perhaps because so many adventures are wrapped in various kinds of humor and irony that the physical aspects of some of these adventures are often glossed over. Even his horse is subject to beatings, a clear reflection of the woes of his master. Shortly after Don Quijote fights with the Yangüeses, this time with the assistance of Sancho Panza, using their sticks, the Yangüeses knock Sancho to the ground as well as Don Quijote. The text reads "donde se echa de ver la furia con que machacan estacas puestas en manos rústicas y enojadas (I, XV, 64b). There is no doubt left in the mind of the reader that Don Quijote and Sancho get the worst in this fight with the results being compressed on their bodies.

Another episode that is often cited within the scope of the theme of freedom is that of the galley prisoners being led to the galleys. The ironic intent of the author is to catalogue the different planes on which Don Quijote and the prisoners function. Very much in the same vein of the episode dealing with Andrés and Haldudo, Don Quijote places his chivalric obligations at the service of his sword and demands that the prisoners be freed, asking in return only that they go to the Toboso to inform Dulcinea of this act done in her name. As Don Quijote persists the prisoners become impatient to the point of stoning Don Quijote and Sancho Panza. The stones rain down on Don Quijote "No se pudo escudar tan bien Don Quijote, que no le acertasen no sé cuántos guijarros en el cuerpo, con tanta fuerza, que dieron con él en el suelo" (II, XXII, 101b). The episode recalls Mark Twain's statement that no good deed goes unpunished. As a result, Don Quijote's body will reveal that ideal conduct can bring with it severe bodily punishment.

As far as blood is concerned, there is no better example than the interpolated novella, the "El curioso impertinente." The central aim of the tale is to deal on the one hand with human foolishness and on the other to treat the theme of truth. The story is well known: Anselmo wants his best friend to test the virtue of his new wife. He does all he can to convince his friend to participate, but his friend remains steadfast in his friendship until both the friend and the wife consume their passion. The human comedy begins at this point where the characters feign a game in which playacting is performed before the hidden husband. This also includes a scene of staged stabbing and the shedding of blood in an attempt at showing the husband, who has conveniently hidden himself, that what is going on before his eyes is the truth. But of course, it is not. The husband seeing the blood cannot but accept the scene as true. Blood is, as Camporesi believes, the "juice of life" with its Christly associations, and Lotario's blood is supposedly the seal of truth and veracity. The guilty couple uses the symbol to its advantage knowing that its presence bestows credibility to their actions. For Cervantes, the blood is the symbol of his own disaster. Is he himself not also a sacrificial lamb of the battle of Lepanto, whose military purposes bore religious principles in the battle between a Christianity convinced of its righteousness and a supposedly malevolent Mohammedanism? We must sense that the use of blood derives from Cervantes's reminiscences of his own debilitating experience in Lepanto buried inside him but never forgotten.

In the 37th chapter of the first part we read of the beheading of the monster; i.e., Don Quijote mistakes the leather jugs of wine for a monster.

The foregoing regarding the religious qualities attached to wine in a Christian culture also applies to this experience. In Don Quijote's mind the wine becomes changed into monsters with the mere color of the wine providing the connective link between the wine and the imagined blood. In Don Quijote's mind all it takes is a sign or symbol upon which to engage his *proyecto vital*, no matter how erroneous it is to the eyes of others.

The chapters devoted to the adventures of the Captive are often described as the very adventures that Cervantes underwent in the *bagnio*. No doubt they supplied the reality base of the adventure. But instead of developing the "real" bases of the situation, Cervantes uses the theme of love as the generative force of the Captive's experiences. Once again, Cervantes hides the true sense of what an experience in the *bagnio* was: one of torture, pain and death. Once again, reality is buried because it is so painful which we can easily infer. Love, the true generative core of the work becomes the most important part of the episode. It is love and the victory of Christianity over Mohammadanism, a sure Counter-Reformation sign. Given what we know about the "truth" of the *bagnios*, the treatment given to the Captive's experiences is a dream world-whitewash as can be read in some of the lighter details of the episode—the lowering of the love notes on a long pole and similar flights of the imagination.

One of the peccadillos of our British brethren Hispanists is to view a number of works of the Golden Age as aspects of "the funny book syndrome," the work of literary art as an exercise in making the public laugh. This narrow view is one to which none other than one of the most distinguished French Hispanists, M. Marcel Bataillon fell when he saw the *Lazarillo* as a "livre pour faire rire."[24] This narrow point of view is one which demands clarification. To be sure, there are episodes in Don Quijote which provoke laughter and were written by Cervantes for that reason. But when the quality of the experiences in their totality are reviewed one can see that even some of the funniest episodes can be viewed through the lens of painful and often malicious actions. One such episode is when women in the inn (I,XLIII) ask Don Quijote to offer up his hand. Don Quijote is

---

[24] Bataillon, Marcel, introduction to Morel Fatio, A. Transl. *La vie de Lazarillo de Tormes*. (*La vida de Lazarillo de Tormes*.). Paris: Aubier, 1958. See also Joseph H. Silverman's criticism of Bataillon's belief that the Lazarillo is a "funny book": *Romance Philology*, XV (1961): 88-94.

standing on Rocinante with his hand tied to the opening. "Con todo esto, tiraba de su brazo, por ver si podía soltarse; mas él estaba tan bien asido, que todas sus pruebas fueron en vano. Bien es verdad que tiraba con tiento, porque Rocinante no se moviese; y aunque él quisiera sentarse y ponerse en la silla, no podía sino estar en pie, o arrancarse la mano" (I, XLIII, 220a). Having Don Quijote be in such a position can only be looked upon as a joke in execrable taste, especially when one sees the practical joke as a form of hostility, a hostility whose results are bound up with hurting and pain. It is easy then to see why I do not consider this and other episodes as "funny."

In terms of our subject, the first part ends with the battle Don Quijote has with the goat shepherd in which both Don Quijote and the *cabrero* are mutually beaten. A detail of this episode should not escape us, however. As in the episode where Don Quijote is left tied to the window, the narrator registers the reaction of some of the people present. In keeping with Cervantes's wish to present all aspects of life, beautiful and ugly, the narrator notes, "Reventaba de risa el Canónigo y el Cura, saltaban los cuadrilleros de gozo, zuzaban los unos y los otros, como hacen a los perros cuando en pendencia están trabados" (I, LII, 253b-254a). Both participants come out fairly well beaten. It is not idle for the narrator to compare the two men to dogs in a dogfight. The human level is lowered to the canine one in one of the episodes that brings us into some proximity to Mateo Alemán's view of life.

In the second part of the work, distanced by ten years from the first there will be similar episodes of pain and wounding. During this time we note a particular transference between Don Quijote and Sancho Panza. Don Quijote refers to the time when Sancho was blanketed. Don Quijote says: "Querrás tú decir ahora, Sancho... que no me dolía yo cuando a ti te manteaban? Y si lo dices, no lo digas, ni lo pienses; pues más dolor sentía yo entonces en mi espíritu que tú en tu cuerpo" (II, II 275b). This seemingly small observation accentuates the tangibility of the kind of experiences that Cervantes's characters have. It also highlights the fact that the blanketing to which Sancho is subjected is another form of a punishing practical joke, maliciously applied.

The episode of Basilio and Quiteria is the twin episode to the bloody chapter of "El Curioso Impertinente." Once again, Cervantes teases the reader who will fix upon the saintly and religious aspects of the blood. The rich Camacho wishes to marry the beautiful Quiteria, although she is loved by the poor Basilio. In the middle of the wedding festivities Basilio appears and impales himself: "Y diciendo esto, asió del bastón que tenía hincado en el suelo, y quedándose la mitad dél en la tierra, mostró que servía de vaina a un mediano estoque que en él se ocultaba; y puesta la que se podía llamar empuñadura en el suelo, con ligero desenfado y determinado propósito se arrojó sobre él, y en un punto mostró la punta sangrienta a las espaldas, con la mitad del acerada cuchilla, quedando el triste bañado en su sangre y tendido en el suelo, de sus mismas armas traspasado" (II,XXI, 343a,b). As with the "El curioso impertinente" Cervantes uses blood as a bludgeon over the characters and the readers. Blood, has, as we noted above, tremendous powers of conviction. Its very presence speaks in its silence. In this episode no one dares to question the significance of Basilio's gesture; the blood he draws seals any doubts. It is only because of the power of blood that Basilio can get away with his trick. Expiring on the ground, seemingly, Basilio asks that Quiteria marry him as the last act of his life, which she does, thinking that she was performing an act of charity for Basilio's last earthly wish. Most of the people watching are convinced that Basilio is on his last breath—, except Sancho who begins to smell a rat. The convincing quality of the episode is to be read in the following: "Estando, pues, asidos de las manos Basilio y Quiteria, el Cura, tierno y lloroso, los echó la bendición y pidió al cielo diese buen poso al alma del nuevo desposado; el cual así como recibió la bendición, con presta ligereza se levantó en pie, y con no vista desenvoltura se saca el estoque, a quien servía de vaina su cuerpo. Quedaron todos los circunstantes admirados, y algunos de ellos, más simples que curiosos, en altas voces, comenzaron a decir: "¡Milagro, milagro! Pero Basilio replicó: —¡No milagro, milagro, sino industria, industria! (II, XXI, 344b).

It is left to the reader to imagine the gimmick which Basilio used, but without the presence of blood, this trick could not have taken place. Blood lends the final credibility to Basilio's game. Without it, I do not believe that anyone would have allowed Basilio to marry Quiteria and, once married, and the trick exposed, Quiteria interestingly accepts the gimmicked marriage as fact, much to the disappointment of the rich Camacho. Blood, therefore, not only has symbolic meanings but it also has an intimate meaning for Cervantes who spent six months in Messina nursing the very wounds that put him in the hospital. Blood, then, possesses for Cervantes multiple meanings.

In view of all we have said about the Algerian experience of Cervantes, it should come as an interesting detail that Merlin should dictate that

Sancho Panza should give himself 3,330 lashes. The subject of torture and punishment should have had numerous reminiscences for Cervantes. To judge by what Fray Diego de Haedo says, it would have been a miracle that anyone would have survived a whipping of that dimension or even less. What is important for me in the context that I am studying is the suggestion of harm or damage that the mere utterance of 3,330 lashes could mean for someone. Once again, Cervantes cloaks the seriousness of the significance in a humorous or light reference. We know that Sancho Panza will not give himself those lashes, but the significance is still difficult to ignore.

As Cervantes continues to confound the reader who is unable to predict the outcome of things, he narrates the story of Claudia Jerónima and her experience with Vicente Torellas. Cervantes redoes the Basilio/Quiteria episode which deals with blood. There are no games this time, no *industria, industria*, as Basilio says when he miraculously comes alive when Quiteria marries him in a deathbed marriage. The same thing happens here with Claudia and Vicente, but the reader must wait to see if there will be any life-saving theatrics; but there are none. Cervantes returns the concept of blood to its original connection with disability or death; in this case, death. This episode, like several others we have discussed, involve wounding, bleeding and death. However, the concept of wounding is preserved through the presence of blood and the destruction of the body.

As any reader of Don Quijote knows, Sansón Carrasco finally succeeds in defeating Don Quijote who must now return to his home. Don Quijote falls into a deep depression and slowly dies. His body is the accumulation of all the blows, cuts, breaks, twists and turns he has suffered. The body, once obviously frail and debilitated by age at the beginning of the work, goes on a decline until his life terminates. His depression is the mental illness, the mental wound that will affect the fatal decline of the body until he is deceased.

One might say that in the novels of chivalry, against which Cervantes inveighs, there is a great deal of fighting and bloodletting. Many of these are so exaggerated as to be ignored for their lack of any verisimilitude. But we know the life of the author and the crucial experiences Cervantes underwent with his wounds. The adventures of the Amadises, Belianises and other knights errant are literature, that is, the product of the imagination; Cervantes's experiences, which he transfers to his characters, is vital; experiences he underwent painfully. There is a big difference between literature and life in this case, and I am convinced that the various episodes which I have discussed, with the accent on wounding and bloodletting, have their origin in Cervantes's crucial and traumatic wounding in Lepanto and his stay in the *bagnio* of Algiers. His crucial traumatic experience is very much like the one that Iñigo de Loyola underwent in Pamplona and with many of the same effects on his life that Iñigo de Loyola had on his. They are, if I may be permitted the pun, brothers under the skin.

9
History, Society, and Economics of the 16th and 17th centuries with Reference to *Don Quijote*

DUE TO THE NATURE of Don Quijote's mission, involved as it is in fantasy, one might not associate it with mundane subjects such as politics and history, not to mention economic ones. However, Anthony Close does not believe that there is a historical background to *Don Quijote*[1]. He believes that we should "question the commonly presented image of him as a writer deeply critical of the political regime and, by extension, social system and ideology, of the Spain in which it was his lot to live" (*Comic Mind,* 30). He modifies his position slightly by referring to some episodes and characters that have an obvious political character but then he returns to his belief that they "do not warrant that conclusion" (30) of a Cervantes with a political and social axe to grind. On the other hand, I see certain political and economic features of the fifteenth, sixteenth and seventeenth centuries that serve as a frame for *Don Quijote,* but in order to accept this, one must go the end of *Don Quijote* and see where and how the politics and the economics of that era frame the work, especially the sad ending of the work.

The trajectory of Don Quijote's quest begins with his desire to become a knight-errant. In this period his spirit is bright and encouraging. He goes through numerous adventures, some good, some bad, some funny, some sad. But when the reader compares the positive spirit of the beginning of his quest with the destruction of his lifetime project (*proyecto vital*) at the hands of Sansón Carrasco, one must acknowledge that the final act, so to speak, of Don Quijote's life is not a pleasant one, and most likely belongs to the aesthetics of Tridentine demands on Cervantes, as it was for his contempo-

---

[1] See Anthony Close's *Don Quijote and the Comic Spirit*.

raries. The end of *Don Quijote,* compared with the encouraging beginning, becomes a work of *desengaño.*[2]

My purpose becomes very obvious, and that is to coordinate the sad and tragic finale with the general state of affairs in Spain during the fifteenth, sixteenth and seventeen centuries, especially between the years 1547 and 1616, the date of Cervantes's death.

If we took the example of other writers who flourished generally during Cervantes's time we would see a similar situation between history and creativity.[3]

It is my profound belief that life, society, politics, and economics promote creativity. One need only examine the work of American authors such as Richard Wright, Ralph Ellison, James Baldwin, Rolando Hinojosa Smith and others to see how one's *circunstancia* molds the nature and meaning of one's work. It is with this spirit that I enter into a consideration of how *Don Quijote* in its central dimension of *desengaño* forms the work. The phrase "siglo de oro" conjures up a series of very affirmative images that tend to obscure some of the more realistic features of those two centuries. Perhaps this is the reason don Américo Castro preferred the praise "el siglo conflictivo" or "la edad conflictiva." His phrase allows for the obverse side of the conventionally accepted picture of the Golden Age. No one knew this better than the author of *Lazarillo de Tormes.* In the final words of the work, the author compares Lázaro's miserable moral degradation with the Empire of Charles V. I cannot imagine anyone who would not see the strongly implied suggestion that the imperial edifice, so grand on the outside, was corroded on the inside. The unknown author of *Lazarillo de Tormes* already saw how Spain was in a decline. Little did he know where this decline would end. I say this because if *Don Quijote* is read as a "funny book," as Mr.Close would have us do, then important extra-

---

[2] I admit that there is a very wide difference between the baroque prose (and its narrative substance) of Cervantes and that of, for example, Mateo Alemán and others. This does not negate that Cervantes has written a work that has shades of *desengaño.* Like his contemporary, Lope de Vega, Cervantes had one foot in the Renaissance and another the Baroque.

[3] See my *Cervantes's Novelas ejemplares: Between History and Creativity.* Stephen Gilman once said that you either believed that art created art or life creates art. I am of the latter. There are, of course, examples where art does create art, and that occurs largely in poetry.

literary factors are simply glossed over.

In a very early moment the stage is set for a rocky future in spite of some of the aura of the Isabeline and Fernandine union.[4] In the short view the notion of a modern state with a double perspective of a Castilian, Aragonese base and an expansionist foreign policy was so novel that the Catholic Kings could not predict what the downside of such a policy was.

The era of Charles V also presaged economic problems that would come to bitter fruition years later. Charles's expansion on several continents called for a massive infusion of money to support such ventures. That these ventures were successful on its face no one can deny. Altamira says, "Almost the whole of the task of conquest was achieved during the reign of Charles I. Among the many who greatly distinguished themselves by their military achievements in carrying it out were Hernán Cortés, Pizarro, Almagro, Valdivia, Alvarado, Montejo" (363-364). Altamira's is a momentary look at the brighter side of Charles V's achievements. The consequences of such achievements become tarnished.[5] Elliott says: "It was, therefore, the deviation from the guiding principles of the heroic age of greatness which was the true source of disaster. Like other societies Castile had created an image of itself and of its past, which had helped to shape its expectations and its goals. The disappointments and reverses of the late sixteenth and early seventeenth centuries created a crisis of confidence, because they implied that Castile was falling short of the goals—essentially military and religious—which it had set itself. This failure was then set into the context of *declinación* [Emph. his]," (*ibid.*, 51). Vilar focuses interestingly on this problem of the decline and *Don Quijote* when he says, "It has often been said that it would be fruitless to look to Cervantes for an interpretation of the 'decadence' of his country 'because he could not have foreseen it'. This is to misunderstand completely the chronology of events. For if the word 'crisis' really means the passage from rise to collapse, then it is certainly between 1598 and 1620, between its greatness and decadence, that

---

[4] Mártir Rizo says: " 'Empires are easily preserved with the customs they acquired at the start, but when idleness replaces hard work, luxury replaces sobriety, and arrogance steps in where justice should prevail, then fortune and manners are changed, and empires are undone unless a remedy is found.' Elliott, "Self-Preservation," 51. Admittedly Mártir Rizo wrote this in 1626, but I am sure that there is an implication of an earlier time, a time closer to Cervantes's.
[5] Kamen also wonders how an "undeveloped country could suffer a decline" (29).

we must locate the decisive crisis of Spanish power, and with even greater certainty, the first great crisis of doubt of the Spanish people. Now the two parts of *Don Quijote* were published in 1605 and 1615" (100).

There were other crises to be recognized in the sixteenth century. Thompson points out that "In other ways, however, war contributed to a crisis of the social order which, while neither initiated nor resolved in this period, was made more acute by the events of the 1590s" (III, 270).

As I hope to show below the sixteenth and seventeenth centuries in Spain were rife with crises of different kinds and some which must have affected Cervantes's life. Some historians are loath to subscribe to the generally accepted notion of decadence, particularly Henry Kamen and Carla Rahn Phillips.

For Kamen, a notion such as "decadence" owes much to the "Black legend," which propagated an idea of a Spain that was poor and backward" ("Decline," 25). Kamen suggests that there could be no decline if there were not a rise in the fortunes and state of things in Spain. Economically, Spain was involved with Europe but rather in a colonialized way. It was, according to Kamen, "a colony of European interests" (*ibid.*, 44). In fact, other markets dictated Spain's economy. He prefers to see these times as a matter of lost opportunities and "the change of fortunes" in Spain (*ibid.*, 27), rather than an outright decline; a matter of lost opportunities and not decay. Kamen believes that the era of Ferdinand and Isabel represented Spain's great moment and the arrival of Charles V whose status as a "foreigner" caused quite a bit of resentment. For Kamen, by 1517 all opportunities in Spain had been missed (*ibid.*, 29). Rather than see the state of Spain in decline, Kamen notes a state of "frustrated hopes" (*ibid.*, 30). In Kamen's view there are four flaws to the "decline" theses: 1) when did it begin and when did it end; there were military defeats and plague years; reverses attributed to Spain were a part of the greater European picture; and there was a general confusion between Spain and Castile (*ibid.*, "Decline," 48). Very important in Kamen's view is the question of how the economic phenomenon of Europe affected and coincided with Spain's. It is easy to understand Kamen's position but some of the historical facts (see below) would show that Spain went through a descent, that is, if you take, as many historians do, the era of the Catholic Kings as the apex of Spanish power. The seeds of Spanish descent were sown during the reign of Charles V, and from then on it went lower.

Carla Rahn Phillips in a perceptive essay, discusses the state of the

Spanish economy and politics. She suggests a Malthusian approach to the subject ("the cycle of boom and bust" [562]). For Phillips, the "rise of the Spanish economy began in the politically chaotic fifteenth century" (532). Many of the negative opinions on the question of Spanish decay and decadence may proceed from its economy. She notes that there is a diversity of production between the various regions, not all were examples of " 'dry' Spain" (535). Phillips prefers to see the era as one of crisis in different parts of Europe. For her, things changed, and a person like Cervantes was probably changing with the various changes. Phillips is not in agreement with the notion that bad things began during the era of Charles V and worsened under Philip II. What Phillips sees is a normal and natural historical process whereby the seeds of decline are always present in the historical process. She decries the work of English-speaking writers who look at Spain and only see the worst.[6]

These two historians, Kamen and Phillips, represent a dissenting voice before the chorus of those that labeled the period between the Catholic Kings and Philip IV as a period of decadence.

My own inclination is to review the "problem areas" that present themselves during the span of Cervantes's lifetime and to see if in fact one could speak of decadence, or, keeping in mind the possibility that the problem here is one of semantics, finding the right word to describe the political, economic and "human" situation of Spain in those centuries. The word most commonly used is "decadence," but like other clichés, namely those propagated by the *Leyenda negra*, the word must suffice, if no other reason, for purposes of argument.

I was also pleased to see a statement by Phillips: Referring to Cervantes's *Don Quijote* she says, "[*Don Quijote*] always seemed to me the perfect exemplar of the early 17th-century disillusionment."[7]

As I said above I believe that Cervantes's time was a time of disillusionment in so many areas, and this is the path I wish to follow. The great promises of the Catholic Kings and the Emperor Charles V wither in the face of events, happenings, and situations of the years of Cervantes's life,

---

[6] Focusing on inland Castile, Andalucia and the Southwest coast, she says, "Yet these same areas could produce very well under the right circumstances" (535). These areas had been traditionally labeled "problem areas."

[7] I have gleaned Phillip's opinion through an article and personal correspondence between us.

many events in which Cervantes participates.[8]

There were other commitments as well. People tend to glorify his ultramontaine policies, especially the conquest of the New World. Essentially, Charles V sowed the seeds for many of the problems that would appear later.

Focusing on the reign of Philip II, Parker notes the wars between Spain and France (later the Netherlands) during his reign, and the costs that Spain bore, because of these Philip had to face the fact that there was an earlier attempt to recover Tripoli and this ended in utter disaster (*Philip II*, 65). Philip was faced with the Turks as an adversary on one side and the Dutch on the other. While generally inflexible on most issues, Philip was totally inflexible on religious issues; at best Protestant enclaves were merely tolerated. His contacts and policies with regard to Holland were financially onerous, taxation to cover the battles being the most onerous of all. Philip was also facing other problems which troubled the waters, e.g., the Morisco problem.[9] While bullion came to Spain (see below for more information on this subject), the administrative functioning of the New World was also problematic and therefore a preoccupation to him.[10]

There is another area which must be considered in understanding the economic background of Philip II's reign: he was beset by natural disasters which had a negative effect on the economy of Spain.[11]

---

[8] See Elliott, *Imperial*, (332), see also 44-45 where he suggests that their greatest achievement, the New World enterprise and discoveries, was profitable to all of Spain, not to mention Castile. Whereas the case of Charles V is more complicated and less simple to understand. Elliott reminds us that "From the moment of his Imperial election Charles V found himself saddled with enormous commitments" (Imperial, 191).

[9] On the subject of Moriscos, see Maravall (87 *et seq.*) and Márquez Villanueva (*Personajes*), and others.

[10] "It was becoming clear that Spain's grip on the New World had become seriously weakened. In 1566 the king advised by Cardinal Espinosa, decided to set up a committee of inquiry into the way in which America was administered" (Parker, *Philip II*, 113).

[11] "On top of all this, the year 1571 brought with it a succession of natural disasters: flooding, plague, harvest failure and, in the end, the worst winter in many years" (Parker, *Philip II*, 119). Also, Domínguez Ortiz adds an interesting insight to Philip II's reign. Domínguez Ortiz says, "Hoy empezamos a conocer mejor estas realidades; pero este conocimiento no será completo si despreciamos la parte del azar (por ejemplo, la muerte prematura de la reina María, que de haber vivido más tiempo pudo consolidar la restauración del catolicismo en Inglaterra) y si no

At the same time Domínguez Ortiz sees the Escorial as a sign of the beginning of the end.[12] What was characteristic of Philip II's rule was his absolutism; joined to this was his distance from his people. Kamen says, "Since Philip almost never visited his people, it followed that their allegiance remained formal rather than rooted in the direct love enjoyed by the Catholic Kings" (*Spain*, 194). Kamen further says, ""The new king was in character a contrast to his dominating father, but his several firm policy decisions suggest that he was less pliant than he has usually been painted. A pious Catholic, he was actively concerned to restore the military fortunes of the nation. Unlike his father, he was willing to give initiative to his ministers" (*ibid.*, 198).

But in spite of Philip II's assiduous pursuit of administration, the very institution of which he was a product, the monarchy, was rotten to the core. Lynch explains the situation in the following way: "Monarchy, then, was absolute. But his absolutism was qualified by conditions, and its power was less imposing in practice than it was in theory. It was restricted in the first place by inefficiency; the bureaucracy, which was not large by present-day standards, never entirely succeeded in overcoming the obstacles of distance involved in governing Spain and in applying central decisions over the length and breadth of the country. It was also restricted by the existence of local forces; the aristocracy with their feudal jurisdiction" (*ibid.*, 196).

It is obvious that King Philip II's life was not one of ease and leisure. He assiduously maintained a lively correspondence and left behind a massive amount of memoranda. He was threatened by war on all sides. Stradling describes it in the following way: "During Philip II's last decade, his empire for the first time came under pressure on all major frontiers simultaneously. This mighty challenge to its power and influence was a foretaste of the total war which was to engulf the monarchy in the course of the next century. Most of Philip's defense problems stemmed from his early mishandling of the Flemish protest movement; now, a generation later, the organized and powerful Dutch rebel provinces held together the threads of a web of resistance to Spain, in which were woven the interests of England, France,

---

tenemos en cuenta la psicología personal de sus gobernantes" (*Antiguo*, 293).

[12] "Felipe II fue criticado en su tiempo a causa de los tesoros que gastó en el Escorial" (Domínguez Ortiz, 337). He also says, "Los eternos apuros financieros de Carlos V le impidieron [a Felipe II] construir un palacio a la medida de su grandeza" (*ibid.*, 336).

Venice, and even the Ottoman empire" (30).[13]

To complete the picture of the historical background during Cervantes's lifetime we should also examine some of the features of the reign of Philip III.

It became obvious that the Spanish government could not subsist, and under Philip III it was strongly suggested that reform take place. Casey says, "Under Philip III and Philip IV plans for retrenchment concentrated above all on restricting *mercedes* [Emph. his] or favours paid to individuals; but outgoings here were not always easy to separate from the general costs of the army and the administration itself" (*Early*, 81).[14]

Philip II's successor also had different problems dealing with economic issues. Domínguez Ortiz notes, "También fue de efectos muy perjudiciales la alteración de moneda, única forma de inflación monetaria que conoció aquella centuria. La comenzó Felipe III, labrando moneda de vellón y duplicando el precio de la que ya existía; la incrementó en términos insostenibles Felipe IV y la terminó la drástica deflación de 1680, una de las fechas claves de nuestra historia económica" (*Antiguo,* 352).

Domínguez Ortiz also focuses on another problem that made Philip III's reign difficult: "Sin embargo, los 23 años de reinado de este soberano inepto (1598-1621) son de brillante apariencia, y muchos lo recordaron después con nostalgia. Es que, si bien estaba rodeado de una corte corrompida, todavía existía en la administración un magnífico plantel de funcionarios, militares y diplomáticos formados en la gran escuela del siglo anterior y penetrados de las ideas de grandeza imperial" (*Antiguo,* 364).

What Domínquez Ortiz is alluding to is a court that outstripped in its costs the very revenue that is supposed to have allowed such a brilliant

---

[13] Stradling makes more precise the nature of some of Philip II's problems: "The expedition to Ireland was a fiasco; the army of Flanders was badly mauled in pitched battle with the Dutch at Nieuwpoort (1600); an attempt on the great pirate capital of Algiers never even reached its destination (1601)" (31).

[14] Casey continues: "The Venetian ambassador Mocenigo (1626-31) calculated that 1,000,000 ducats a year were needed for the court and another 2,000,000 for administration generally, together with just under 5,000,000 for war. But the crippling burden was really the snowball effect of anticipating revenue year after year, leading to periodic bankruptcies and consolidations of the government debt. There in turn generated inexorable increases in the amounts needed to meet payment of interest. Between 1573 and 1606 interest on the government bonds or *juros* doubled to 4,000,000 ducats a year, and rose to 9,147,341 by 1667" (*ibid.*, 81).

court to flourish, like the author of *Lazarillo de Tormes* who read the external glory of his government but which was vacuous. Philip III will govern over the further dismanteling and decadence of the government.

That Spain was in a serious state was seen clearly by the *arbitristas*. Casey says, "Though political and military defeat could be staved off for several more generations, it was from 1600 that a group of Spanish writers—the famous *arbitristas*—began to highlight the underlying economic weakness of their country: depopulation, decline of agriculture, collapse of manufactures" ("Spain Failed," 209).

González de Cellorigo was one of such *arbitristas* that alerted the country to the fact that the country was declining: "This hardly seemed likely, and one of the most acute of the *Arbitristas*, González de Cellorigo, devoted the first chapter of his book, published in 1600, to the theme of " 'how our Spain, however fertile and abundant it may be, is subject to the *declinación* to which all republics are prone' " (Elliott, "Self-Perception," 48).[15]

Furthermore, Elliott adds, "Behind the phrase *decline of Spain* [Emph. his] there lurk different, although interrelated phenomena. The decline of Spain can, in the first place, be regarded as part of that general setback to economic advance which mid seventeenth-century Europe is said to have experienced, although the Spanish regression may well prove to have been more intense or to have lasted longer. Secondly, it describes something more easily measured: the end of the period of Spanish hegemony in Europe and the relegation of Spain to the rank of the second-rate powers. This implies a deterioration in Spain's military and naval strength, at least in relation to that of other states, and a decrease in its ability to mobilize the manpower and credit required to maintain its traditional primacy in Europe" ("Decline" 56).

To the name of Cellorigo, Elliott adds the names of Moncada and Fernández Navarrete who attempted to put forth suggestions toward resolving questions that were a result of problems and deficiencies in Spanish government. Elliott says, "Royal expenditure must be regulated, the sale of offices halted, the growth of the church be checked. The tax system must be overhauled, special concessions be made to agricultural

---

[15] See generally Elliot, 41-45 on this problem of self-awareness of a decline. See also "The Decline of Spain, 53."

labourers, rivers be made navigable and dry lands irrigated" ("Decline" 65).[16]

For Altamira, "The most conspicuous external expressions of the decline were military defeats and the abandonment of enterprises great in themselves but not in the best interests of Spain, such as retention of the Low Countries of Northern Europe (Holland)" (393).[17]

A common way of trying to exculpate Spain concerning the defeat of the Armada was that "Castile had provoked the divine wrath, and was paying the price of its sins" (Elliott, "Self-Perception," 46). Yet the Jesuit Pedro de Ribadeneyra thought the opposite, that "The disaster was, he argued, yet another sign of God's favour, since it would oblige Castilians to strengthen their faith, purify their intentions and reform their manners and morals" (*ibid.*, 46). Would that it had been that easy. "All that can be said at present with any certainty is that Olivares was making heavy demands on the manpower of a country whose population had lost its buoyancy and resilience, and had ceased to grow" (Elliott, "Decline" 60). Olivares was a combination of a desire for reform and a desire for war (Elliot, *Imperial*, 320).

In attempting to examine the socio-political state of Spain during the years of Cervantes's flourishing, we must note that not everything was bad. Spaniards, especially Cervantes, could look back with pride on Lepanto. However, there were other less felicitous events for which there was less pride. Cádiz is one such event where the British forces successfully attacked and sacked that city: "Because most troops were deployed abroad the peninsula itself was never completely secure, and the English were imaginative enough to exploit the weakness" (Kamen, *Spain,* 163). Part of the scenario at Cádiz was that "Sir Francis Drake and a small English fleet

---

[16] The problem of "decline" continued on into the administration of Olivares, just as it was earlier. See "Self-Perception," 58-61.

[17] Yet in the face of great failures, there is a sensitivity to the splendid life of the privados. Domínguez Ortiz points out that Lerma was in favor of terminating the draining war in Flanders (*Antiguo*, 368), but at the same time as Elliott says, "All that can be said at present with any certainty is that Olivares was making heavy demands on the manpower of a country was yet to come. There was the case of Flanders which depleted Spain's revenue which Domínguez Ortiz perceptively explains: "Con ser graves estos hechos, mucho más lo era el comienzo de las guerras de Flandes, que iban a hipotecar toda la política española durante ochenta años" (*Antiguo*,302).

sailed around the world, plundering Spanish shipping all along the way" (Parker, *Philip II,* 146). Fernández Alvarez and Díaz Medina explain the meaning of the Armada succinctly when they state "Es la época que contempla el arrollador avance del Imperio español, cuyo ocaso parece anunciarse presisamente en los últimos años del siglo, cuando sobreviene el desastre de la Armada invencible, en un año que marcaría a toda una generación en 1588. Y a poco se incubaría la vision melancólica del mundo, que rezuma del *Don Quijote,* junto con la desgarrada irrupción de la novela picaresca, fruto de una sociedad que entra en decadencia" (Austrias, 1).[18]

The effect that the Armada defeat had on the population was extreme. Parker says that "The feeling it caused in all of Spain was extraordinary...Almost the whole of Spain went into mourning...People talked about nothing else" (*Philip II,* 155). Therefore one cannot say that someone like Cervantes could have avoided being impressed by the defeat. Another aspect of this defeat was the blow it dealt the economy. Lynch observes that "The Indies trade felt the impact more than any other section of the Spanish economy, not only because of the number of ships it had committed to the campaign but because they were its biggest, youngest, and best ships—precisely those on which it had relied so much" (165).[19]

The pressing economic situation in Spain owes much to its bankers. Vicens Vives points out that thanks to Charles V, the "Genoese gained control of Spanish finance and commerce" (336). Money lending was not limited to the Genoese and other European bankers. Vicens Vives cites the case of Simón Ruiz and Francisco de la Presa y Burgos who gave up a mercantile enterprise to concentrate on lending (340). Elliott enumerates ways of controlling the Spanish economy, one of which was to rid itself of

---

[18] Fernández Alvarez y Díaz Medina are not the only ones to turn to literature to exemplify history. See Elliott ("Self-Perception"), in which he states that the theater of the Siglo de Oro: "The rustic virtues were idealized in the increasingly urbanized Madrid of the early secenteenth century by a theater which glorified the independence and integrity of the peasant rural community—the only uncontaminated part of the commonwealth" ("Self-Perception" 52). Altamira does something similar (401). Fernández Alvarez and Díaz Medina also point out that the Spanish Armada was inferior to the English navy in many ways, which helps understand Spain's failure in this singular event (281).

[19] Cfr. Stradling, "The Invincible Armada alone, for example had cost a year's gross revenue" (38). Elliott also addresses the question of disillusionment, *Imperial,* 293.

"its humiliating dependence on foreigners, on the Dutch and the Genoese, be brought to an end" ("Decline," 65).[20]

Bankruptcy was one of the major causes of the depression of the Spanish economy and hence the depression of Spanish life. Debts were paid through loans and raising taxes. Elliott cites bankruptcy as a fundamental part of the 1580s and 1590s ("Self-Perception," 46).[21]

Another area of concern on the question of the status of the Spanish economy dealt with agriculture. According to Casey, the late 16th century was a time of great difficulty as far as agriculture was concerned (*European*, 211). Casey also notes that Philip II acknowledged to his father in 1545, 'The infertility of these realms is well known to Your Majesty, and one bad year can throw our people into poverty' " (*Early*, 9).

The need for soldiers badly affected the agricultural area because shepherds were sent off to war notwithstanding the damage that this did to the agricultural economy, e.g., neglecting the fields (Vicens Vives, 349). Unlike Portugal which was able to rehabilitate itself, as Vicens Vives notes, there were several reasons as to why the Spanish economy foundered: "entailment of property; increase in mortmain; vagrancy; deforestation; an excessive number of ecclesiastics; scorn for work and for the liberal arts; indiscriminate charity; monetary chaos and oppressive taxation" (*ibid.* 463).[22]

There was also a stagnation of agriculture. Lynch believes that so long as Philip II was determined to continue a strategy of wars, it was unlikely that the economy could improve.[23]

---

[20] Due to the increased costs of governance and the decline in revenues, some bankers refused to issue new loans (Domínguez Ortiz, *Antiguo*, 296-297).

[21] See also Vicens Vives, p. 375 for similar remarks: Bankruptcy and the increased taxation occasioned "the collapse of financial and economic activity" (375), and the inability of the government to pay its debts with its interest (383). The crown was reduced to sequestering the treasures of individuals who welcomed the income from abroad as well as the devaluation of currency (436). There were instances when the payment of interest had to be postponed in favor of other pressing affairs (Stradling, 39).

[22] See pg. 464 for other reasons.

[23] Elliott leads us to believe that the Cortes during the reign of Philip II were well aware of the crisis ("Decline," 58). See also Kamen's "anti-decline" position as it touches upon the question of decay ("Decline," 35).

Along with the precarious state of the Spanish economy, the national debt posed a great problem to recuperation from its economic problems. Crushed by its debt, declared itself bankrupt to withhold the payment of its obligations (Vicens Vives, 383).[24]

Kamen believes that Spain was never able to shake off the enormous debts that Charles V had accumulated (*Spain,* 90), and the importation of silver, which should have been a boon to Spain's steadily deteriorating economy was used to help pay off its debts (*ibid.,* 101).[25]

Added to the various "decadent" phenomena of the period is the problem of depopulation (alluded to above). Casey states, "A basic test is population, perhaps the chief victim of the ravages of the 1590s. The population of Spain as a whole probably rose from 7½ to 8½ million people between 1541 and 1591, then fell to 6½ million by 1650" (*European,* 209).

A census of population showed "depopulated or underpopulated areas in many regions, a state of things which many contemporaneous documents deplored" (Altamira, 386).[26]

Besides some of the difficulties I have named above, one of the crucial ones is the state of the economy during the 16th and 17th centuries. Casey says, "The misery created by the fatal decade of the 1590s, though, hastened on structural transformations in other areas: the peasants lost more and

---

[24] Kamen also refers to it as "the insurmountable debt a direct cost of the war" (*Philip II,* 309). He furthers avers, "The debt, consisting of money owed by the crown to financiers and other creditors, was consuming over two-thirds of ordinary income. Extraordinary sources of money, such as silver from America were infrequent and unreliable" (*Philip II,* 87).

[25] Parker also notes a similar thing. As he says, "In the course of his reign, therefore, Philip II's revenues tripled, but the size of the public debt almost quadrupled. In almost every year, debt interest absorbed half or rather more than half of the crown's available income, leaving insufficient funds to meet its military and other needs, and making further borrowing unavoidable" (*Philip II,* 179). Stradling also states: "To some extent, all these factors were present in the years leading up to 1607, forcing Philip III in that year to utilize the *decreto y medio real* [Emph. his] not improperly rendered as a 'bankruptcy' by most historians" (39).

[26] Casey observes that for the various undertakings, military primarily, manpower was needed to keep the military machine going (*Early,* 24). See also Vicens Vives, 413. To this he adds the expulsion of Moriscos as a further geographic problem of depopulation, 464. See Domínguez Ortiz, *Antiguo,* 360, for his views on depopulation. Kamen refers to the loss of manpower through people going to America ("Decline," 30).

more of their land, the artisans sank further and further into dependence. Possibly this was anyway an inevitable outcome of the growth of the population and commerce earlier in the century. The problem was that this transition was frozen: peasants and artisans were both pauperized, but they stayed by and large in control of agriculture and manufactures, a handicap for future growth" (Casey, "*European*," 224).

Elliott approaches the question of decline through a series of indicators whereas there were others that pointed to a decline. As he says, "These indicators were essentially economic and fiscal. They included the state of the crown's finances, which a minister described in 1629 as having been in 'continuous *declinación*' [Emph. his] during his thirty nine years in the royal service; the fiscal burden, especially on the peasantry; the excess of imports over exports and the consequent ruin of domestic industry; the disorders of the debased *vellón* coinage; and perhaps the most alarming of all the indicators in the eyes of contemporaries, the decline of population" ("Self-Perception," 53).[27]

Vicens Vives points out that the importation of foreign cloth "merely revealed and emphasized the inferiority of national industry, which then faced competition from cheaper products on its own territory" (354).[28] Domínguez Ortiz reminds us that the importation of precious metals merely went from Spain to Italy, England and Flanders, creating more economic problems for the country (296).[29] In the light of this difficult situation, Domínguez Ortiz points out that c. 1596 the government resorted to a novel step, that of the use of religious means to increase revenue, (*Antiguo*, 313). At the same time the precariousness of the situation can be seen in some statistics that Domínguez Ortiz shows: On the death of Philip II in 1598 the importation revenue was 10 million but the national debt was 68 million (313), and he lays the blame solidly on the Habsburg rulers (350). Another aspect was the demoralization that ensued: that the people who

---

[27] Elsewhere Elliott states "Some Spaniards therefore, were beginning to see decline in terms of economic backwardness relative to other contemporary societies" ("Decline," 57).

[28] Vicens Vives also highlights the fact that in 1575 after the declaration of bankruptcy by Philip II there was "a rise in the alcabala sales tax from 1.2% to 10%. Both measures meant the collapse of financial and economic activity" (375). Elsewhere Vicens Vives alludes to a state of monetary chaos (463).

[29] See also pp. 299-300 for the emergency measures that were enacted to keep the country afloat.

were suffering as a result of these economic problems could see that royalty, *privados* and other highly placed people were living lavish lives (365).

That Spain was living in a precarious state can be seen when Thompson says, "The consequences were to become obvious when the returns of 1588 came in. Over 10 million gold ducats had gone on preparations for the fleet in the first three quarters of 1587, but all the time disease, corruption and decay were eating away at the resources so painstakingly built up. To continue spending at that rate was out of the question" (V, 202). To show just how precarious the situation developed, Thompson informs us that the Duke of Medina Sidonia contributed an enormous amount of his own money (8 million *maravedís*) to support the venture (V, 210).[30]

Kamen notes with his usual acuity that Spain had to contend with another issue and that was trade was being taken over by foreigners (*Spain*, 161). Spain became, as Kamen notes, an economic entity controlled by international capitalism, and he quotes Tomás de Mercado who criticized " 'our senseless subjection to foreigners in giving them control of all the most important things in the country, something that informed people have lamented for years' " (*ibid.*, 171). It was under Philip II that "there were clear signs that the sun was giving away to shadow. Imperial destiny inculcated, as in all empires, a hubris that revealed itself in contempt for other nations" (*ibid.*, 193).

Parker observes that Philip II came into more money c. 1577: "on August 1577 a fleet of fifty-five ships arrived at Seville from the Indies bearing over two-million ducats for the King in bullion... And on 5 December Philip came to an agreement with his bankers whereby he agreed to honor the debts outstansing since the bankruptcy decree of 1575, in return for a new loan of five million ducats payable in Italy, by installments, in 1578 and 1579" (133). This proof shows yet again that the bullion merely was used to pay off loans.

There is another datum of importance in this survey of Spain's economics. Traditionally, craft guilds were a basis of sound economic practice. But they often were functioning with antiquated rules of production and, as Lynch says, "Far from showing concern for methods of production, training and technique, they were more concerned with trying to remove competition, both regional and foreign" (116). Moreover, for

---

[30] See also Thompson, VIII, 7a for his statements regarding the agricultural failures of the time.

comparative effects, Lynch notes that Spain did not follow the pattern of the industrial revolution as it occurred in England (119).[31]

Stradling points out an interesting strategy on the part of the Spanish government, "During the 1590's, the crown's revenues were running at a figure of about ten million ducats per annum. This was more than a threefold increase over the levels of the beginning of Philip II's reign, the result of rocketing silver imports and greatly increased (Castilian) taxation. In the quinquenium 1596-1600, more silver reached the royal coffers from the mines of the New World colonies than at any other time in their history. Nevertheless, the costs of war were escalating even more quickly. The Invincible Armada alone, for example, had cost a year's gross revenue. Expenditure on this scale necessitated the invention of a heavy new sales tax (the *millones*) and not long afterwards, monetary manipulation (through the issue of copper, or *vellón*, coinage), (Stradling, 38).

Elliott notes that the decline of Spain can be associated with a general regression that occurred in the rest of Europe. Spain's decline could also signal "the end of the period of Spanish hegemony in Europe and the relegation of Spain to the rank of second-rate powers. This implies a deterioration in Spain's military and naval strength, at least in relation to that of other states, and a decrease in its ability to mobilize the manpower and credit required to maintain its traditional primacy in Europe" ("Decline," 56). He further notes that Castile could no longer afford to be the imperial force that it had been.[32]

On the other hand, Kamen pleads for the opposite of what people are saying. As stated above, he is opposed to the idea of a decadent and declining Spain. He says, "The point is not that Spain did not suffer crises and reverses, for the contrary is obviously true. The real questions are: did these reverses represent the collapse of a once highly flourishing society? Were the reverses so extensive as to cover nearly two centuries, and so universal as to embrace all aspects of activity? The answer in both cases is

---

[31] Lynch also comments on the effects of misplaced funds that came from the New World. He states, "Thanks to the Imperial defenses provided by Philip II the colonial revenue continued to inject some life into the economy of the mother country. But this income was not invested productively and therefore it continued to cause inflation" (346).

[32] Elliott points out that the Habsburgs depended on the wealth of Castile, but such wealth was beginning to be seriously depleted ("Past and Present" 60).

a firmly negative one that must throw serious doubt on the relevance of 'decline'. The main consideration to bear in mind is that Spain had never been an economically strong nation" ("Decline," 35). Elsewhere he denies that there was a decline in imports, (*ibid.,* 39). Thompson/Yun attempt to set down clearly the numerous problems facing Spain at that time: "Thus the failure of the Spanish economy has in a long tradition that extends from the seventeenth century to the second half of the twentieth been explained in terms of arbitrary government, a bad religion, the tyrannical Inquisition, reactionary *hidalgo* values, the wretched laziness of the people, the absence of a capitalist and entrepreneurial spirit and other failings of the national character, as much as in terms of objective economic analysis" (3).

Yet another problem that faced the Spanish people was the shortage of food at that time. Vicens Vives describes the situation in the following way: "As a symptom of the growing food shortage, we should keep in mind that after 1570 agricultural prices, which had always stayed far below industrial ones, became equally high and in many cases higher. Thus the specter of famine hovered over the whole Peninsula, cutting into demographic growth. After 1550 the terrible scourge of plague reappeared periodically, further damaging normal population development" (347).

In spite of what Kamen says in his defense of the "integrity" of Spain, he does say on this question, "Philip returned only to plunge into severe problems at home. There were food shortages. In 1599 torrential spring rains fell, the river Duero flooded, and Southern Castile was suffering from grain scarcity" (*Philip II,* 79).[33]

Parker avers, "Capital starvation and overtaxation were two of the reasons for Spain's economic crisis in the 1590's and both were the direct result of Philip II's imperialism" (*Philip II,* 180).

For Lynch, "The acute shortage of cereals in Spain can be attributed to two basic conditions in her economic life. As the population was increasing, so there were mouths to feed, and domestic production could not keep pace with the growing demand. This failure was due, in turn, to the neglect of arable resources in favour of pasture farming" (114).[34]

---

[33] Elsewhere Kamen refers to the "failure of the grain harvest" (*Philip,* 317).
[34] Cfr. also, "The periodic shortages of grain suffered by Spain and other Mediterranean countries—particularly acute from 1586 to 1590—gave them [the Northern maritime countries] their card of entry and opened the area to Dutch and English shipping" (*ibid.,* 234). He also states, "The price of grain rose by more than 50 per cent. in Castile and Andalucía between 1595 and 1599. Prolonged neglect of

Elliott addresses the problem of food shortages in the following way. He says, "In the last years of the century, the harvests failed. The price of a *fanega* (1.6 bushels) of Andalusian corn rose from 430 *maravedís* in 1595 to 1,041 in 1598," (*Imperial,* 292).

Accompanying the problem of food shortages was the problem with goods. Casey observes that at one point in time Spanish goods were noted for the high standard of quality but, as he says, "by the 1580s the vital woolen manufactures—in Cordoba, in Segovia—were beginning a slow decline, though recession only became marked from around 1620," (*European,* 216-217). Elliot observes an interesting turn-about. He says, "If, as Sancho de Moncada wrote 'experience has shown that republics which used to be poor, like France, Flanders, Genoa and Venice, have prospered by producing their own manufactures; while Spain, rich in fruits and silver fleets, has grown poor by its failure to do so', then the answer was to go and do likewise" (*"Self-Perception, 56*-57). Lynch brings another consideration into the picture. He addresses the idea of competition and says, "other European countries, less affected by the price rise than Spain, could produce cheaper goods, against which Castilian manufacturers were unable to compete and to which they eventually lost the colonial market" (107). While some goods were imported, a rise in prices closed some markets, both national and international. Some thought that the rise of prices was due to increased exports. Vicens Vives says, "Naturally the results of these measures were the opposite of what had been hoped for: the authorized import of foreign cloth merely revealed and emphasized the inferiority of national industry, which then faced competition from cheaper products on its own territory" (354).

Concurrent with the above-mentioned problems was the problem of depopulation. Lynch notes the fluctuations of population. He observes the increase after Spain's civil wars (101). In fact, he notes that some agricultural problems are aggravated in some places by the increase in population. The negative results were due to the agricultural problems (114). Perhaps the Spain that one thinks of, its days of Imperial hegemony were in some ways due to its robust population (Elliott, "Decline," 57).[35] However, the need for

---

agriculture and growing reliance of foreign grain, the supply of which was more precarious during wartime, culminated in a food shortage which left the country on the verge of famine" (346).

[35] See Domínguez Ortiz, *Antiguo,* for more useful information on depopulation (360).

soldiery called for more and more recruits. Elliott notes that the fall of population could be accounted for in providing troops for the forces in the New World and elsewhere between 1530-1594 (*ibid.*, 57-58).[36]

Poverty was also another problem that had to be acknowledged as a part of the mosaic of decline. Altamira observes, "All this wealth very soon melted away, chiefly in consequence of the wars. Accordingly, not long after Philip II's death, and most particularly at the close of the seventeenth-century, a condition of industrial decline and poverty was brought about which was in sad contrast to former prosperity" (391). Kamen states that in a letter to his father, Philip II noted, " 'And after debating and arguing with them on the matter, and about the great distress and poverty in which these realms are' " (*Philip*, 19). Lynch points out that "On the other hand, the price revolution brought impoverishment to those who lived on fixed incomes and small rents, for these did not keep pace with prices," (127), and he continues by showing that wages were not on the same level as prices so that the ability to meet certain demands could easily lead to impoverishment (127).[37] All of this perforce brings us to the question of prices.

As a part of the hunger question several historians discuss cases of famine, noting that Castile suffered from the effects of hunger and disease in the 1590s. Casey goes on to say that "Mortality reached a paroxysm in 1599, when plague and famine carried off about one person in ten in the region, or 8 per cent of the Spanish population as a whole" (*European*, 211).[38] For Elliott, "The late 1580s and the 1590s seem in retrospect the critical years: the years of major reverses in Spain's north European policies, of another official 'bankruptcy' in 1597, of the death of the old king himself in 1598, and of the famine and plague which swept through Castile and Andalusia at the end of the century, and claimed perhaps half a million

---

[36] Kamen sees the decline of populations among the major problems of Castile ("Decline," 35).

[37] Fernández Alvarez and Díaz Medina say, "El hambre se mantiene como un mal endémico a lo largo de todo el siglo, se agudiza al producirse una mala cosecha, y se convierte en crisis de carácter catastrófico cuando la climatología hace que esas malas cosechas se vayan encadenando" (26). While Casey notes, "This last piece of evidence is particularly surprising, because it was Castile which suffered most from the ravages of hunger and disease in the 1590s" (*European*, 211).

[38] Casey notes, "This last piece of evidence is particularly surprising because it was Castile which suffered most from the ravages of hunger and disease in the 1590s" (*European*, 211).

victims out of a population of the order of six million" ("Self Deception," 46).

Vicens Vives presents a sharply worded description of this problem when he says, "As a symptom of the growing food shortage, we should keep in mind that after 1570 agricultural prices, which had always stayed far below industrial ones, became equally high and in many cases higher. Thus the specter of famine hovered over the whole Peninsula, cutting into demographic growth. After 1550 the terrible scourge of plague reappeared periodically, further damaging normal population development" (347).[39]

According to Kamen, "The king's long illness, economic problems, rising taxes, the failure of the grain harvest, lent substance to the feeling of popular dissatisfaction. A reign of triumphs, but also of disappointments, was ending in disillusion, the keynote of the following century. Madrid had its own particular problems. The plague epidemic which had affected the northern provinces reached the capital in the autumn of 1598. In 1599 the death rate soared" (*Philip II*, 317-318).[40] Stradling adds his name to those who detected the plague, and studies its ravages: "By 1599, when a potent virus of bubonic plague arrived in Spain, successive years of malnutrition had reduced the physiological resistance of the unprivileged masses to a low ebb. For five years, the epidemic raged along an axis from north to south of Castile" (34).[41]

---

[39] Elsewhere Vicens Vives states, "Famine appeared in Castile, and conditioned Philip II's external policy to such an extent that he even had to apply to his chief enemies—the English and Dutch—to transport 'bread from oversea,' grain which came from Sweden and Poland after a roundabout route through hostile seas" (461).
[40] See also Fernández Alvarez and Díaz Medina who say, "Por ello Luis de Mercado, catedrático de la Universidad de Valladolid, recibe el encargo de Felipe II de escribir un tratado sobre los medios para combatir la peste. La obra se publicó en 1598, momento en el que la enfermadid azotaba duramente a Castilla, divulgándose rápidamente por todo el Reino" (31). See also Parker, "On top of all this, the year 1571 brought with it a succession of natural disasters: flooding, plague, harvest failure and, in the end, the worst winter in many years" (119).
[41] Elliott provides an interesting note to the question of the plagues. He says, "At this moment, in the summer of 1519, the city of Valencia was struck by plague, which a preacher in Valencia Cathedral pronounced to be a divine chastisement for prevailing immorality" (146). See also 292 for another allusion to the plague. He says, "The epidemic made its first appearance in northern Spain in 1596, and moved steadily southwards, ravaging in its passage the densely crowded cities of Castile. The great plague of 1599-1600 probably wiped out at a single blow the 15 per cent population increase of the sixteenth century, and opened a new era in Castilian

Nature also showed its negative face by inflicting floods upon Spain. Such natural catastrophes touched upon other aspects of Spanish life. Parker states, "On top of all this, the year 1571, brought with it a succession of natural disasters: flooding, plague, ..." (119).

As a part of the various economic difficulties that beset the peninsula, there was the question of prices and how they affected Spaniards of the era that we are studying. Food shortages, mentioned above, tended to push up prices (Vicens Vives, 347). As prices rose for different goods, sales decreased, especially of wool (*ibid.,* 49). Again he notes that "In contrast to the regressive tendency of the 15th century, Spanish prices underwent a sharp rise in the 16th, with an index of 100 in 1501 climbing to 412 in 1600" (*ibid.,* 377). Kamen acknowledges Hamilton's thoughts on the subject, which he accepts with some qualification: "In recent times the causal connection between American bullion and Spanish inflation was most persuasively argued by Hamilton. The pace of price inflation, it seemed to him, closely followed the level of gold and silver imports" (*Spain,* 99). Kamen also notes that concerning the question of bullion imports from 1515 to 1551, high prices made profits for some, and this was not to the best interests of Spanish merchants (101).[42]

The problem of rising prices is studied by Fernández/Díaz Medina, and they aver "Más que los remedios que proponen estos tratadistas nos interesa su diagnóstigo de la situación económica que estaban viviendo, y en la que dos cuestiones aparecen constantemente destacadas: elevación de precios y huída de metales preciosos" (53).

The repercussions of price inflation is seen by Lynch as "The income from rents increased with the rise in prices, with the result that the nobility, who despised work and regarded business as debasing, was one of the few sectors of Spanish society that did not suffer from the price revolution" (104).[43]

Apparently no one saw the causal relationship between prices and the

---

demographic history: an era of stagnation, and perhaps of demographic decline" (292). See also Kamen, "Decline," 48, for further observations on the plague as well as Thompson, 202; for further material on epidemics, Domínguez Ortiz, *Antiguo;* Kamen, *Philip II,* 176.

[42] Kamen also mentions that "Castile under Philip was therefore suffering not only a price revolution but a tax revolution as well" (*Spain,* 167).

[43] He further says, "Spain's industrial difficulties however, can be attributed above all to the price revolution and the burden of taxation" (119).

influx of precious metals. Lynch says, "The Spanish government, like its neighbours in the rest of Europe, did not understand the causal connection between the influx of precious metals and the rise of prices, and was thus hampered in its economic and financial policies" (123).[44]

Focusing on the reign of Charles V as representing economic expansion, Elliott notes that "the first clear signs of a check to this expansion appear in 1548, when the country was experiencing one of the five-year periods of highest price increase for the entire sixteenth century" ("Decline," 61). Elsewhere Elliott also notes complaints that domestic goods bore high prices during the early years of Charles V's reign. As it appeared, Castilian goods were more expensive than imported goods (*Imperial*, 182), which would tend to affect the purchasing power of local as well as outside goods.

Production was bound to be affected by the various problems that we have been studying. Casey notes the fall in grain output c. 1590 (*Spain*, 212) and the drop in wheat production which fell by one fifth, barley and wine by even more, over the last quarter of the century (*European* 212). Around that time there was a decline in wool manufactures (217). In some cases the importation of foreign goods led to the "decay" of local textile goods (*ibid.*, 218). Philip III turned to copper, known as the *vellón*, and with it began a veritable revolution in Castile and Europe (Vicens Vives, 446).[45]

For Vilar, the "pouring cheap silver into Europe, the Spanish Conquest founded a new society. Such a society, however, could only develop with increased productive forces and with new social relationships" (105). But the arrival of new silver, as Kamen explains it, did do some help but the king still had to resort to new taxes (*Philip II*, 109). Lynch clarifies that the treasure was mostly silver and less gold from the New World which had little effect on prices (121).

It is tempting to think of this influx of silver and other precious metals as enriching Spain, but unfortunately, it did not because "this constant influx of precious metals still remained insufficient to meet the enormous

---

[44] Elsewhere Lynch notes, "The Seville merchants, knowing from experience that a rise of prices in Spain created a presumption in favor of a rise of prices in the Indies, increased their exports in the expectation of heavy returns. Heavy returns of bullion in turn raised prices and trade still further" (160). He also points out that "The price of grain rose by more than 50 per cent in Castile and Andalucía between 1595 and 1599" (346).

[45] Vicens Vives states that Philip II followed an economic system "which at least would provide him with abundant and immediate supplies of silver (453).

cost of Habsburg policy" (Lynch, 134).

One fact was clear, the cost of running the government and revenues were out of balance; therefore during the 1590s new taxes were created, e.g., *millones* and the issuance of copper coinage (the *vellón*), thereby affecting prices.[46]

The other source of economic problems was taxes. For Casey, increased tax levies lent great difficulties to the situation (219). On top of this the imposition of the *millones* was "a response to the disaster of the Armada two years before" (*Euroepan* 220).[47]

Vicens Vives stresses "the absence of productive investments, or the predominance of unproductive ones, for the first capital sums amassed" (381).[48] Elliott takes as one of the basic problems of the Spain of that time, the problem of productivity ("Decline" 57). He also pinpoints as one of the bases of the drop in production was dependence on foreign goods and for its food supply as well and that parts of its population devoted itself to generally non-productive activities (65).[49]

Currency played a particularly important role in the developing situation regarding the economy of Spain. Philip II tried to avoid devaluating currency, but when American silver began to dwindle, Philip III turned to copper, the *vellón*, and with it began a veritable revolution in Castile and Europe (Vicens Vives, 446).[50] For Vilar, "by pouring cheap silver into Europe, the Spanish Conquest founded a new society. Such a society, however, could only develop with increased productive forces and with new social relationships" (105). But the arrival of new silver, as Kamen explains it, did render help but the king still had to resort to new taxes

---

[46] Cfr. Kamen, "Decline", 35, for a denial of charges of decline and also to point to the fact that bullion imports could not make up the balance of trade (35). Elliott also sees the situation as one of the manipulation of coinage. The *vellón* (copper) was authorized in 1599 and did much to create an inflationary situation later (*Imperial*, 299).

[47] In another item, Casey notes the lack of products like hay and oats (Early, 12).

[48] See Domínguez Ortiz who says, "Esto, traducido al lenguaje actual, podríamos resumirlo diciendo que España estaba falta de inversiones productivas" (*Antiguo*, 359).

[49] See Kamen, "Decline," 41, for further statements on the dependency on foreign markets.

[50] Vicens Vives states that Philip II followed an economic system "which at least would provide him with abundant and immediate supplies of silver" (453).

(*Philip II*, 109). Lynch clarifies that the treasure was mostly silver and less gold from the New World which had little effect on prices (121).

It is tempting to think of this influx of silver and other precious metals as enriching Spain, but unfortunately, it did not because "this constant influx of precious metals still remained insufficient to meet the enormous cost of Habsburg policy" (*ibid.*, 134). One fact was clear, the costs of running the government and revenues were out of balance.[51]

The other source of economic problems was taxes. For Casey, increased tax levies lent great difficulties to the situation ("*European*," 219). On top of this the imposition of the *millones* was a response to the losses incurred by the Armada (*ibid.*, 220).[52]

For Vicens Vives, "oppressive taxation" was one of the causes of Spain's economic woes (463).[53]

As was mentioned earlier taxes formed the basis for some of the economic difficulties of the time. Kamen articulates this problem very clearly when he cites a presentation concerning the people of Castile: "With what they owe for other things, the common people who have to pay the taxes are reduced to such extremes of misfortune and poverty that many of them go naked without clothing. And the misery is so universal that it afflicts not only Your Majesty's subjects but even more those of the nobility, for they cannot pay their taxes nor have the means to do so. The prisons are full, and all are heading for ruin. Believe me, Your Majesty [Charles V], if this were not true I would not dare write it to you' " (*Philip*, 18).

---

[51] Cfr. Kamen, "Decline, 35, for a denial of charges of decline and also to point to the fact that bullion imports could not make up the balance of trade. Elliott also sees the situation as one of the manipulation of coinage. The *vellón* (copper) was authorized in 1599 and did much to create an inflationary situation later, *Imperial Spain*, 299).
[52] Casey also refers to other taxes which assisted in bringing about bankruptcy. e.g., the *alcabala* (the royal tax), 220.
[53] Cfr. Domínguez Ortiz, "Pero eran tales los gastos que acarreaba una politica internacional de dimensiones casi planetarias que estos incrementos resultaron insignificantes, como vamos a ver, y la Hacienda castellana siguió atenida a los mismos recursos de emergencia: emisiones de Deuda Pública, arbitrios diversos, bancarrotas periódicas y, hacia el fin del reinado [Philip II's], imposición de la contribución llamada vulgarmente de *Millones* que tanta y tan adversa influencia había de tener en la economía castellana" (*Antiguo*, 299-300). Domínguez Ortiz also points out that on the death of Philip II revenue was 10 million ducats but the national debt was 68 million (313). See also his observations on the effects of doubling the value of the *vellón*.

Circumstances necessitated that taxes be raised as other problems became dire. Kamen notes that "In broad terms, government tax revenue in Castile in 1577 was about 50 per cent higher than in 1567. The increase was extremely unpopular. Discontent was aggravated by the drought conditions prevailing in Castile in 1577" (*ibid.*, 158).[54] Parker states the problem in the following way, "From a total of 750,000 ducats received in the biennium 1566-1567, the tax revenue rose to 4.4 million in 1570-71. The cost of the Netherlands to Spain fell in precise proportions: 2 million ducats arrived from the Castilian treasury in 1566-1567, but only 550,000 in 1570-71. The 'Netherlands problem' appeared to be well on the way toward its final solution" (97).[55]

But this situation of rising taxes and the various impositions it imposed could not go without some response. Parker notes, "In 1590, as previously noted, they had voted the 'millones' to pay for the Armada. In 1592, they were called back to vote more money for the wars with France, England and the Dutch, but this time there was a solid core of deputies, led by those from Burgos and Seville, who refused: they opposed every crown proposal for raising money with arguments about the depopulation and impoverishment of the countryside. They even presented memorials criticizing the king's expensive foreign policy: one deputy suggested that the war in the Netherlands alone had cost Castile 115 million ducats, and that this was too much" (184).

Lynch lays the blame bluntly on taxes, "Spain's industrial difficulties, however, can be attributed above all to the price revolution and the burden of taxation" (119).

What was remarkable about the economic situation was the multiple increase of taxes.[56]

---

[54] Elsewhere Kamen says, "The King's long illness, economic problems, rising taxes, the failure of the grain harvest, lent substance to the feeling of popular dissatisfaction" (*ibid.*, 317).

[55] Parker also says, "Capital starvation and overtaxation were two of the reasons for Spain's economic crisis in the 1590's, and both were the direct result of Philip II's imperialism" (180).

[56] Stradling says, "During the 1590s, the crown's revenues were running at a figure of about ten million ducats per annum. This was more than a threefold increase over the levels of the beginning of Philip II's reign, the result of rocketing silver imports and greatly increased (Castilian) taxation. In the quinquenium 1596-1600, more silver reached the royal coffers from the mines of the New World colonies than at

The degree of increase alluded to above was often very high. Elliott notes that "At Medina del Campo, for instance, the tax on sales, which had previously stood at only 1.2 per cent rose to ten percent with serious consequences for trade at the fairs" (*Imperial*, 263).

The tax burden fell heavily on Castile as compared to other parts of the peninsula (*ibid.*, 280).[57] Of all of the factors that had affected Spain negatively war had to be one of the biggest causes for discontent and a failing economic situation.[58]

The groundwork for the wars Spain undertook can begin with the era of Charles V which carried on wars in various fronts as well as pursued an intercontinental policy in the New World. Such enterprises when passed on the subsequent monarchs created various crises. Casey points out that, "But it was the continuing burden of providing manpower for the upkeep of empire which represented the really significant drain on the country's resources" (*Modern Spain*, 24).

In spite of the great cost to the country, Thompson avers that "The wars of the 1590s were wars which nobody really won. Reputations evaporated, even of the greatest (Essex, Parma, Medina Sidonia). Universal failure exposed the pitiless waste of resources. Even the wealth of the Indies could achieve nothing; nor could divine providence be relied upon to depend its cause" (III, 275-276).

The demise of the Armada is well known to historians, and this was due in large measure to its great deficiencies.[59] One of the basic preoccupations of Philip II was the Ottoman threat (Kamen, *Philip II*, 87). The edifice

---

any other time in their history. Nevertheless, the costs of war were escalating even more quickly. The Invincible Armada alone, for example, had cost a year's gross revenue" (38).

[57] Allied with the question of taxes is the question of trade. There was a visible decline of trade and imports, along with a decline of agriculture (Elliott, "Self-Perception," 53). The theme of how foreigners took over a great deal of the trade is discussed by Kamen, "Decline," 30).

[58] In view of the foregoing, Thompson says, "Fiscal exhaustion was rather a 17th- than a 16th- century phenomenon. Before the 1630s the tax burden was neither unremittingly excessive nor, in the broad view, exceptional. Less than 9 per cent of national income compares favourably with 17th-century rates, not only in Spain but in other European states as well" (II, 19).

[59] See Thompson, VIII, 17a. He also adds, "By 1588, men were beginning to laugh at the King of Spain and his Armada. It had already cost millions of ducats and was costing a further 900,000 ducats a month" (*ibid.*, VIII, 18ab).

of the Empire begins to crack with the debacle of Djerba (88).[60] Philip II wanted peace and this depended largely on the fact that wars were very costly and the Castilian treasury was overwhelmed with the costs of such wars, but Philip II nevertheless continued to wage war in spite of the onerous costs to the nation. Kamen says, "At the time Philip must have seen 1568-9 as possibly the worst year of his reign. Though the situation in the Netherlands seemed to be stabilizing, it was at the cost of men, money and the understanding of other countries" (*ibid.*, 129). Spain's luck seemed to be running out when Drake's ships had taken Santo Domingo. The British continued their depredations in Cartagena and the Florida coast (*ibid.*, 265).

One of the principles that fueled Philip II's actions was the strict confirmation to Catholic goals and standards. He saw war as a part of the larger religious picture. Philip II felt compelled to fight all religious heresy and he believed that the Protestant schism of which Netherlands was a part, had to be fought.[61]

Philip II's tenure was marked by series of wars and ended with the death of the monarch himself in 1598. As was said above, the Turks were Philip II's prime enemy, and Philip tried to recover the city of Tripoli. However, the campaign turned out to be a disaster (Cfr. Parker, 65). But the Turks were not the only enemy; Spain faced the French, the Dutch and English as well: "The cost of the war in the Netherlands had become intolerable. Finance was fast becoming Philip II's principal problem and he was more and more obsessed by the need to raise money (*ibid.*, 121).[62]

Lynch sums things up in the following way: "Starved of native production, hit by war, and damaged by fiscal policy, Spanish commerce began to limp badly in the second half of the sixteenth century. This, however, did not apply to the Indies trade, the greatest trade in the world and the economic life-line of its owner" (Lynch, 147). It seems that Spain would not extricate itself from the effects of war (see *ibid.*, 169). It was hardly possible for Spain to recover economically so long as Philip II

---

[60] See Lynch for further comments on the relations with the Turks, 232.
[61] See Kamen, *Spain*, 36. For costs of war to Spain, see Kamen, *Spain*, 164; see also Parker, 68, 74, 75.
[62] Parker notes, "there was little that either man could do, either to save Spain from bankruptcy or to win her wars. After the mutinies and the military failures there was really no prospect of a Spanish victory in either the Netherlands or in the Mediterranean" (125). See also 195 for similar remarks.

continued with prolonged warfare (*ibid.*, 346).

As if things were not bad enough under Philip II, Elliott says, "The new regime of Philip III ordered a fresh military effort to be made in Flanders at the start of the new century and sent a half-hearted expedition to Ireland in 1601, but war could not be fought without resources, and the resources were draining away. In 1607— a mere ten years after the decree of suspension of payments of 1596—the Spanish crown was forced to repudiate its debt once again, and two years later Spain signed its twelve-year truce with the Dutch" (*Imperial*, 285).[63]

To return to my original hypothesis, life in Spain during Cervantes's life, was full of disasters, plagues, crop failures, and a foreign policy that failed. In sum, behind the gloss of the crown, there was a terrible picture economically and politically. It could only have made Cervantes's life more difficult, and history—as far as what we know about Cervantes's life—made for a difficult time.

Many episodes call for some qualification, e.g., the sumptuous feast of Basilio during the episode of the pastoral marriage event was probably largely an invention of Cervantes's, although there were wealthy people in rural areas. Other episodes like that of the Captive, resonate with historical truth, because Cervantes is using them in certain ways in an altered and fictional framework that does coincide with historical fact as we can read it.

I fear that I may have presented too dark a picture of Spain in those years. Kamen and Rahn Phillips stand fast in their assertion that there was no decline. However, when one takes the historical evidence together, it is very difficult to deny that life in Spain in those years was difficult and become even more difficult in the years after Cervantes's death.

The *desengaño* of which I spoke above was almost an obligatory ending for *Don Quijote*. What was there to boast about in a country collapsing under the weight of bad foreign policy, agricultural scarcity, a land ravaged by nature, and the depopulation which ensued in the wake of the various poorly thought-out historical incidents?

The kind of summary view of the political and economic state of Spain between these two dates that I wish to make would, I believe, leave room for doubts concerning a point of view that would cut *Don Quijote* away from the very events of the time of *Don Quijote's* gestation and birth. That *Don Quijote* is not a "funny book" I have developed in an earlier chapter.

---

[63] For further discussion of war and the Olivares' regime, see 320.

Were it to be a funny book, then one would have to reconcile the "funny book" syndrome with the sad historical, economic terms of the times.

It seems that if Don Quijote and Cervantes took umbrage in the fantasy life of the romances of chivalry, perhaps it was because to gaze directly at reality would force an escape from it.

Concluding Remarks

MY APPROACH TO READING Cervantes in his *Don Quijote* has stressed the supremacy of the experiential mode with respect to the characters. Cervantes does not appeal to an external reality, as might occur in the works of Quevedo, who looks to God and Heaven as a panacea to the woes of the individual on earth. All actions are seen as the interaction between characters and their contingency on others. Don Quijote makes an existential decision to undertake a metamorphosis and to act on that choice. In the same arena of action are the lives of others who either interact with other characters or plunge ahead in life on their own, but whose actions originate in the inner being of that individual.

As can be expected, such a determination is carried out in an historical frame, and it is for this reason that I have surveyed the social, historical and economic situation in the Spain of that time. The individual does not live floating in an ether detached from others; their interdependency is stressed by Cervantes because the characters share an epochal time and space. This also includes the conflict of *castas*, as Castro would have it. Cervantes invents situations in which the experiental factors of one group impinges upon those of another.

My approach has focused precisely on the human and the experiential, in order to avoid falling into the pit of artificiality as does the *Amadís*, which is of greater fantasy than the created fiction of Cervantes. When Don Quijote imagines and "creates" he does so always from a fairly credible perspective. Human lives are uncovered because of their tangibility and these are reflective of the realities and human situation of the very readers to whom Cervantes aims his book.

Don Quijote delves into lives as matters of substance and not of artificial pretenses and inventions. No wonder a writer with theological pretensions like Alfonso de Valdés and others would decry the chivalric genre as a waste of time and a danger to public morals. Yet when Valdés does a survey of sinners in the first part of his *Diálogo de Mercurio y Carón*, he does so in a very human vein, including the characters that wear the cloth.

The greatest contribution that Cervantes makes with his work is the reconsideration of the relativity of truth and objective reality. Faced with a rationalism that often defies contact with more human relationships, Cervantes suggests very strongly that there is no such thing as objective truth and reality; that all human actions are subject to personal interests and biases; that we cannot take comfort in attaching ourselves to an exterior reality, since all relationships are complex and involve personal interests over public ones.

No work approaches life as lived more than does *Don Quijote*, and perhaps it is for this reason that it has captured the imagination of the public, and will continue to do so for the future.

Selected Bibliography

Abbott, Jack Henry. *In the Belly of the Beast: Letters from Prison*. New York: Random House, 1981.

Ascunce Arrieta, José Angel. *El Quijote como tragedia y la tragedia de don Quijote*. Kassel: Reichenberger, 2005.

Avalle Arce, Juan Bautista. *Nuevos deslindes cervantinos*. Barcelona: Ariel, 1975.

———. *Don Quijote como forma de vida*. Madrid: Castalia, 1976.

———. with E.C. Riley. *Suma Cervantina*. London: Tamesis, 1973.

Allen, J.J. *Don Quijote: Hero or Fool? A Study in Narrative Technique*. Gainesville: University of Florida Press, 1969.

Altamira, Rafael. *A History of Spain: From the Beginnings to the Present Day*. Translated by Muna Lee. N.Y.: Nostrand, 1949.

Auerbach, Eric. "The Enchanted Dulcinea," in Nelson, Lowry, Jr., ed. *Cervantes: A Collection of Critical Essays*. N.J.: Prentice-Hall, 1969, 98-122.

Bataillon, Marcel., ed. Introduction to A. Morel-Fatio's edition of *La Vie de Lazarillo de Tormes* [*La vida de Lazarillo de Tormes*], Paris: Aubier, 1958.

Bordoy Cerda, Miguel. *Mallorca, Lepanto y Cervantes*. Palma de Mallorca: Cort. 1971.

Bowers, Fredson., ed. *Vladimir Nabokov. Lectures on Don Quijote*, with an introduction by Guy Davenport. N.Y.: Harcourt Brace Jovanovich, 1983.

Camporesi, Piero. *The Juice of Life. The Symbol and Magic Significance of Blood*. Foreword by Umberto Eco. Translated by Robert R. Barr. N.Y.: Continuum, 1995.

A.J. Cascardi. "The Archaeology of Desire in *Don Quijote*," in *Quixotic Desire. Psychoanalytic Perspectives on Cervantes*. El Saffar, Ruth Anthony and Diana de Armas Wilson, eds. Ithaca: Cornell UP, 1993, 37-58.

Casey, James. *Early Modern Spain: A Social History*. London: Routledge, 1999.

——— " Spain: A Failed Transition," *in The European Crisis of the 1590s: Essays in Comparative History*. London: Allen & Unwin, 1985, 209-228.

Castro, Américo. *El pensamiento de Cervantes*. Anejo VI, *RFE*. Madrid: Hernando, 1925. See also a revised edition of this work edited by Rodríguez Puértolas.

———. *De la edad conflictiva*. Madrid: Taurus, 1961.

———. *Cervantes y los casticismos españoles*. Madrid-Barcelona: Alfaguara, 1967.

Cervantes, Miguel de. *El ingenioso hidalgo Don Quijote de la Mancha*. Prólogo de Américo Castro, Séptima Edición. México, D.F. : Porrúa, 1967.

Close, Anthony. *Cervantes and the Comic Mind of his Age*. Oxford: UP, 2000.

———. *The Romantic Approach to* Don Quijote. *A Critical History of the Romantic Tradition in Quijote Criticism*. Cambridge: UP, 1978.

Combet, Louis. *Cervantès ou Les Incertitudes du Désir*. Lyon: Presses Universitaires de Lyon, 1980.

Creel, Bryant. *Don Quijote, Symbol of a Culture in Crisis*. Valencia: Albatros (Hispanófila, 47), 1988.

Crowley, Robert and Geoffrey Parker. *The Reader's Companion to Military History*. Boston: Houghton Mifflin, 1996.

Croce, Benedetto. "The Sympathy of Don Quijote," in Flores, Angel and M.J. Benardete, *Cervantes Across the Centuries*. New York: Dryden, 1947, 179-182.

Damasio, Antonio. *Descartes' Error: Emotion, Reason and the Human Brain*. New York: Putnam, 1994.

Dennett, Daniel. *Kinds of Minds: Toward an Understanding of Consciousness*. New York: Basic Books, 1996.

———_. *Diccionario general ilustrado de la lengua española*. Barcelona : Spes, 1953 and 1973.

Domínguez Ortiz, Antonio. *El antiguo régimen: Los Reyes Católicos y los Austrias*. Madrid : Alianza-Alfaguara, 1977.

Durán, Manuel. *La ambigüedad en el Quijote*. Xalapa : Universidad Veracruzana, 1960.

Edie, James M., ed. *Merleau Ponty. The Primacy of Perception and Other Essays on Phenomenological Psychology, the Philosophy of Art, History and Politics*. Evanston: Northwestern UP, 1964.

Efron, Arthur. *Don Quijote and the Dulcinated World*. Austin: University of Texas Press, 1971.

El Saffar, Ruth A. and Diana De Armas Wilson, eds. *Quixotic Desire. Psychoanalytic Perspectives on Cervantes*. Ithaca: Cornell UP, 1993.

Elliott, J.H. *Imperial Spain, 1469-1719*. London: Arnold, 1963.

———. "The Decline of Spain," Past and Present, 20 (1961): 52-75.

———. "Self-Perception and Decline in Early Seventeenth-Century Spain," *Past and Present,*" 74 (Feb.1977): 41-61.

———. *Encyclopedia of Philosophy*. New York: Macmillan, 1972.

Felman, Shoshana. *Writing and Madness*. (Literature/Philosophy/Psychoanalysis). Translated by Martha Noel Evans. Ithaca: Cornell UP, 1985.

Fernández Alvarez, Manuel y Ana Díaz Medina. *Historia de España : Los austrias mayores y la culminación del Imperio (1516-1598)*. Madrid: Gredos, 1987.

— —. *La sociedad española en el siglo de oro*. Madrid: Gredos, 1987.
Finello, Dominic K. *Pastoral Themes and Forms in Cervantes's Fiction*. Lewisburg: Bucknell UP, 1994.
Foucault, Michel. *Madness and Civilization. A History of Insanity in the Age of Reason*. Translated by Richard Howard. N.Y.: Vintage, 1973.
Garcés, María Antonia. *Cervantes in Algiers*. Nashville: Vanderbilt UP, 2002.
Gaylord, Mary M. "The Whole Body of Fable with All of its Members," in *Quixotic Desire*. 117-199.
Gilman, Stephen. *The Novel According to Cervantes*. Berkeley: University of California Press, 1989.
Girard, René. *Deceit, Desire and the Novel. Self and Other in Literary Structure*. Translation by Yvonne Freccero. Baltimore: Johns Hopkins University, 1961.
Grinberg, León and Juan Francisco Rodríguez, "Cervantes as Cultural Ancestor of Freud." In *Quixotic Desire*, 23-33.
Grotjahn, Martin. *Beyond Laughter*. New York: Blakeston, 1957.
Greenblatt, Stephen. "Mutilation and Meaning" in *The Body in Parts. Phantasies of Corporeality in Early Modern Europe*. Hilman, David and Carla Mazzio, eds. New York: Routledge, 1997, 221-241.
Guillén, Claudio. "La disposición temporal del *Lazarillo de Tormes*," *HR*, 25 (1957): 264-279.
Haedo, Fray Diego de. *Topografía e historia general de Argel*. Madrid: Sociedad de bibliófilos españoles, 1927; vol. II, 1929 ; vol. III, 1929.
Hays, Peter L. *The Limping Hero: Grotesques in Literature*. N.Y.: New York UP, 1971.
Husserl, Edmond. *The Phenomenology of Internal Time-Consciousness*. Heidegger, Martin, ed. Translated by James S. Churchill, introduction by Calvin O. Schrag. Bloomington, IN: Indiana UP, 1966.
———. *Phenomenology and the Crisis of Philosophy. Philosophy as Rigorous Science and Philology and the Crisis of European Men*. Translation with notes and introduction by Quentin Laure. N.Y.: Harper, 1965.
Johnson, Carroll B. *Don Quijote. The Quest for Modern Fiction*. Boston: Twayne, 1990.
Kamen, Henry. *Spain 1469-1714. A Society of Conflict*. London: Longman, 1983.
———."The Decline of Spain: A Historical Myth? *Past and Present*, 81 (Nov. 1978): 24-50.
———. *Philip of Spain*. New Haven, CT: Yale UP, 1997.
Kundera, Milan. "The Depreciated Legacy of Cervantes," in *The Art of the Novel*. Translation by Linda Asher. N.Y.: Grove, 1988, pp. 3-20.
———. *Testaments Betrayed. An Essay in Nine Parts*. Translated by Linda Asher. N.Y.: Harper-Collins, 1995.

Langer, Suzanne K. *Philosophy in a New Key*. Cambridge: Harvard UP, 1978.
Levin, Harry. "The Example of Cervantes," in Lowry Nelson, Jr. *Cervantes*, 34-48.
Lodge, David. *Consciousness and the Novel*. Cambridge: Harvard UP, 2002.
Lynch, John. *Spain under the Habsburgs*. Vol. I (Empire and Absolutism 1516-1598). New York: Oxford UP, 1964.
Maldonado de Guevara, Francisco. "La pesadilla de Cervantes: Lepanto," *Anales cervantinos*, 15 (1976): 247-48.
Mancing, Howard. *The Chivalric World of Don Quijote. Style, Structure and Narrative Technique*. Columbia, MO: University of Missouri Press, 1982.
Mann, Thomas. "Voyage with Don Quijote," in *Cervantes*, Lowry Nelson, Jr., 49-72.
Maravall, José Antonio. *Poder, Honor y Elites el Siglo XVII*. Madrid: Siglo veinteuno de España, 1979.
Márquez Villanueva, Francisco. *Personajes y temas del Quijote*. Madrid: Taurus, 1975.
———. *El problema morisco: desde otras laderas*. Madrid: Libertaria, 1998.
Martínez Bonati, Félix. *Don Quijote and the Poetics of the Novel*. Translated by Diane Fox. Ithaca: Cornell UP, 1992.
McCrory, Donald. *Miguel de Cervantes: The Captive's Tale (La historia de El Cautivo), Don Quijote, part 1, chapters 39-41*. Westminster, England: Aris and Phillips, 1999.
Medina Molera, Antonio. *Quijote e Islam. El Quijote a cielo abierto*. Barcelona : Escanera, 2005.
Meissner, S. J. W. W. *The Psychology of a Saint. Ignatius of Loyola*. New Haven, CT: Yale UP. 1992.
Meyerhoff, Hans. *Time in Literature*. Berkeley: University of California Press, 1960.
Navarro Ledesma, Francisco. *Cervantes. The Man and the Genius*. New York: Charterhouse, 1973.
Nelson, Jr. Lowry. *Cervantes. A Collection of Critical Essays*. New Jersey: Prentice-Hall, 1969.
Parker, Geoffry. *The Grand Strategy of Philip II*. New Haven, CT: Yale UP, 1998.
———. *Philip II*. Boston: Little, Brown, 1978.
Parr, James. *Don Quijote, Don Juan and Related Subjects. Form and Tradition in Spanish Literature, 1330-1630*. Selinsgrove: Susquehanna UP, 2004.
———. *Don Qwuijote: An Anatomy of Subversive Discourse*. Newark, DE.: Juan de la Cuesta, 1988.
Phillips, Carla Rahn. "Time and Duration: A Model for the Economy of Early Modern Spain," *American Historical Revue*, 92, #3 (1987):531-562.
Puller, Jr. Lewis B. *Fortunate Son. The Autobiography of Lewis B. Puller, Jr*. New York: Grove Weidenfeld, 1991.

Redondo, Augustin. *Otra Manera de Leer el Quijote. Historia, Tradiciones Culturales y Literatura*. Madrid: Castalia, 1997.

Ricapito, Joseph V. *Cervantes's Novelas ejemplares: Between History and Creativity*. W. Lafayette, IN.: Purdue UP, 1996.

———. *Formalistic Aspects of Cervantes's 'Novelas ejemplares'*. Lewiston, N.Y.: Mellen, 1997.

———. "La teatralidad en la prosa de el *Quijote*," in *Theatralia* : El teatro de Miguel de Cervantes ante el IV centenario, Maestro, Jesús G., ed. Pontevedra: Mirabel, 2000, 315-327.

Riley, E.C. *Cervantes's Theory of the Novel*. Oxford: Clarendon, 1968.

———. *Don Quijote*. London: Allen & Unwin, 1986.

Riquer, Martín de. "Cervantes y la caballeresca," in *Suma Cervantina*, Avalle/Riley, 273-292.

Russell, P.E. " 'Don Quijote' as a Funny Book,' " *MLR*, 64 (1969): 312-326.

Sieber, Harry. *Las novelas ejemplares*, 2 vols. Madrid: Cátedra, 1980.

———. "Literary Time and the 'Cueva de Montesinos'," *MLN*, 86, #2 (Mar. 1971): 268-273.

Silverman, Joseph H. Review of Bataillon's edition of *Lazarillo de Tormes*, *RPh*, 15 (1961): 88-94.

Slattery, Dennis Patrick. *The Wounded Body. Remembering the Marking of the Flesh*. Albany: SUNY Press, 2000.

Smith, Paul Julian. "The Captive's Tale: Race, Text and Gender," *in Quixotic Desire*, 227-235.

Sola, Emilio and José F. de la Peña. *Cervantes y Berbería. (Cervantes, mundo turco-berberisco y servicios secretos en la época de felipe II)*. México-Madrid : Fondo de Cultura Económica, 1995.

Spitzer, Leo. "*On the Significance of Don Quijote*," Lowry Nelson Jr., *Cervantes*, 82-97.

Starobinski, Jean. *Fragments for the History of the Human Body*, Part II, Feher, Michael, Ramona Nadaff, and Nadia Tazi, eds. New York: Zone, 1989.

Stiker, Henri-Jacques. *A History of Disability*. Translated by William Sayers. Ann Arbor: University of Michigain Press, 1999.

Stradling, R.A. *Europe and the Decline of Spain*. London: Allen & Unwin, 1981.

Sullivan, Henry. *Grotesque Purgatory. A Study of Cervantes's Don Quijote, part II*. University Park: Pennsylvania State UP, 1996.

Thompson, I.A.A and Bartolomé Yun Casalilla, eds. *The Castilian Crisis of the Seventeenth Century. New Perspectives on the Economic and Social History of Seventeenth-Century Spain*. Cambridge: UP, 1994.

———. *War and Society in Hapsburg Spain. Selected Essays*. Aldershot, Great Britain:

Variorum, 1992.

Vicens Vives, Jaime. *An Economic History of Spain*. Translated by Frances M. López Morillas. Princeton: Princeton UP, 1969.

Vilar, Pierre. "*The Age of Don Quijote*," in *Essays in European Economic History, 1560-1800*, Oxford: Clarendon, 1974.

Wardropper, Bruce. "The Pertinence of the Curious Impertinent," *PMLA*, 72 (1957): 587-600.

Waterman, David. *Disordered Bodies. Disrupted Borders. Representations of Resistance in Modern British Literature*. Lanham: UP of America. 1999.

Wilson, Edmund. *Triple Thinkers and The Wound and the Bow*. Foreword by Frank Kermode. Boston: Northeastern UP, 1984.

Zimic, Stanislas. "Un eco de Lepanto en la ironía cervantina, " *RoNotes*, 12, #1, (1970): 174-176

Printed in the United States
132641LV00007B/78/A